FGF Studies in Small Business and Entrepreneurship

More information about this series at
http://www.springer.com/series/13382

Dennis Brüntje • Oliver Gajda
Editors

Crowdfunding in Europe

State of the Art in Theory and Practice

Springer

Editors
Dennis Brüntje
Technische Universität Ilmenau
Ilmenau
Germany

Oliver Gajda
European Crowdfunding Network
Brussels
Belgium

ISSN 2364-6918 ISSN 2364-6926 (electronic)
FGF Studies in Small Business and Entrepreneurship
ISBN 978-3-319-18016-8 ISBN 978-3-319-18017-5 (eBook)
DOI 10.1007/978-3-319-18017-5

Library of Congress Control Number: 2015947507

Springer Cham Heidelberg New York Dordrecht London

Printed on acid-free paper

Springer International Publishing AG Switzerland is part of Springer Science+Business Media (www.springer.com)

Multifaceted and Interdisciplinary Perspectives on Small Business and Entrepreneurship Research: Introducing the FGF Studies in Small Business and Entrepreneurship

Understanding entrepreneurship and entrepreneurial phenomena in new ventures, small businesses, and established corporations is of crucial importance for entrepreneurs, corporate managers, and policymakers alike. The Förderkreis Gründungsforschung e.V. (FGF) has from its inception in 1987 strongly supported the development of research on these important topics and is today the largest and leading association of entrepreneurship and innovation scholars in Germany, Austria, Switzerland, and Liechtenstein. Today, FGF provides an established platform for the exchange of ideas and results of entrepreneurship research and related phenomena such as innovation, small and medium-sized enterprises (SMEs), and family businesses. In doing so, FGF pursues a number of important goals and its members strive to provide evidence-based answers to questions such as the following:

- How can we effectively support start-ups in order to strengthen employment and innovation in the economy?
- Where do administrative and regulatory barriers to entrepreneurship and innovation exist and how can they be successfully reduced?
- What needs to be done to effectively organise knowledge and technology transfer out of universities, research institutes, and other types of higher education institutions?
- What can be done to improve educational programmes in schools and institutions of higher education that want to foster entrepreneurship and innovation?
- How do we strengthen values and beliefs that are the foundation of an entrepreneurial culture and what can be done to improve individual entrepreneurial spirit?
- What measures need to be taken to advance the collaboration of entrepreneurial small businesses and institutions of higher education?
- How can SMEs and family businesses survive in the modern, globalised economy?
- How can large, established firms benefit from corporate entrepreneurship and corporate venturing?

To support those researchers, teachers, practitioners, and policymakers who work on finding rigorous answers to these questions, FGF developed and continues to develop a plethora of measures. By organising national and international conferences on entrepreneurship, innovation, and small and medium-sized enterprises, it provides scholars from various disciplines such as management, economics, psychology, sociology, or economic geography with numerous opportunities to network and collaborate with each other. Various work groups and networks within the FGF address topics such as the development of entrepreneurship research, entrepreneurial finance, cultural entrepreneurship, sustainable entrepreneurship and innovation, corporate entrepreneurship, or entrepreneurship education. Based on this, recommendations for policy- and decision-makers are developed and disseminated widely.

The latest endeavour in this regard are the FGF Studies in Small Business and Entrepreneurship, a book series devoted to those phenomena that are at the heart of FGF's activities and which we are happy to start with the present edited volume on crowdfunding. The aim of the FGF Studies in Small Business and Entrepreneurship is to showcase exceptional scholarly work in small business and entrepreneurship research. The book series will have an interdisciplinary focus and will include works from management, finance, innovation, marketing, economics, sociology, psychology, and related areas reflecting the breadth of different approaches to small business, innovation, and entrepreneurship research. We will publish research monographs, edited volumes, and handbooks or reference books, depending on what particular format suits the topic under investigation best. Equally, the FGF Studies in Small Business and Entrepreneurship acknowledge that small business and entrepreneurship phenomena occur at various levels of analysis and hence the series is concerned with a plethora of levels including the analysis of individuals, organisations, networks, economies, and societies.

Through this, we are confident that the book series will serve as an important vehicle to help academics, professionals, researchers, and policymakers, working in the fields of small business, innovation, and entrepreneurship, to disseminate and obtain high-quality knowledge, thereby adding to achieving FGF's overall goal of fostering an entrepreneurial and innovative culture and making entrepreneurs more successful in their endeavours.

We are happy to be able to start the series with an edited volume that achieves all of the goals that we have in mind with the series in an exceptional way. How we think about entrepreneurial finance has changed dramatically since the first platforms to finance new ventures with the help of a crowd of small and widely dispersed investors emerged on the Internet. Given its recent timeliness, the phenomenon is not understood very well yet from an academic perspective—and the large number of players entering and leaving the market indicates that we are still in a phase of experimentation from a practical viewpoint. Knowledge on for instance how best to arrange such platforms or what makes a particular crowdinvesting campaign successful is desperately needed from a practical perspective. The first volume is thus highly relevant from both a practical and academic perspective. We are therefore very thankful to the editors of this particular volume for accepting the challenge of collecting what is state-of-the-art knowledge on crowdfunding. Readers will find a useful combination of rigorous, evidenced-based academic perspectives and seasoned professionals' views on crowdfunding. This unique combination of timeliness and perspectives makes the volume really stand out in the emerging stream of literature on crowdfunding—which is why we are convinced that it will develop to become a standard reference for everyone interested in this exciting phenomenon.

Hohenheim, Germany Andreas Kuckertz
Trier, Germany Joern H. Block

Preface

While the world economy was brought to its knees in 2008 by the financial structures created in search of profit maximisation, approved by the world's leading economists and policymakers, the brunt of the crisis was borne by the common citizen, the tax payer. In some countries, the impact was more visible than in others, but the result has been a deep distrust of financial institutions and economic theory across the board by many citizens. This created a welcome breeding ground for the idea of crowdfunding: a collaborative, Internet-based solution of allocating money and resources, across geographies, directly to the projects of interest, circumnavigating the incumbent financial services firms.

If 2008 signposted a significant increase in crowdfunding activity, leading to a market worth billions of Euros in Europe alone within only a few years, 2013 was the year crowdfunding received worldwide recognition and captured the interest of established financial services industry, economists, politicians, and corporations. Institutions like the World Bank, the European Commission, the U.S. Government, as well as some of the world's largest banks, corporations, and top universities jumped on the bandwagon. Until then, the crowdfunding sector had to a great extent been driven by entrepreneurs, many with a broader understanding of the social need for innovating financial services and power structures within our economies. Crowdfunding was a democratic tool to take back the decision power from banks and corporations over where to put our own money and what products should be created and sold within a collaborative economy.

Simultaneously, the scientific research underpinning this phenomenon has been gaining ground. Since 2010, crowdfunding has been explored from different perspectives in various disciplines, such as the social sciences, psychology, information technology, economics, and entrepreneurship research. But we are far away from an elaborated research field. In 2013, there was hardly any relevant academic discussion on this topic. The first papers had started to appear here and there, and a few conferences picked up this topic as a side issue, but the data available for relevant studies were limited and the scope of the academic discussion was negligible.

On this basis, the concept for this publication was conceived in late 2013 and we set out to convince a cross-selection of academics, who had worked on crowdfunding, to act as our editorial board, double-peer reviewing all received contributions. In the process of forming this group, many questions were raised about the proposed aim and vision of the publication, and it did not only find support. The end result, however, was the formation of an editorial board that fully subscribed to our vision. The result left us happy and unconventional.

We are proud to have the following distinguished persons involved as members of this volume's editorial board:

- Prof. Dr. Ralf Beck, Fachhochschule Dortmund, Germany
- Prof. Ali Dardour, KEDGE Business School, France
- Dr. Dan Marom, Hebrew University of Jerusalem, Israel
- Prof. Ivana Pais, Università Cattolica del Sacro Cuore, Italy
- Prof. Dr. Andreas Will, Technische Universität Ilmenau, Germany

The European Crowdfunding Network (ECN), the pan-European interest group of crowdfunding platforms, issued two open calls for papers in early 2014, one for academics and one for practitioners. Researchers from all academic institutions and fields were welcome to participate with their scientific work in this publication. We especially wanted to encourage young scholars and Ph.D. candidates to contribute to the edited volume with their research findings. If crowdfunding was disrupting established beliefs of how modern markets should work and how financial services should be designed, then we needed a disruptive view of academic research on crowdfunding, too.

Instead of inviting the big names in entrepreneurship research, who so far had not realised the value of crowdfunding to our society, we aimed to give the floor to academics who still had to prove themselves. We believe that it will be this new generation of academic researchers who will be the thought leaders of tomorrow. But in reality, today's young academic researcher is as likely to be an innovator in the real economy tomorrow, leaving his university days behind in order to add value to a business or another organisation. In order to broaden the scope and to answer related requests, we decided to set up a second open call, welcoming also practitioners to enlarge the scientific perspective by a few selected practical issues. And in the end, our open call also encouraged leading scientists in their research field to contribute to our volume, a fact of which we are very proud.

Welcome were both shorter (e.g. summaries of existing or forthcoming works) and longer contributions (e.g. new examinations). All submissions were double-blind peer reviewed by our editorial board, following certain evaluation criteria to ensure the volume's high quality. Those articles where reviewers had significantly differing opinions were then submitted to a third reviewer. Contributions with potential, but which could not convince the board completely, were returned to the authors with the request that they rework these papers. After another review by the editorial board, the accepted papers were sent to an external proofreader for general language checks. Together with the reviewer's detailed feedback, we asked the authors to do another revision of their articles. Last but not least, we did a final check of all articles prior to the final revisions by the authors.

We very much appreciate that Prof. Dr. Joern Block and Prof. Dr. Andreas Kuckertz invited us to publish our edited volume on crowdfunding as the first edition of the *FGF Studies in Small Business and Entrepreneurship* showing its high relevance for both research and practice. This first compendium on crowdfunding theory and practice highlights relevant current and future issues. It could be used as a guideline and will advance classification in an emerging research field.

Our overall motivation and objective in 2014 was the foundation of an interdisciplinary scientific work group on crowdfunding within the European Crowdfunding Network. With this research group, we wanted to contribute to a better comprehension of crowdfunding, encourage further fundamental research, and contribute to a systematisation of this research field. But mostly we wanted to bring together scientists conducting research on crowdfunding in Europe. This volume is just the first step towards identifying the key European actors in crowdfunding research.

Since then, we have collaborated with numerous scholars, universities, and academic initiatives in order to further scientific research into crowdfunding. In October 2014, the ECN Scientific Work Group joined FGF's annual scientific conference G-Forum 2014 in Oldenburg—the largest conference on entrepreneurship research in Germany, Switzerland, and Austria with more than 300 academic participants—organising two inspiring panels on crowdsourcing and crowdfunding, as well as a panel discussion with practitioners. Further publications and activities such as conferences and meetings are planned. Thus, interested scholars are invited to join this group at any time.

We would like to thank our editorial board, the series editors, and Springer for their support and, of course, the authors who contributed to this volume for their excellent work.

Ilmenau, Germany
Brussels, Belgium
February 2015

Dennis Brüntje
Oliver Gajda

Contents

Introduction

Ralf Beck, Dennis Brüntje, Ali Dardour, Oliver Gajda, Dan Marom, Ivana Pais, and Andreas Will

Abstract Crowdfunding is part of the world's progress towards a global and digital society. The idea behind crowdfunding is not new, it is the idea of people pooling their resources in order to realise a common goal, sharing tasks and responsibilities. Yet there is a noticeable lack of scientific research on crowdfunding. This work is a collaborative effort by a new generation of forward-looking academics and practitioners from around Europe to better understand the growing phenomenon of crowdfunding, its triggers and motivations, and how it may be harnessed by organisations and individuals alike to better our lives, to strengthen our economies and to optimise our use of resources. This introductory chapter focuses crowdfunding's relevance for research, society and the economy, and provides an overview of the book's contents and its objectives.

Keywords Innovation • Digitisation • Economy • Crowdfunding • Crowdsourcing

Tomorrow The word itself holds such promise and excitement. Think of the possibilities that tomorrow can bring: the start of a new day, a new era, a new age.

Scientific Work Group at the European Crowdfunding Network AISBL

R. Beck
Fachhochschule Dortmund, University of Applied Sciences and Arts, Dortmund, Germany

D. Brüntje (✉) • A. Will
Technische Universität Ilmenau, Ilmenau, Germany
e-mail: dennis.bruentje@tu-ilmenau.de

A. Dardour
KEDGE Business School, Bordeaux, France

O. Gajda
European Crowdfunding Network AISBL, Brussels, Belgium
e-mail: oliver.gajda@eurocrowd.org

D. Marom
Hebrew University of Jerusalem, Jerusalem, Israel

I. Pais
Università Cattolica del Sacro Cuore, Milan, Italy

D. Brüntje, O. Gajda (eds.), *Crowdfunding in Europe*, FGF Studies in Small Business and Entrepreneurship, DOI 10.1007/978-3-319-18017-5_1

Still, we hardly ever notice when we are in the midst of a paradigm shift. The world seems to change gradually all around us and it is not until much later that we look back and realise the magnitude of the change that our world underwent and its importance in our lives. In fact, one might feel it is hard to notice or even get excited about innovation at all, with so many seemingly ground-breaking achievements vying for our attention every day.

So when you hear about this new concept called crowdfunding that is going to revolutionise your life, you may not be so impressed, and understandably so. After all, what is so exciting about a bunch of people paying for something they want, or need, or believe in? You have probably already heard ten better ideas before breakfast, right?

Wrong. Crowdfunding is the next step in the world's progress towards a globalised society promoting cultural and geographical diversification, towards pacification and education of all people, towards economic stability and equality, in our efforts to close distances and bridge gaps—crowdfunding is what is next.

The idea behind crowdfunding itself is not a novel concept; it has been around for centuries, even millennia. The idea of people pooling their resources in order to fund a common goal is as old as people living in communities, sharing tasks and responsibilities. The use of collective funds and resources is the driving force of local community efforts. It is a key factor behind civil society, arts or cultural projects and all grass-roots movements. Even the Statue of Liberty on Staten Island was partly funded by the masses following a public call for financial support in the newspapers, not unlike a modern-day crowdfunding project.

So why has this idea of pooling resources become a hot topic all of a sudden? Why is crowdfunding more important today than it was when Lady Liberty was being constructed? The answer is, of course, the Internet, the World Wide Web. This is the backbone of the global digital revolution, which has created new avenues of communication and cooperation.

Crowdfunding is, as part of the digital revolution, in essence a democratic, internet-based mechanism, utilizing elements of free trade and collaborative wisdom, to pool people and communities around a common cause. By giving money and support to a project on crowdfunding websites, people are shaping society by deciding which idea is worthwhile pursuing and which is not, and they are doing so by managing their own resources and time, investing their own money.

This book, perhaps in fitting symbolism of its subject matter, is a collaborative effort by a new generation of forward-looking academics and practitioners from around Europe, all learned in their respective fields, to better understand this growing phenomenon, its triggers and motivations, and how it may be harnessed by organisations and individuals alike to better our lives, to strengthen our economies and to optimise our use of resources.

Today, governments, companies, investors and banks are beginning to realise the potential for financial growth that crowdfunding offers in modern economies. Indeed, crowdfunding is not just a mechanism for acquiring resources, but also for managing them, and as such it can be adapted for a multitude of applications.

Crowdfunding came to the fore during turbulent economic times, and did so with little interference from formal authorities, answering the need for disintermediation of the rights (as innovators, investors and shapers of society) of citizens. However, in order to ensure that this trend continues in a positive, constructive direction we must learn to shape its growth.

To that end, we must rely on the three pillars of Regulation, Education and Research (De Buysere, Gajda, Kleverlaan, & Marom, 2012). We must ensure appropriate rules and measures are in place so that people and organisations have the security they need in order to engage in crowdfunding freely and unreservedly. We must educate entrepreneurs of all shapes and sizes on the best ways to run successful crowdfunding campaigns, and we must educate funders on the best practices for investing their money in order for crowdfunding to reach its full potential. But, perhaps most importantly, we must research and study every aspect of crowdfunding so that our regulators and educators have the information they need to do their part. This book is a first step in this direction.

In Part I this book elaborates crowdfunding's *status quo as an emerging research field*. Gierczak, Bretschneider, Haas, Blohm and Leimeister start off by providing a deeper understanding of the rise of crowdfunding as an alternative funding opportunity. Moritz and Block continue with a state-of-the-art overview of crowdfunding literature and present directions for future research. Gossel, Brüntje and Will complete this section by outlining a research programme on the societal relevance and the potential of crowdfunding.

Part II explores the different *regional examinations on crowdfunding*. Hagedorn and Pinkwart analyse the process of equity-based crowdfunding in Germany from the perspective of a capital seeker. Guerzoni, Peirone, Pais and Miglietta provide an analysis of geographical and socio-economic characteristics of crowdfunders on the Italian market. Ramos and González present a first attempt to measure the jobs created by projects funded through crowdfunding in Spain. Looking beyond Europe, Torkanovskiy makes a preliminary exploration of the underlying economics of Russian crowdfunding and its relationship with the international crowdfunding community. And Funk analyses the World Bank Report on Crowdfunding's 2013 procedural methods and their applicability to China.

Part III of this book attempts to address the far-reaching effect of crowdfunding in different settings with an *analysis of specific application areas in crowdfunding*. Hooghiemstra and De Buysere explore regulatory obstacles, and propose remedies for crowdfunding regulation. Kirilova examines the impact of debt crowdfunding for civic projects on the optimal portfolio of a socially responsible investor. Marelli and Ordanini set out to deepen the understanding of crowdfunding campaigns through an investigation of 500 Kickstarter projects, in order to deduce success factors. Joenssen and Müllerleile discuss the theoretical effects of scarcity management in the crowdfunding context, and investigate this empirically via an analysis of 42,996 projects from Indiegogo.com. Lastly, Gholamzadeh Nasrabadi analyses the most relevant aspects of equity crowdfunding beyond the obvious financial sphere.

This volume concludes with *selected case studies on crowdfunding practice* (Part IV) from research and practice. By using their best practices from Austria with a crowdsourcing and a crowdfunding platform, Willfort and Weber introduce the crowdpower 2.0 concept, which combines open innovation approaches with the latest crowd technologies. As an academic, Banhatti focuses on using crowdfunding for financing the initial phases of a social enterprise, presenting a case study of the Glow project. Again, with a crowdfunding industry background, Risterucci provides with his "Ten Commandments of Crowdfunding" a self-assessment approach, including essential rules to take into account when considering whether to use crowdfunding as a marketing and funding tool.

In the world of research, this book is indeed just the first step, but one of many to come. It is the first stone of our ongoing efforts to support the three pillars that are the framework for crowdfunding. And like crowdfunding itself, this is an enterprise that benefits from the power of many. The more people who get involved in relevant research, the faster and better this industry will grow. This is a new frontier and we need as many hands and minds as we can gather to explore it. So whether you are a newcomer to this field, a veteran explorer, or just curious, consider this an open call for collaboration and knowledge sharing.

While this book aims to enlighten and introduce people to the subject of crowdfunding, it is also meant to raise the level of discussion in this field in academic circles and beyond. It wants to provoke thought and inspire debate on this exciting topic. It is also meant to provide tools to people who see potential in the crowd-empowered phenomenon. Most importantly, it is a call to developers, investors, entrepreneurs, CEOs, researchers, academics, community leaders, government officials and the general public, to join the conversation and enrich it by contributing their knowledge and experience. Help us to realise the possibilities of our tomorrow.

Reference

De Buysere, K., Gajda, O., Kleverlaan, R., & Marom, D. (2012). *A framework for European crowdfunding*. Retrieved from http://www.eurocrowd.org/files/2013/06/FRAMEWORK_EU_CROWDFUNDING.pdf

Part I
Status Quo of an Emerging Research Field

Crowdfunding: Outlining the New Era of Fundraising

Michael M. Gierczak, Ulrich Bretschneider, Philipp Haas, Ivo Blohm, and Jan Marco Leimeister

Abstract Crowdfunding is increasingly gaining attention in theory and practice. Various platforms have emerged, offering entrepreneurs and project owners the possibility to raise money from an undefined group of online users ("crowd"). In this article we aim to provide a deeper understanding of the rise of crowdfunding as an alternative funding opportunity by discussing its main characteristics, the market development, different classification approaches, its fields of application and by providing directions for future research.

Keywords Crowdfunding • Crowdinvesting • Crowdsourcing • Crowdfunding types • Crowdfunding platforms

1 Introduction

The development of Web 2.0 technologies within the past decade has enabled the evolution of new and innovative business models, in which the digital user plays an increasingly important role by changing the way goods are being used and consumed (Brenner et al., 2014). This digital user is no longer located at the end of the value chain. He is an integral part of it, a co-decision-maker. This change requires whole industries to think and act differently—leading to a fundamental transformation from offline business models to digital ones. In this context, crowdsourcing is a striking example. It describes the outsourcing of various tasks to an undefined group of people using information technologies (Blohm, Leimeister, & Krcmar,

M.M. Gierczak (✉) • U. Bretschneider
Information Systems, Kassel University, Pfannkuchstraße 1, 34121 Kassel, Germany
e-mail: michael.gierczak@uni-kassel.de

P. Haas • I. Blohm
Institute of Information Management (IWI), University of St. Gallen, Müller-Friedberg-Strasse 8, 9000 St. Gallen, Switzerland

J.M. Leimeister
Information Systems, Kassel University, Pfannkuchstraße 1, 34121 Kassel, Germany

Institute of Information Management (IWI), University of St. Gallen, Müller-Friedberg-Strasse 8, 9000 St. Gallen, Switzerland

D. Brüntje, O. Gajda (eds.), *Crowdfunding in Europe*, FGF Studies in Small Business and Entrepreneurship, DOI 10.1007/978-3-319-18017-5_2

2013; Leimeister, 2012). It helps companies to develop new ideas and innovations by including customers' needs and requests in the innovation process (Chesbrough, 2006). Crowdsourcing approaches often aim to benefit from the wisdom of the crowd (Surowiecki, 2004) and from collective intelligence (Leimeister, 2010).

One of the main crowdsourcing forms—besides crowdvoting and crowdcreation—is crowdfunding (Howe, 2006; Leimeister, 2012). It can be defined as an open call—mostly through the Internet—for the provision of financial resources by a group of individuals instead of professional parties either in form of donations, in exchange for a future product or in exchange for some form of reward (Belleflamme, Lambert, & Schwienbacher, 2014; Schwienbacher & Larralde, 2012). Using a proverb, crowdfunding can be described as "many a little makes a mickle", meaning that a large amount of money can be raised by accumulating small contributions from a large group of backers. Therefore, using Internet platforms as intermediaries between individuals, start-ups or companies on the one hand, and potential backers on the other, the process of fundraising is sourced out to the crowd (Moritz & Block, 2014).

Being referred to as an innovative method of funding, the basic idea of crowdfunding is not a new phenomenon. A frequently cited example of early crowdfunding is the pedestal of the Statue of Liberty. In 1885, Joseph Pulitzer, at that time publisher of New York's newspaper "World", asked the citizens of New York for a financial contribution to the pedestal of the statue. In return, he offered to print the name of each backer in his newspaper. After 5 months, the "World" announced that the donation campaign had reached US$102,000. Remarkably, the funds of New Yorkers who donated less than US$1 made up for 80 % of the grand total (Harris, 1986). More recent examples include the 2008 election campaign of US-president Barack Obama. Obama's team managed to raise three-quarter of a billion USD by crowdfunding. Of note, about half of the overall donation sum was raised by contributions under US$200 (Kappel, 2009). Up-to-date various ventures, start-ups and individuals have already applied the method of crowdfunding (Bradford, 2012). Successful examples of crowdfunding campaigns reaching wide public attention are, for instance, the movie *Stromberg* (2011), a cinematic version of a German sitcom (BRAINPOOL Artist & Content Services GmbH, 2013) which raised 1 million euros in total in less than 1 week and *Coolest Cooler*, a portable cooler that includes extra-functions (e.g. an integrated blender and bluetooth speakers). *Coolest Cooler* was funded on *Kickstarter* attracting 62.642 backers and raising US$13,285,226 (Kickstarter, 2014a).

Since 2007 crowdfunding is gaining attention both in theory and in practice. Different researchers from all over the world investigated crowdfunding by providing new insights in this emerging research field and thus creating different views. The purpose of this article is to consolidate some of these research streams by providing a holistic view on crowdfunding and crowdfunding-related topics as well as shedding light on the crowdfunding market in general, discussing current views on crowdfunding and its types and principles, identifying common fields of application and discussing potential future research directions. Our article will help to understand crowdfunding as a new and important possibility of fundraising that has a great economic and social value.

2 The Crowdfunding Market

The crowdfunding market is still growing. The modern, digitised form of crowdfunding has its roots in the beginning of this century. Many of today's largest crowdfunding platforms are from the US and were launched from 2005 onwards. In 2010, the crowdfunding wave swapped over to Europe. From this moment on, crowdfunding started to particularly gain momentum in the UK, Germany and the Netherlands, the most mature European crowdfunding markets. The overall market numbers indicate an impressive development of crowdfunding. According to the Crowdfunding Industry Report 2013, over 800 crowdfunding platforms are currently active or in the process of being built (Massolution, 2012). The total volume is projected to US$5.1 billion in 2013 (Massolution, 2012). The biggest crowdfunding platform, *Kickstarter*, has already reached a total of US$1 billion of funds in 2014 (Kickstarter, 2014b). Nevertheless, crowdfunding has not yet reached its full potential. The growth of the crowdfunding market is not only limited to the US. Current figures from the European market show an increase in demand (Für-Gründer.de, 2014). In Germany there are 66 active crowdfunding platforms over which 19 million euros has been raised in 2013 (Blohm, Leimeister, Wenzlaff, & Gebert, 2013). Compared to 2012, the funding volume has doubled. With a share of 25 % of the global crowdfunding volume, the European crowdfunding market is the second largest in the world (Massolution, 2012).

The overall results of a Delphi study carried out by the University of St. Gallen in early 2014 show that the growth of the crowdfunding market will continue in the next years (Blohm et al., 2014). In this study, 70 experts were asked in two rounds on the future development of the crowdfunding industry in Germany, Switzerland and Austria. In detail, the experts think that the global crowdfunding volume will rise up to US$35 billion in 2020. In the same period, the crowdfunding volume of the German market is expected to rise up to 359 million euros (median). The most significant growth is expected in profit-oriented models, such as equity-based and lending-based crowdfunding. According to the experts, these two models will reach a market share of around 60–80 %, both globally and in Germany. Looking at the years ahead, the experts are convinced that crowdfunding in Germany will be able to continue to grow, in particular helping creative projects (97 %), start-ups (87 %) and young growth companies (92 %) to raise money (see Table 1).

Table 1 Development of the fields of application of crowdfunding by the year 2020 (Blohm et al., 2014)

	German-speaking market (Germany, Switzerland, Austria)				Global market			
Crowdfunding for...	Very likely (%)	Likely (%)	Unlikely (%)	Very unlikely (%)	Very likely (%)	Likely (%)	Unlikely (%)	Very unlikely (%)
Private persons	4	28	**64**	4	4	**53**	40	2
Creative projects	40	**57**	2	0	**64**	36	0	0
Start-ups	**51**	36	11	2	**70**	23	6	0
Young growth companies	13	**79**	9	0	19	**74**	6	0
Small and medium enterprises	6	36	**57**	0	9	40	**51**	0
Large corporations and multinational groups	0	0	36	**64**	0	0	40	**60**

3 A Classification of Crowdfunding

3.1 *Crowdfunding Principles*

Crowdfunding typically contains three participating stakeholders: the project initiators who seek funding for their projects, the backers who are willing to back a specific project, and the matchmaking crowdfunding platforms acting as intermediaries (Belleflamme et al., 2014). Figure 1 illustrates the crowdfunding principle, containing the three mentioned stakeholders. Each stakeholder type shows differentiating characteristics, which have to be considered by attempting to describe basic principles of crowdfunding. Based on these basic principles, three archetypes of crowdfunding can be derived.

3.1.1 Project Initiators and Backers

Most frequently, project initiators and backers are private persons (Gerber, Hui, & Kuo, 2012; Verstein, 2011). However, organisational project initiators, like start-ups or non-governmental organisations (NGOs) can be found as well (Belleflamme et al., 2014; Bradford, 2012; Schwienbacher & Larralde, 2012). Furthermore, the recent adoption of the JOBS Act in the USA indicates that there are also organisational backers (Mollick, 2014; Ordanini, Miceli, Pizzetti, & Parasuraman, 2011).

Most research on the crowdfunding stakeholders refers to backers. Studies find that the investment decision of backers is influenced by social networks (Lin, Prabhala, & Viswanathan, 2013; Zvilichovsky, Inbar, & Barzilay, 2013), herding (Burtch, 2011) and free-riding behaviour (Burtch, Ghose, & Wattal, 2013). Lin, Boh, and Goh (2014) summarise that crowdfunding is manifold and addresses diverse interests. Backers also differ in their motivation for participation

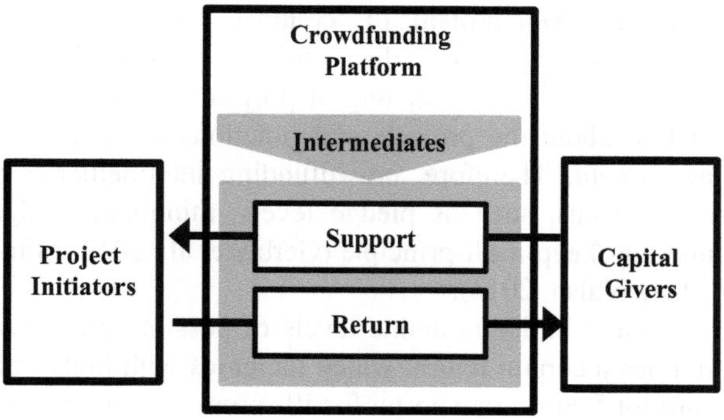

Fig. 1 The crowdfunding principle (Haas, Blohm, & Leimeister, 2014)

(Bretschneider, Knaub, & Wieck, 2014). In the crowdfunding context, backers observe and are aware of the decisions from other backers and are influenced by their behaviour (Bretschneider et al., 2014). Family and friends are often important groups of backers in crowdfunding projects (Agrawal, Catalini, & Goldfarb, 2011). Agrawal et al. (2011) argue as follows: Backers could be motivated to support projects to which they have an emotional relationship, projects with which they are familiar, or projects that are initiated by somebody they have a friendship identification with. This is discussed as the direct identification-motive. Another motive theoretically discussed in the crowdfunding literature is regional identification. This motive is based on the geographical proximity between a project initiator and a backer (Agrawal et al., 2011; Lin & Viswanathan, 2013). It is argued that investors have a "home bias" in the allocation of credit (Lin & Viswanathan, 2013). The return-motive is primarily discussed in the context of equity-based crowdfunding. Bretschneider et al. (2014) discuss this motive in view of a backers' goal of obtaining profit and/or capital gains on the invested capital. Further, there is the recognition-motive. In general, recognition is found to be a basic human need, as it gives people a sense of self-esteem (Nerdinger, 2006). This motive was discovered, for example, by Hars and Ou (2002) in open source software communities. In these communities, users expect positive reactions from other participants and feel proud when third parties acknowledge their contributions. Applied to the crowdfunding case, Bretschneider et al. (2014) argue as follows: The fact that backers are prominently visualised on a crowdfunding platform through their names may be perceived by these backers as an opportunity to receive recognition. More generally speaking, backers may invest in a project to receive recognition for their investment from other people, the community and the society (Bretschneider et al., 2014).

3.1.2 Crowdfunding Platform

Assessing the intermediary crowdfunding platform, several distinctive characteristics can be found. They refer to the funding mechanism, the fundamental specialisation of the crowdfunding platform and the type of support/return (Haas et al., 2014).

Funding Mechanism In contrast to traditional financial intermediaries, crowdfunding platforms do not borrow, pool, and lend money on their own account. They focus on the matching of project initiators and backers by providing information about the projects and functionalities, e.g. for reducing the risks of the investment. Therefore, crowdfunding intermediaries provide particular funding mechanisms, such as pledge levels, minimum pledge amounts and the all-or-nothing-/keep-it-all-principle (Gerber et al., 2012; Mitra & Gilbert, 2014; Mollick, 2014; Walsh, 2014).

Project initiators define levels of possible pledge amounts. Each pledge level implies a certain return, which increases with higher pledge amounts (e.g. a postcard for 5 euros, or a poster for 10 euros). A minimum pledge amount represents the lowest possible sum, which can be pledged by the backers. The minimum level of the pledge amount varies widely from almost zero, e.g. for charity projects, up to 100 or 1,000 euros for start-up funding. Central to most crowdfunding platforms is the all-or-nothing-principle (Cumming, Leboeuf, & Schwienbacher, 2014). Following the all-or-nothing-principle, project initiators are only paid out the collected amount in case they reach their pre-defined funding goal. This is based on the assumption that backers are only able to accomplish their project and to deliver the promised returns if they have the complete resources required for doing so. However, some crowdfunding platforms are based on a keep-it-all-principle in which project initiators receive any collected sum (Gerber et al., 2012). This funding principle is particularly used for charitable projects or projects which use crowdfunding as a subordinate source of funding (Blohm, Leimeister, Wenzlaff, et al., 2013).

Specialisation The Internet economy is characterised by so-called hyperspecialisation (Malone, Laubacher, & Johns, 2011). Serving the highly heterogeneous needs and requirements of project initiators and backers, crowdfunding platforms focus on specific niches and serve a particular segment of the crowdfunding market. Thus, crowdfunding platform specialisation may reach from innovative and creative projects or products (Agrawal, Catalini, & Goldfarb, 2010), start-ups and new businesses (Ahlers, Cumming, Günther, & Schweizer, 2012; Schwienbacher & Larralde, 2012) to sustainability and charity projects (Burtch et al., 2013).

Support and Return Type The most obvious characteristic of a crowdfunding platform is the type of return provided by the project initiator. In crowdfunding, project initiators offer a bandwidth of possible returns, reaching from altruistic returns to financial compensation. From a legal perspective, Bradford (2012) distinguishes five returns: (1) No compensation—The backer makes a donation in order to support projects for the greater good. (2) Reward—The backer receives a non-monetary return. (3) Pre-ordered product—The backer's support is a prepayment for a product. (4) Interests—The backer participates in a loan. (5) Profit shares—The backer receives equity shares from the project (e.g. a start-up). The degree of complexity for the provision of capital and the resulting returns increase from donation, rewards, pre-selling, lending and equity, as shown in Fig. 2 (Hemer, Schneider, Dornbusch, & Frey, 2011).

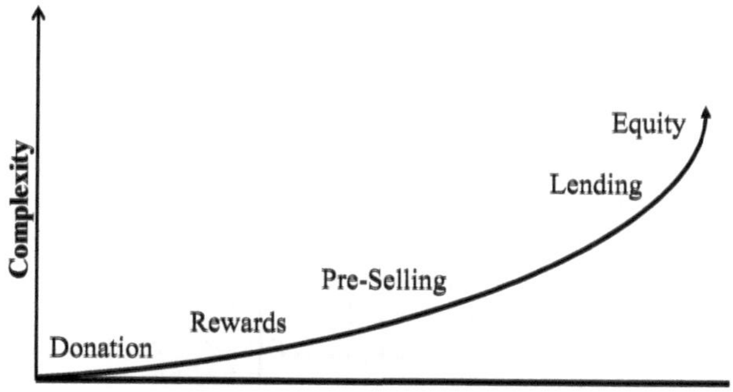

Fig. 2 Complexity of return/support types (according to Hemer et al., 2011)

3.2 Crowdfunding Types

To summarise these differentiating characteristics, crowdfunding platforms differ on multiple dimensions. Thus, it is not surprising that different types of crowdfunding exist. In order to systemise crowdfunding and to develop a classification scheme for crowdfunding, researchers presented multiple approaches in the last few years. All of them are based on the return type offered for the backers' support. Beyond Bradford's (2012) legal distinction, researchers and practitioners have proposed different classifications of crowdfunding. Hemer (2011) distinguishes the seven types of donation, sponsoring, pre-ordering, membership fees, crediting, lending, and profit-sharing. Belleflamme et al. (2014) identify the two poles pre-ordering and profit-sharing. Further, the consulting agency Massolution (2012) developed the most common classification so far that differentiates between reward-based crowdfunding (subsuming rewards and pre-ordering), crowdlending, crowdinvesting and crowddonation.

All these classifications are based on one single aspect—the return type. This neglects that crowdfunding platforms differ on many dimensions, which have to be considered when distinguishing crowdfunding types. In this respect, Haas et al. (2014) identified 13 differentiating characteristics of crowdfunding platforms by linking crowdfunding to the theory of financial intermediation. Applying cluster analysis, they examine three generic crowdfunding archetypes. By taking a holistic view and considering multiple characteristics, these archetypes can be differentiated by their pursued value proposition, determining which project initiators are attracted in order to satisfy the backers' specific demands, e.g. regarding project type, return, risk, and platform functionalities for matchmaking. In total, Haas et al. (2014) identify three distinct types of crowdfunding, as shown in Fig. 3—Hedonism, Altruistic and For Profit.

Hedonism The hedonic value proposition primarily describes a crowdfunding type where backers pledge for innovative and creative projects and products, such as the well-known *Pebble* smart watch or the Oscar-winning movie *Inocente*, and receive a non-monetary return in form of pre-ordered products or rewards. Funding mechanisms are quite rigid, in order to reduce the risk of underfinancing and in order to motivate backers to spend more money. These platforms mostly apply the all-or-nothing principle and set minimum pledge amounts and pledge levels. Typical

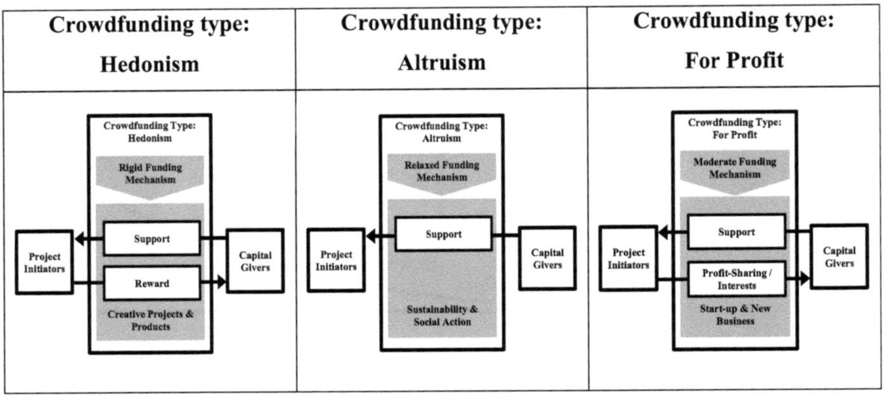

Fig. 3 Overview over crowdfunding types (Haas et al., 2014)

crowdfunding platforms within this type are *Kickstarter* or *Indiegogo*. These platforms have in common that they try to address a sense of interest or joy and thus strive to create hedonistic value that is realised by supporting such projects.

Altruism With the focus on charitable projects, this types prevailing form of support are donations. Thus no compensation is offered. Backers support projects of this kind for the "greater good" or altruistic reasons. Typical platforms, pursuing an altruistic value proposition include *Crowdrise* and *Kiva*. Loose funding mechanisms ensure greatest possible support for these projects. Therefore, these platforms do not use minimum pledge amounts or pledge levels and apply a keep-it-all principle.

For Profit A crowdfunding type with a profit-oriented value proposition often focuses on the funding of start-ups, but also on the granting consumer credits. Therefore, backers are offered monetary returns, like interests or profit shares. The value proposition aims at the profit orientation of backers. Representative platforms with a profit-oriented value proposition are *FundedByMe* which offers a profit-sharing model or the peer-to-peer-lending platform *Prosper*. Funding mechanisms are of moderate rigidity, in order to ensure enough flexibility for the individual requirements of start-ups. Therefore, these platforms apply pledge levels as well as minimum pledge amounts and use the keep-it-all and all-or-nothing principle alternatively.

4 Potentials and Challenges of Crowdfunding

4.1 Potentials

The potentials of crowdfunding may highly vary due to the diversity of crowdfunding projects and platforms.

Fundraising The main potential of crowdfunding is the acquisition of capital. In this regard, crowdfunding may help to overcome an early-stage gap of start-ups, provide small- and medium-sized enterprises with capital to fund certain projects, or enable the realisation of creative, altruistic, ecological, and social projects (Belleflamme, Lambert, & Schwienbacher, 2010). All of these projects frequently reflect some sort of niche project or projects that have a strong regional focus. As a consequence, crowdfunding offers not only the possibility of raising money for start-ups and new ventures but also makes funding possible for niche projects which perhaps are perceived as non-profitable, and thus are not able to raise money from traditional sources. Therefore, crowdfunding not only enables prominent and lucrative projects to be funded but also helps to develop less prominent projects. Thus, crowdfunding may be described as an emerging long tail offer in the financial service industry.

(Pre-)Sales This form of application of crowdfunding involves businesses collecting payments in advance for products to be delivered at some later point of time (Hemer et al., 2011). Doing so, the fix costs of producing a product can be financed before production starts. In most cases, project initiators collect money to develop a future product, which usually exists only in form of a prototype. The project initiator guarantees the delivery of the final product in return for the contributor's pledge. The value of the pledge is determined by an assessment of the market value of the product. During the campaign, products might be offered at a discounted price to encourage potential backers to support the crowdfunding campaign.

Marketing Crowdfunding is heavily based on social media and online communication, radically simplifying the sharing of information about a crowdfunding project across geographical borders (Agrawal et al., 2010). For backers, promoting crowdfunding projects by forwarding information to friends and other interested parties is very easy and much faster than using offline techniques due to decreased transaction costs. Due to their financial investments, backers frequently show a high level of involvement, making use of the available communication tools in order to create awareness for projects. As a consequence, crowdfunding enables the creation of viral marketing effects.

Market Research Due to the fast, easy, and not geographically limited access to capital, the rapid exchange of information with potential backers allows for an initial testing of business ideas (Mollick, 2014; The World Bank, 2013). In this regard, successfully funded or even overfunded projects may serve as acceptance tests of potential products and value propositions. As potential customers do have to invest their money, crowdfunding might be more apt to elicit the true beliefs regarding a product or a service than rating scale based product evaluations and other crowdsourcing approaches (Riedl, Blohm, Leimeister, & Krcmar, 2013).

Co-creation Many crowdfunding projects have benefited from the crowd's feedback. This feedback can reach from simple questions regarding a future product or service, to concrete suggestions for improvement, or even innovative new ideas. Crowdfunding, therefore, is based on the fundamental idea of co-creation, in the sense that customers or backers are directly integrated into value creation (Blohm, Leimeister, & Krcmar, 2013).

4.2 Challenges

Besides the manifold potentials, crowdfunding as a source of financing may also pose some challenges. Uncertainty and risk for backers and cost of capital for the project initiator are the most important ones.

Uncertainty and Risk Usually, the investment decisions of backers are not based on solid financial data but influenced by a high degree of emotionality and various decision biases, such as herding or supporting regional projects (Agrawal et al., 2011; Burtch et al., 2013). As a consequence, the funding usually implies risk and uncertainty. For instance, backers may not receive the return as specified. In this regard, start-ups going bankrupt or delayed delivery of pre-sold products are among the most prevalent problems (Gierczak, Bretschneider, & Leimeister, 2014). However, crowdfunding does not only include uncertainty for backers but also for project initiators. For instance, many project initiators who use crowdfunding as pre-sales mechanisms do not possess scalable production facilities. As a consequence, many products and other rewards are delivered with delay, potentially damaging the reputation of the project initiator. This may also decrease profitability of the project due to unforeseen extra costs.

Cost of Capital In sum, crowdfunding—compared to other forms of financing—exhibits high costs of capital (Agrawal, Catalini, & Goldfarb, 2013). On average, crowdfunding platforms request about 10 % of the raised capital and frequently charge additional fees for due diligence of projects or insurances reducing uncertainty and risk for the backers. Further, project initiators need to account costs for the potential returns such as interests, shared profits, discounts, or other types of rewards. Conducting crowdfunding campaigns frequently requires high efforts with respect to preparing a video and other information supporting the campaign, the management of the campaign itself (e.g. responding to questions of potential backers), and potentially increased investor relation efforts after the end of the project.

5 Future Research Directions

In view of the relatively new crowdfunding phenomenon, research lacks a deeper knowledge on crowdfunding and crowdfunding related topics. Therefore, no or only limited statements can be made with regard to a wide variety of questions (Burtch, Benedetto, & Mudambi, 2014), as for, for instance, backers' motivation to support a crowdfunding campaign as well as project initiators' motivation to start a project, the influence of diverse facets of perceived risk on the funding behaviour and crowdfunding as an alternative fundraising method for small and medium enterprises. Crowdfunding research efforts cover inter alia topics on the effective use of crowdfunding (Schwienbacher & Larralde, 2012), different types of customers (Ordanini et al., 2011), the project-specific selection of crowdfunding platforms (Belleflamme et al., 2014), determinants of project success and failure, e.g. success factors (Mollick, 2014) or the influence of creativity and hedonic value (Schulz, Haas, Blohm, & Leimeister, 2015), investment decisions of backers, e.g. geographic barriers (Agrawal et al., 2010), the prevalence of herding behaviour (Burtch, 2011) or free riding behaviour (Burtch et al., 2013).

5.1 Backers' Motivation

In view of this, research still lacks a deeper knowledge about backers' motivation for participating in crowdfunding initiatives. In particular, empirically validated knowledge on what motivates the crowd to invest in certain projects is very limited, even though the motives to participate in other forms of crowdsourcing initiatives have been well investigated. For example, Bretschneider, Leimeister, and Mathiassen (2015) investigated why the crowd develops ideas for firms in crowdsourcing for innovation communities. However, there are calls to investigate a crowd's motivation for crowdfunding separately (Lehner, 2012; Moritz & Block, 2014), since it is expected that backers' crowdfunding motives differ significantly from motives for engaging in other forms of crowdsourcing initiatives. According to this and as presented in Sect. 3.1, preliminary research results discusses a few possible motives but they are still incomplete and just derived from theory and—as already mentioned—not empirically validated. For example, Bretschneider et al. (2014) discuss herding behaviour as a possible influencing motive for participation in crowdfunding. Banerjee (1992) describes herding behaviour as "everyone doing what everyone else is doing" (p. 798). Backers' motives already discussed in literature are not an exhaustive list of motives. Certainly, there are a lot more motives to be detected and to be derived from theory. Hence, crowdfunding researchers should focus on insights from motivation research and carefully analyse and screen the body of knowledge in this field. These efforts would certainly reveal further possible motivation factors that are relevant and applicable to the crowdfunding context. Also, there is the need for empirically validating backers' motivation factors in crowdfunding.

5.2 Project Initiators' Motivation

One further possible direction is strongly related to the preceding remarks. It is still unclear why project initiators are motivated to use crowdfunding. One might be tempted to assume that it is of course the need for capital, which motivates project initiators to engage in crowdfunding. Even if this is right in many or most cases, it is by no means the only reason. Why project initiators are actually using crowdfunding might be the most basic question in this field, as it refers to the fundamental purpose of crowdfunding, which is the starting point and value proposition for any crowdfunding business model. As shown in the discussion about the fields of application of crowdfunding, combining the wisdom of the crowd (Surowiecki, 2004) with an efficient resource allocation mechanism (Belleflamme et al., 2014; Mollick, 2014; Schwienbacher & Larralde, 2012), which overcomes information asymmetries (Ahlers et al., 2012; Burtch et al., 2013) and transaction costs (Agrawal et al., 2010; Bakos, 1998) on an entertaining platform, reveals manifold opportunities, which address diverse project initiator's motives. A differentiated view on project initiators' motives is necessary in order to understand them. Therefore, project initiators' motives should be studied with respect to the different crowdfunding types, as they might differ a lot. Future studies should examine project initiators' motives to use crowdfunding instead of other forms of funding. This will highlight new insights into crowdfunding and new facets of this topic. Studying project initiators' motives provides a better understanding of different crowdfunding types, as it focuses on the value for the users not on how it works. Any business model should take a customer-centred perspective, rather than a functional perspective. Therefore, functionalities should serve the purpose of building proper crowdfunding business models, in order to get a better understanding of the principles and their correlations. Studying project initiators' motives will have important practical implications as well, as it provides insights in what actual crowdfunding platforms have to offer in order to satisfy customer needs. Knowledge about project initiators' motives will reveal manifold niches for new crowdfunding platforms as well as new fields of application for crowdfunding in general.

5.3 *Risk in Crowdfunding*

A further research direction should focus on what influences a customer's decision on whether or not to support a crowdfunding initiative financially. One possible direction derived from e-commerce and human behaviour literature could be the empirical investigation of perceived risk in crowdfunding (Gierczak et al., 2014). For practitioners, risk has been widely considered to be one of the important factors that influence customers' buying behaviour. To adequately assess and reduce these risks, it is crucial for project initiators and intermediaries to know which risk dimensions are of greatest concern to consumers. Risks mainly occur due to information asymmetries in transactions, in which the seller usually possesses more information than the buyer (Pavlou & Gefen, 2004). In general, perceived risks play a crucial role in all types of consumer behaviour (Mitchell, 1992). The more risks occur, the less likely a consumer is to purchase (Forsythe & Shi, 2003).

Therefore, according to Mitchell (1999), perceived risks are powerful at explaining consumers' behaviour because "consumers are more often motivated to avoid mistakes than to maximise utility in purchasing" (p. 454). Knowing the risks that arise in a crowdfunding campaign will help to systematically design and implement potential risk-reducing elements and strategies into the crowdfunding platforms and projects in order to attract the crowd to invest and therefore to increase their success (Mollick, 2014). Doing so can further help to convert some visitors into backers and thus helps to retain and expand the base of backers.

5.4 *Crowdfunding for Small and Medium Enterprises*

Small and medium enterprises (SME) seeking financial support from traditional funding opportunities—bank loans and credits—might now face more challenges upon their request than several years ago. Due to the financial market crisis and the resulting regulations, these requests seem to be significantly more difficult. In this regard, crowdfunding is seen as a valuable alternative to the traditional funding opportunities in order to provide SME with the financial resources required (Rossi, 2014). Nevertheless, crowdfunding research still lacks deeper understanding in this field. Answering questions on how to use crowdfunding for SME, when to use it, for what purpose as well as specifying general conditions on how platforms should be designed to ensure success of a crowdfunding campaign will help to strengthen this funding method for SME, irrespective of the crowdfunding type applied. In the case of researching on the applicability of crowdfunding for SME, it is important to note that SME differ a lot, particularly due to their size.

Beside these open research questions, there are further questions that need to be answered. Among these are issues relating to the following questions: How could SME and other crowdfunding stakeholders systematically use all potentials of crowdfunding, not only in terms of fundraising? Which business models are necessary to enable all these potentials? How should marketing, sales or product development processes as well as IT-systems be adjusted to ensure the use of crowdfunding?

These above-mentioned potential future directions for research represent only a minute proportion of potential research directions. Crowdfunding in general still lacks deeper understanding. Answering these and further questions on crowdfunding will help to increase its success for all involved parties (Mollick, 2014) and help to ensure the long-term efficiency and sustainability of crowdfunding in total (Burtch et al., 2013).

6 Conclusion

The aim of this article was to create a better understanding of the continuously changing field of crowdfunding by discussing different fundamentals and potential future research directions in order to make the term "crowdfunding" become more accessible for backers, project initiators and intermediaries as well as for other interested parties. Crowdfunding is an umbrella term that basically describes the funding of a project or venture by many individuals (the crowd) using the Internet. Through crowdfunding, all kinds of projects that would otherwise eventually not receive funding get the possibility of raising money. Therefore, crowdfunding is currently gaining—and will gain in the future—a lot of attention from practice and theory. This emerging importance is already evident from current market figures and the predicted future development. In the near future, the funding volume will increase significantly, new crowdfunding platforms will be established and others will be withdrawn from the market. In total, this fragmented crowdfunding market will consolidate. As we have stated in this article, crowdfunding provides a lot of potentials. Besides its actual function of fundraising, there are further fields of interest, inter alia using crowdfunding for the purpose of (pre-)sale marketing and market research as well as for co-creating with possible future customers. There are still uncertainties and risks that may appear before, during and after a campaign. However, there is precious little knowledge about these potential risks and uncertainties. Thus, future research must examine, inter alia, the risks and uncertainties carefully and research questions on what motivates backers to participate in a crowdfunding campaign as well as what drives project imitators to call a project into being. Doing so will help to understand and bring forward this emerging field.

Acknowledgements Our thanks go to Oliver Englisch for his excellent support and valuable comments. This paper was developed within the project "The Open Innovation Project (IOIT)", funded by the European Union INTERREG IVB NWE Programme (Funding code: 166F-IOIT).

References

Agrawal, A., Catalini, C., & Goldfarb, A. (2010). *The geography of crowdfunding* (NET Institute Working Paper No. 10-08). doi:10.2139/ssrn.1692661

Agrawal, A., Catalini, C., & Goldfarb, A. (2011). *Offline relationships, distance, and the Internet: The geography of crowdfunding.* http://pages.stern.nyu.edu/~atakos/ResearchCamp/agoldfarbpaper.pdf

Agrawal, A., Catalini, C., & Goldfarb, A. (2013). *Some simple economics of crowdfunding* (NBER Working Paper Series No. 19133). doi: 10.3386/w19133

Ahlers, G. K., Cumming, D., Günther, C., & Schweizer, D. (2012). *Signaling in equity crowdfunding.* doi:10.2139/ssrn.2161587

Bakos, Y. (1998). The emerging role of electronic marketplaces on the Internet. *Communications of the ACM, 41*(8), 35–42. doi:10.1145/280324.280330

Banerjee, A. V. (1992). A simple model of herd behavior. *The Quarterly Journal of Economics, 107*(3), 797–817.

Belleflamme, P., Lambert, T., & Schwienbacher, A. (2010). *Crowdfunding: An industrial organization perspective.* Prepared for the Workshop Digital Business Models: Understanding Strategies, Paris, France.

Belleflamme, P., Lambert, T., & Schwienbacher, A. (2014). Crowdfunding: Tapping the right crowd. *Journal of Business Venturing, 29*(5), 585–609. doi:10.1016/j.jbusvent.2013.07.003

Blohm, I., Leimeister, J. M., Wenzlaff, K., & Gebert, M. (2013). *Crowdfunding-Studie 2013/2014: Analyse, Perspektiven und Erfolgsfaktoren innovativer Unternehmens- und Projektfinanzierungen*. Berlin: epubli GmbH.

Blohm, I., Leimeister, J. M., & Krcmar, H. (2013). Crowdsourcing: How to benefit from (too) many great ideas. *MIS Quarterly Executive, 12*(4), 199–211.

Blohm, I., Sieber, E., Schulz, M., Haas, P., Leimeister, J. M., Wenzlaff, K., et al. (2014). *Delphi-Studie Crowdfunding 2020—Komplement oder Substitut für die Finanzindustrie?* Norderstedt: Books on Demand.

Bradford, C. S. (2012). Crowdfunding and the federal securities laws. *Columbia Business Law Review, 2012*(1), 1–150.

BRAINPOOL Artist & Content Services GmbH. (2013). *Stromberg—Der Film*. Retrieved August 15, 2013, from http://www.myspass.de/specials/stromberg-kinofilm/

Brenner, W., Karagiannis, D., Kolbe, L., Krüger, J., Leifer, L., Lamberti, H.-J., et al. (2014). User, use & utility research. *WIRTSCHAFTSINFORMATIK, 56*(1), 65–72. doi:10.1007/s11576-013-0394-y

Bretschneider, U., Knaub, K., & Wieck, E. (2014). *Motivations for crowdfunding: What drives the crowd to invest in start-ups?* Paper presented at the 22nd European Conference on Information Systems (ECIS 2014), Tel Aviv, Israel.

Bretschneider, U., Leimeister, J. M., & Mathiassen, L. (2015). IT-enabled product innovation: Customer motivation for participating in virtual idea communities. *International Journal of Product Development, 20*(2), 126–141.

Burtch, G. (2011). *Herding behavior as a network externality*. Paper presented at the International Conference on Information Systems, Shanghai.

Burtch, G., Benedetto, C. A., & Mudambi, S. M. (2014). Leveraging information systems for enhanced product innovation. In F. J. Martínez-López (Ed.), *Handbook of strategic e-business management* (pp. 211–216). Berlin: Springer.

Burtch, G., Ghose, A., & Wattal, S. (2013). An empirical examination of the antecedents and consequences of contribution patterns in crowd-funded markets. *Information Systems Research, 24*(3), 499–519.

Chesbrough, H. W. (2006). *Open innovation: The new imperative for creating and profiting from technology*. Harvard: Harvard Business School Press.

Cumming, D., Leboeuf, G., & Schwienbacher, A. (2014). *Crowdfunding models: Keep-it-all vs. all-or-nothing*. doi: 10.2139/ssrn.2447567

Forsythe, S. M., & Shi, B. (2003). Consumer patronage and risk perceptions in Internet shopping. *Journal of Business Research, 56*(11), 867–875. doi:10.1016/S0148-2963(01)00273-9

Für-Gründer.de. (2014). *Crowdfunding-monitor*. Retrieved September 2, 2014, from http://www.fuer-gruender.de/fileadmin/mediapool/Unsere_Studien/Crowdfunding-Monitor_H1_2014_F%C3%BCr-Gr%C3%BCnder.de.pdf

Gerber, E. M., Hui, J. S., & Kuo, P.-Y. (2012). *Crowdfunding: Why people are motivated to post and fund projects on crowdfunding platforms*. Paper presented at the ACM Conference on Computer Supported Cooperative Work, Vancouver, BC, Canada.

Gierczak, M. M., Bretschneider, U., & Leimeister, J. M. (2014). *Is all that glitters gold? Exploring the effects of perceived risk on backing behavior in reward-based crowdfunding*. Paper presented at the International Conference on Information Systems (ICIS), Auckland, New Zealand.

Haas, P., Blohm, I., & Leimeister, J. M. (2014). *An empirical taxonomy of crowdfunding intermediaries*. Paper presented at the International Conference on Information Systems (ICIS), Auckland, New Zealand.

Harris, J. (1986). *A statue for America: The first 100 years of the statue of liberty*. New York: Simon & Schuster.

Hars, A., & Ou, S. (2002). Working for free? Motivations for participating in open source projects. *International Journal of Electronic Commerce, 6*(3), 25–39.

Hemer, J. (2011). *A snapshot on crowdfunding* (Working Papers Firms and Region, No. R2/2011). Karlsruhe: Fraunhofer Institute for Systems and Innovation Research ISI.

Hemer, J., Schneider, U., Dornbusch, F., & Frey, S. (2011). *Crowdfunding und andere Formen informeller Mikrofinanzierung in der Projekt- und Innovationsfinanzierung*. Stuttgart: Fraunhofer Verlag.

Howe, J. (2006). *The rise of crowdsourcing*. Retrieved June 10, 2014, from http://archive.wired.com/wired/archive/14.06/crowds.html

Kappel, T. (2009). Ex ante crowdfunding and the recording industry: A model for the U.S. *Loyola of Los Angeles Entertainment Law Review, 29*(3), 375–385.

Kickstarter. (2014a). *COOLEST COOLER: 21st century cooler that's Actually Cooler*. Retrieved August 30, 2014, from https://www.kickstarter.com/projects/ryangrepper/coolest-cooler-21st-century-cooler-thats-actually

Kickstarter. (2014b). *Kickstarter stats*. Retrieved April 18, 2014, from http://www.kickstarter.com/help/stats

Lehner, O. M. (2012). *Crowdfunding social ventures: A model and research agenda*. Paper presented at the 2012 Research Colloquium on Social Entrepreneurship, University of Oxford, Skoll Center of SAID Business School UK.

Leimeister, J. M. (2010). Collective intelligence. *Business & Information Systems Engineering (BISE), 4*(2), 245–248.

Leimeister, J. M. (2012). Crowdsourcing: Crowdfunding, crowdvoting, crowdcreation. *Zeitschrift für Controlling und Management, 56*, 388–392.

Lin, Y., Boh, W. F., & Goh, K. H. (2014). *How different are crowdfunders? Examining archetypes of crowdfunders and their choice of projects*. Retrieved November 19, 2014, from 10.2139/ssrn.2397571

Lin, M., Prabhala, N. R., & Viswanathan, S. (2013). Judging borrowers by the company they keep: Friendship networks and information asymmetry in online peer-to-peer lending. *Management Science, 59*(1), 17–35. doi:10.1287/mnsc.1120.1560.

Lin, M., & Viswanathan, S. (2013). *Home bias in online investments: An empirical study of an online crowd funding market*. doi: 10.2139/ssrn.2219546

Malone, T. W., Laubacher, R. J., & Johns, T. (2011). The big idea: The age of hyperspecialization. *Harvard Business Review, 89*(7/8), 56–65.

Massolution. (2012). *Crowdfunding industry report—market trends, composition and crowdfunding platforms*. Retrieved May 18, 2014, from http://www.crowdsourcing.org/document/crowdfunding-industry-reportabridged-version-market-trends-composition-and-crowdfunding-platforms/14277

Mitchell, V.-W. (1992). Understanding consumers' behaviour: Can perceived risk theory help? *Management Decision, 30*(3), 26–31.

Mitchell, V.-W. (1999). Consumer perceived risk: Conceptualisations and models. *European Journal of Marketing, 33*(1/2), 163–195.

Mitra, T., & Gilbert, E. (2014). *The language that gets people to give: Phrases that predict success on Kickstarter*. Paper presented at the Proceedings of the 17th ACM conference on Computer Supported Cooperative Work & Social Computing, New York, NY, USA.

Mollick, E. (2014). The dynamics of crowdfunding: An exploratory study. *Journal of Business Venturing, 29*(1), 1–16. doi:10.1016/j.jbusvent.2013.06.005

Moritz, A., & Block, J. H. (2014). Crowdfunding und Crowdinvesting: State-of-the-Art der wissenschaftlichen Literatur [Crowdfunding and Crowdinvesting: A Review of the Literature]. *ZfKE—Zeitschrift für KMU und Entrepreneurship, 62*, 57–89. doi:10.2139/ssrn.2274141

Nerdinger, F. W. (2006). Motivierung. In H. Schuler (Ed.), *Lehrbuch der Personalpsychologie* (2nd ed., pp. 385–404). Göttingen: Hogrefe.

Ordanini, A., Miceli, L., Pizzetti, M., & Parasuraman, A. (2011). Crowd-funding: Transforming customers into investors through innovative service platforms. *Journal of Service Management, 22*(4), 443–470.

Pavlou, P. A., & Gefen, D. (2004). Building effective online marketplaces with institution-based trust. *Information Systems Research, 15*(1), 37–59. doi:10.1287/isre.1040.0015
Riedl, C., Blohm, I., Leimeister, J. M., & Krcmar, H. (2013). The effect of rating scales on decision quality and user attitudes in online innovation communities. *International Journal of Electronic Commerce, 17*(3), 7–37.
Rossi, M. (2014). SMEs' access to finance: An overview from Southern Italy. *European Journal of Business and Social Sciences, 2*(11), 155–164.
Schulz, M., Haas, P., Blohm, I., & Leimeister, J. M. (2015). *How idea creativity and hedonic value influence project success in crowdfunding.* Paper presented at the 12th International Conference on Wirtschaftsinformatik (WI2015), Osnabrück, Germany.
Schwienbacher, A., & Larralde, B. (2012). Crowdfunding of small entrepreneurial ventures. In D. Cumming (Ed.), *The Oxford handbook of entrepreneurial finance* (pp. 369–391). Oxford: Oxford University Press.
Surowiecki, J. (2004). *The wisdom of crowds: Why the many are smarter than the few and how collective wisdom shapes business, economies, societies, and nations.* New York: Doubleday Books.
The World Bank. (2013). *Crowdfunding's potential for the developing world.* http://www.infodev.org/infodev-files/wb_crowdfundingreport-v12.pdf
Verstein, A. (2011). Misregulation of person-to-person lending. *The University of California Law Review, 45*(2), 445–530.
Walsh, A. (2014). SEEK!: Creating and crowdfunding a game-based open educational resource to improve information literacy. *Insights, 27*(1), 63–66.
Zvilichovsky, D., Inbar, Y., & Barzilay, O. (2013). *Playing both sides of the market: Success and reciprocity on crowdfunding platforms.* Paper presented at the International Conference on Information Systems, Milan, Italy.

Crowdfunding: A Literature Review and Research Directions

Alexandra Moritz and Joern H. Block

Abstract Crowdfunding has become important in recent years. However, there is no comprehensive overview of the economic literature on this topic. This paper provides an overview of crowdfunding literature, classified in terms of the main actors (capital seekers, capital providers, and intermediaries), and presents important research questions for future research.

Keywords Crowdfunding • Crowdinvesting • New venture financing

1 Introduction and Motivation

In the last few years, crowdfunding has emerged as an alternative source of funding for various types of projects. In the beginning, crowdfunding was mainly used to finance artists from different sectors (Agrawal, Catalini, & Goldfarb, 2013; Harzer, 2013; Meinshausen, Schiereck, & Stimeier, 2012). The establishment of various crowdfunding Internet platforms in the music sector (e.g. ArtistShare, SellaBand) made this form of financing interesting for musicians. Subsequently, other artistic and creative areas (e.g. film, journalism) have adopted the idea. Funding of companies through the crowd[1] has been discussed intensively since 2010 and explored in practice and theory. Crowdfunding is seen as a way to reduce the funding gap in the early stages of new ventures (early-stage gap) (Hemer, Schneider, Dornbusch, & Frey, 2011, p. 30; Meinshausen et al., 2012; Röthler & Wenzlaff, 2011). Funding from venture capitalists and banks is usually available only in the later development

[1] The "crowd" refers to a large number of people who come together at a specific location (here, on the Internet; the "Internet community").

A. Moritz (✉)
Trier University, Trier, Germany
e-mail: moritz@uni-trier.de

J.H. Block
Trier University, Trier, Germany

Erasmus University Rotterdam, Rotterdam, Netherlands

D. Brüntje, O. Gajda (eds.), *Crowdfunding in Europe*, FGF Studies in Small Business and Entrepreneurship, DOI 10.1007/978-3-319-18017-5_3

phases of start-ups (Berger & Udell, 1998; Robb & Robinson, 2014). In the early phases of a company's life cycle (pre-seed/seed stage), funding is typically provided by the founder himself, by his friends and family and, if possible, by business angels. If these funds are insufficient, the venture faces a funding gap (Collins & Pierrakis, 2012). This situation has been exacerbated by the financial market crisis (Block & Sandner, 2009; Duygan-Bump, Levkov, & Montoriol-Garriga, 2011; Fink, 2012; Mach, Carter, & Slattery, 2013).

The purpose of this article is to provide an overview of the academic research on crowdfunding. Given that the term crowdfunding implies raising financial resources from a large number of capital providers ("the crowd") without indicating the purpose of the funding, our review encompasses all types of crowdfunding, which include donation-based, reward-based, lending-based and equity-based crowdfunding[2] (Beck, 2012, p. 15; Collins & Pierrakis, 2012; Giudici, Nava, Rossi Lamastra, & Verecondo, 2012; Leimeister, 2012). Although we account for the scope of crowdfunding as well as for the multidisciplinary nature (Lehner, 2013) of the subject, our main focus is on the economic literature based on new ventures as the capital-seeking party. This literature review is structured according to the main actors in crowdfunding: capital seekers, capital providers, and intermediaries. The results of previous research are then discussed and open research questions are identified.

2 Review of the Scientific Literature on Crowdfunding

There are two literature reviews on crowdfunding. Bachmann et al. (2011) discuss the main results of 43 scientific articles on peer-to-peer lending. Feller, Gleasure, and Treacy (2013) structure research on crowdfunding quantitatively according to the different forms of crowdfunding without considering the specific contents of these studies. There is no comprehensive overview of crowdfunding literature focusing on companies as capital-seeking parties. The following review closes this research gap.

2.1 Literature Research and Selection Criteria

The scientific articles on crowdfunding were identified in the first step in a Google Scholar title keyword search for the terms "crowdfunding" and "crowdinvesting" (patents and citations excluded). The search returned 531 hits.[3] In the next step, the

[2] In German-speaking countries, the term crowdinvesting is often used to distinguish equity-based crowdfunding from other forms of crowdfunding.

[3] July 31, 2014.

search was continued based on the references cited in the articles. Afterwards, specific terms, such as peer-to-peer online lending, P2P lending, social lending and person-to-person lending were investigated.

A keyword-based search (including the various spellings) in several library catalogues (e.g. local and international library catalogues and electronic journal catalogues) completed the search. Due to the fact that this is a new topic, there are few studies published on this subject. For this reason, we included (unpublished) working papers in the review. The final selection of articles and working papers is based on the following criteria:

- We only considered scientific articles and working papers. Practical contributions, information guides and seminars, bachelor's and master's theses were excluded.
- The research papers were classified according to the main actors in the crowdfunding process (capital seekers, capital providers and intermediaries). Only those contributions were taken into account which appeared relevant in this context.
- The main focus was on economic research papers.

Using these criteria, 127 articles and working papers were selected for the literature review.

2.2 *Development of Scientific Research in Crowdfunding*

Crowdfunding is a recent phenomenon. Thus, many research papers on crowdfunding follow a "phenomenon-based approach" (Von Krogh, Rossi-Lamastra, & Haefliger, 2012). This involves developing a definition and description as well as a differentiation to related subjects and concepts. Before the term "crowdfunding" appeared in literature, scientific articles on lending-based crowdfunding used the terms "social lending" (Hulme & Wright, 2006) and P2P lending (i.e. "peer-to-peer") (Freedman & Jin, 2008, 2014; Herzenstein & Andrews, 2008; Klafft, 2008).[4]

The first scientific discussions mentioning "crowdfunding" were mainly focused on the legal issues under U.S. law. In 2009, Kappel analysed the legal restrictions of crowdfunding under the Securities Law from 1933[5] using the music industry as an example. Subsequently, the legal restrictions of crowdfunding dominated U.S. legal literature (see Sect. 2.3.3). Belleflamme, Schwienbacher and colleagues began discussing venture financing through crowdfunding in 2010 (Belleflamme & Lambert, 2014; Belleflamme, Lambert, & Schwienbacher, 2010, 2013a, 2013b; Schwienbacher

[4] The publication of the data of the P2P lending platform Prosper.com in the U.S. in 2007 made an important contribution to the increasing research volume (Bachmann et al., 2011).

[5] Crowdfunding models in the U.S. that provide a financial return for capital providers (lending- and equity-based crowdfunding) are in the scope of the Securities Law of 1933 (Bradford, 2012).

& Larralde, 2012) (see Sect. 2.3). A number of scientific contributions have since emerged, following a descriptive, explanatory or concept-based approach, often in combination with case studies from the respective national context (Giudici et al., 2012; Hemer, 2011; Hemer et al., 2011; Ingram, Teigland, & Vaast, 2014; Klaebe & Laycock, 2012; Kortleben & Vollmar, 2012; Martínez-cañas, 2012; Meinshausen et al., 2012; Mitra, 2012; Tomczak & Brem, 2013; Vitale, 2013; Wheat, Wang, Byrnes, & Ranganathan, 2013).

The first empirical studies are qualitative-empirical and describe the phenomenon. Initial market data were analysed and enhanced with findings from interviews (Aitamurto, 2011; Gerber, Hui, & Kuo, 2012; Hemer et al., 2011; Ley & Weaven, 2011; Röthler & Wenzlaff, 2011). Research based on quantitative data began to emerge after the platforms established themselves as intermediaries and the required transaction volumes became available or first surveys were conducted (e.g. Ahlers, Cumming, Günther, & Schweizer, 2013; Burtch, Ghose, & Wattal, 2013a; Kuppuswamy & Bayus, 2013; Mollick, 2014; Mollick & Kuppuswamy, 2014; Pierrakis & Collins, 2013).

In this paper, we analyse the content of the articles identified, structured according to the main crowdfunding actors (capital seekers (focusing on companies), capital providers, and intermediaries), classified according to their research priorities.

2.3 Crowdfunding Literature with a Focus on Capital Seekers

Crowdfunding literature focusing on the capital-seeking party is predominantly concerned with the motivations for crowdfunding, the determinants of success, and the legal restrictions of equity-based crowdfunding. Table 1 gives an overview of the studies discussed in this paper.

2.3.1 Motivations of Companies for Crowdfunding

In their interviews with crowdfunding-experienced entrepreneurs Belleflamme et al. (2013b) identify three main reasons for choosing crowdfunding to finance projects. All of the respondents stated that collecting funds was the main reason for using crowdfunding. Other motives mentioned were attracting the public's attention and receiving feedback for their products or services. Gerber et al. (2012) come to very similar conclusions. They performed semi-structured interviews with market participants and identified five categories of motivation: financing, forming relationships and networks, self-affirmation, replication of success stories and increased awareness of the product. Crowdfunding offers, according to Hemer et al. (2011), the ability to obtain funding in the early stages of a company's life cycle and thus an opportunity to close the early-stage gap. Further motives for

Table 1 Literature on crowdfunding with a focus on capital seekers

Author(s)	Content	Method	Source
Agrawal, Catalini, and Goldfarb (2011, 2014)	Importance of geographical proximity between entrepreneur and capital providers.	Quantitative	SellaBand
Belleflamme et al. (2013a)	Choice of crowdfunding type as a decision problem (pre-ordering vs. profit-sharing).	Model-based approach	–
Belleflamme et al. (2013b)	Motivations for entrepreneurs and importance of enterprise type to funding success.	Quantitative	44 direct crowdfunding transactions; questionnaires
Belleflamme et al. (2010)	Crowdfunding vs. traditional sources of funding; price discrimination possibilities; enterprise type (profit vs. non-profit).	Model-based approach	–
Bradford (2012)	Exemption proposals from the Securities Act for smaller companies through equity-based crowdfunding.	Legal analysis	Securities Act
Burtch, Ghose, and Wattal (2013b)	Importance of cultural similarities and differences in the investment behaviour of capital providers.	Quantitative	KIVA
Cohn (2012)	Critical consideration of the provisions of the JOBS Act.	Legal analysis	JOBS Act
Cumming, Leboeuf, and Schwienbacher (2014)	Chances of success for crowdfunding projects choosing the "all-or-nothing" (AON) or "keep-it-all" (KIA) model.	Quantitative	Indiegogo
Dorfleitner, Kapitz, and Wimmer (2014)	Suitability of crowdfunding for financing SMEs in Germany.	Market analysis, quantitative	Seedmatch, Companisto, Innovestment, Bankless24
Fink (2012)	Relationship between employment and crowdfunding.	Legal analysis	Securities Act, JOBS Act
Frydrych, Bock, Kinder, and Koeck (2014)	Establishing organisational legitimacy in reward-based crowdfunding.	Quantitative	Kickstarter
Gerber et al. (2012)	Motivations of capital seekers and capital providers for crowdfunding.	Qualitative	Interviews
Giudici, Guerini, and Rossi-Lamastra (2013)	Influence of social capital on the success of crowdfunding projects.	Quantitative	11 Italian platforms
Griffin (2012)	Critical analysis of H.R. 2930 (later JOBS Act).	Legal analysis	Securities Act, H.R. 2930
Hazen (2012)	Disclosure obligation under the JOBS Act under consideration of investor protection.	Legal analysis	Securities Act, JOBS Act

(continued)

Table 1 (continued)

Author(s)	Content	Method	Source
Hekman and Brussee (2013)	Social network analysis; relationship between the success of crowdfunding projects, social networks of initiators and media activities.	Quantitative	Kickstarter, Facebook
Hemer et al. (2011)	Theoretical and practical analysis of crowdfunding as an alternative to early-stage financing of start-ups.	Qualitative, literature review	Interviews, case studies
Heminway (2013a)	Proposal for the reformation of U.S. financial market regulations; regulation of risks.	Legal analysis	Securities Act
Heminway and Hoffman (2011)	Analysis of the financial instruments used in crowdfunding and legal classification.	Legal analysis	Securities Act
Hu, Li, and Shi (2014)	Optimal product and pricing decision in a reward-based crowdfunding mechanism.	Model-based approach	–
Hui, Gerber, and Greenberg (2012)	Analysis of the required effort for the capital-seeking party to prepare and execute a crowdfunding transaction.	Qualitative	Interviews (Kickstarter, Indiegogo, Rockethub)
Hui, Greenberg, and Gerber (2013)	Identification of challenges of network capabilities, activating network connections and expanding network reach.	Qualitative	Interviews (Kickstarter, Indiegogo, Rockethub)
Kappel (2009)	Possibilities of ex ante crowdfunding (compared to ex post facto) in the U.S. record market under consideration of the legal restrictions.	Market and legal analysis	Case studies; U.S. laws
Kassinger, Kaufmann, and Traeger (2013)	Short overview of the CROWDFUND Act and its main points of criticism; description of various U.S. platforms.	Market and legal analysis	CROWD-FUND Act
Kim and Hann (2013)	Examination of how geography affects crowdfunding projects; significance of crowdfunding as an alternative to traditional sources of finance.	Quantitative	Kickstarter
Klöhn and Hornuf (2012)	Analysis of the German equity-based crowdfunding market with a focus on platforms; analysis of the German and U.S. legal situation for equity-based crowdfunding.	Market and legal analysis	German and U.S. laws
Kortleben and Vollmar (2012)	Equity-based crowdfunding and agency conflicts; comparison of legal forms and its suitability for crowdfunding.	Classification and description	Case studies

(continued)

Table 1 (continued)

Author(s)	Content	Method	Source
Lehner (2014)	Process of opportunity recognition, formation and exploitation in crowdfunding for social ventures.	Qualitative	36 crowd-funded social cases
Lehner (2013)	Crowdfunding in the context of social entrepreneurship; derivation of research questions.	Literature analysis	–
Ley and Weaven (2011)	Analysis of agency dynamics and requirements for equity-based crowdfunding.	Qualitative	Interviews (11 - Australian venture capital companies)
Mach et al. (2013)	Analysis of small business loans using P2P lending.	Quantitative	LendingClub
Macht and Weatherston (2014)	Framework of crowdfunding benefits.	Literature review with framework development	–
Martin (2012)	Analysis of the JOBS Act and its key provisions; motives for crowdfunding from a business perspective and its possible consequences for a company.	Legal analysis	JOBS Act
Mollick (2014)	Success factors in crowdfunding.	Quantitative	Kickstarter
Mollick and Kuppuswamy (2014)	Outcomes of crowdfunding campaigns; advantages of crowdfunding beyond financing.	Quantitative	Survey (capital seekers on Kickstarter)
Pope (2011)	Proposals for Securities Law adjustments in the U.S. to enable equity-based crowdfunding.	Legal analysis	Securities Act and its exemptions
Saxton and Wang (2013)	Analysis of the relevant factors for online donations via social media.	Quantitative	Data of 66 non-profit organisations using Facebook
Schwienbacher and Larralde (2012)	Crowdfunding as an alternative to classical start-up financial sources; requirements for companies.	Qualitative and quantitative	Case study, interviews, questionnaires and blog contributions
Stemler (2013)	Equity-based crowdfunding before and after the JOBS Act.	Legal analysis	Securities Act, JOBS Act
Wroldsen (2013)	Regulations of the downside risks; proposals for regulations of upside risks.	Legal analysis, VC comparison	JOBS Act

crowdfunding that were identified were the speed and flexibility of funding, few formal obligations, testing the product on the market, multiplier effects, positive signalling effects[6] and the use of the "wisdom of the crowd" for various company tasks (Hemer et al., 2011; Hienerth & Riar, 2013; Macht & Weatherston, 2014; Surowiecki, 2004).

In recent years, companies have begun using their customers' knowledge for company purposes (Kleemann, Voß, & Rieder, 2008). Crowdfunding now offers consumers the chance to adopt the role of investors (Ordanini, Miceli, Pizzetti, & Parasuraman, 2011). Those who are willing to invest are largely those who believe in the success of the company and its products or services. The company is legitimised by the market (Martin, 2012) if crowdfunding is successful and at the same time it helps to build a customer base. Burtch et al. (2013a) confirm with empirical data that crowdfunding leads to increased visibility and higher product consumption. Mollick and Kuppuswamy (2014) found that crowdfunding is more than just a financing method for companies because it facilitates better access to customers, more press coverage, and greater interest from potential employees and outside funders.

In addition, crowdfunding allows companies to exploit their market potential more effectively (Belleflamme et al., 2010; Hu et al., 2014). Belleflamme et al. (2010) and Hu et al. (2014) show in a theoretical model that reward-based crowdfunding (pre-ordering) allows for price discriminations. Companies have difficulty identifying customers who are willing to pay a premium for a product being available earlier. These customers can be identified through crowdfunding, which allows companies to skim the market for these premiums. Later, Belleflamme et al. (2013a) expanded their model and included a decision problem for companies to choose between crowdfunding as a pre-ordering model and a profit-sharing model.

2.3.2 Determining Factors for Successful Crowdfunding

Companies or projects with a social or non-profit oriented background have a higher probability of receiving crowdfunding. This relationship has been confirmed both theoretically (Belleflamme et al., 2010, 2013a) and empirically (Belleflamme et al., 2013b). Capital providers are primarily interested in the realisation of the project (Belleflamme et al., 2013b). According to Belleflamme et al. (2013b), non-profit organisations have a higher credibility in fulfilling this expectation, in contrast to profit-oriented organisations. Thus, Lehner (2013) suggests that crowdfunding and social entrepreneurship[7] should harmonise.

[6] A successful crowdfunding transaction sends a positive signal about the venture to various market participants.

[7] A social entrepreneur is "a person who establishes an enterprise with the aim of solving social problems or effecting social change." Retrieved May 10, 2014, from http://www.oxforddictionaries.com/definition/english/social-entrepreneur.

Mollick (2014) analysed data from the platform Kickstarter and found that the probability of a successful crowdfunding transaction decreases as the funding amount and duration increases. The size of the capital seeker's social network, the presence of a product video and geographical proximity to capital providers increase the likelihood of successful funding (Frydrych et al., 2014; Giudici et al., 2013; Hekman & Brussee, 2013; Mollick, 2014; Saxton & Wang, 2013). In line with these results, Mollick and Kuppuswamy (2014) found that successful capital seekers had many Facebook friends (as a proxy for the social network), outside endorsements and appropriate backgrounds.

Geographical proximity was also analysed by Agrawal et al. (2011). The authors found while analysing the archival data from the music platform SellaBand that in funded projects, the average distance between the musicians and capital providers was 3,000 miles. However, at the start of funding, a greater proximity between the parties could be determined. Agrawal et al. (2011) explained this result as a family and friends effect.[8] The positive influence of geographic proximity on funding success was also found in P2P lending markets (Burtch et al., 2013b; Lin & Viswanathan, 2013). However, this home bias could not be explained by a family and friends effect. Emotional (Lin & Viswanathan, 2013) and cultural (Burtch et al., 2013b) factors, such as strong preferences for local products and services, seemed to be responsible.

2.3.3 Legal Framework

Equity-based crowdfunding (or crowdinvesting) has been discussed by U.S. legal scholars since 2009. This discussion was triggered by the question of the legality of some business models of crowdfunding platforms and the scope of application of the Securities Act of 1933 (Kappel, 2009). The legal issues, combined with the tremendous speed of growth of crowdfunding[9] and the liquidity shortage caused by the financial market crisis, led to a change in U.S. legislation (Fink, 2012; Stemler, 2013). In 2011, a legislative proposal to increase access to capital for new and small ventures was developed and came into force on April 5, 2012. The main objective of the "Jumpstart our Business Startups Act" (JOBS Act) is to make it easier and cheaper for new and small companies to raise equity capital. Title III of the JOBS Act, called the CROWDFUND Act (Capital Raising Online while Deterring Fraud

[8] This result confirms the assumption that the first people to participate in a crowdfunding transaction are typically family and friends. They know the entrepreneur and want to support the venture and its team (Agrawal et al., 2011).

[9] Crowdfunding activities worldwide increased from US$1.5 billion in 2011 to US$2.7 billion in 2012 and were expected to reach US$5.1 billion in 2013. Massolution Report 2013. Retrieved May 8, 2014, from http://www.crowdsourcing.org/editorial/2013cf-the-crowdfunding-industry-report/25107?utm_source=website&utm_medium=text&utm_content=LP+bottom&utm_campaign=2013CF+Launch.

and Unethical Non-Disclosure Act), determines the rules and requirements for issuers of equity, investors and platforms (Martin, 2012; Wroldsen, 2013). The liberalisation of the Securities Act of 1933 is heavily discussed in legal literature (e.g. Bradford, 2012; Cohn, 2012; Cumming & Johan, 2013; Griffin, 2012; Hazen, 2012; Heminway & Hoffman, 2011). Although the JOBS Act came into force in 2012, the market is still awaiting the final specifications from the Securities and Exchange Commission (SEC) (Heminway 2013a, 2014).[10]

Legal provisions for equity-based crowdfunding are country-specific and very heterogeneous. In most countries—among others in the EU—issuing of shares through equity-based crowdfunding is either prohibited or, due to stringent legal requirements, associated with high transaction costs for the issuer.[11] The measures required to implement equity-based crowdfunding in the EU is discussed by De Buysere, Gajda, Kleverlaan, and Marom (2012), Klöhn and Hornuf (2012) and Röthler and Wenzlaff (2011). A proposal for regulation at the EU level does not yet exist.

2.4 *Crowdfunding Literature with a Focus on Capital Providers*

The behaviour of capital providers is crucial for the success of crowdfunding. Scientific research has mainly focused on the motives of capital providers for participating in crowdfunding and the factors that influence the investment decision. Table 2 summarises the studies focusing on capital providers.

2.4.1 Motivations of Capital Providers

Capital providers in crowdfunding are not just financially motivated. Social reputation and intrinsic motives play a significant role (Allison et al., 2014; Lin et al., 2014). The motives to participate in crowdfunding are heterogeneous and depend on the respective crowdfunding model (Lin et al., 2014; Ordanini et al., 2011). Interviews with founders and employees of three crowdfunding platforms show that capital providers have some common characteristics: they are innovation-oriented, are interested in interacting with others, identify themselves with the company or the product, and are interested in the financial result (Ordanini et al., 2011). These motives were also

[10] The proposal for these specifications was released by the SEC in October 2013 in a 585-page document for public comments. Since the period for comments expired in February 2014, the market has been awaiting final SEC specifications under Title III of the JOBS Act. The proposal is available at http://www.sec.gov/rules/proposed/2013/33-9470.pdf (Accessed 15 May 2014). For further discussion of the proposal, see Guzik (2014).

[11] A discussion of the legal situation in different European Countries can be found in Hornuf and Schwienbacher (2014b). The German situation is discussed in Klöhn and Hornuf (2012) and the publication of the BaFin (BaFin, 2012).

Table 2 Crowdfunding literature with a focus on capital providers

Author(s)	Content	Method	Source
Ahlers et al. (2013)	Identification of signals that facilitate the investment decision	Quantitative	ASSOB
Allison, Davis, Short, and Webb (2014)	Importance of intrinsic and extrinsic cues in entrepreneurial narratives in microlending markets	Quantitative	KIVA
An, Quercia, and Crowcroft (2014)	Analysis of pledging behaviour of crowd investors and development of recommendation strategies	Quantitative	Kickstarter, Twitter
Bachmann et al. (2011)	Literature review on P2P lending until 2010	Literature review	–
Barasinska and Schäfer (2010, 2014)	Investigation of whether women are disadvantaged in online credit markets analogous to traditional credit markets	Quantitative	Smava
Berger and Gleisner (2009)	Importance of intermediaries (group leaders) in P2P lending markets; relevance for granting loans and interest rates	Quantitative	Prosper
Berkovich (2011)	Herding behaviour in P2P lending markets; significance of hard and soft facts for the investment decision.	Quantitative	Prosper
Böhme and Pötzsch (2010)	Significance of soft facts in P2P lending and consideration of data privacy protection	Quantitative	Smava
Brem and Wassong (2014)	Analysis of the factors determining the investment decision of individual investors in crowdfunding	Quantitative, case studies	Survey (221 students)
Burtch et al. (2013a)	Interdependency of investment decisions of capital providers	Quantitative	U.S. platform for online journalism
Duarte, Siegel, and Young (2012)	Trust building through image/appearance and its impact on lending probability and interest rates in P2P lending markets	Quantitative	Prosper
Everett (2010)	Reduction of information asymmetries through relationship building; consequences for default risk and interest rates	Quantitative	Prosper
Freedman and Jin (2008, 2014)	Significance of social networks in reducing information asymmetries in P2P lending markets and its effect on loan performance	Quantitative	Prosper
Gao and Lin (2014)	Analysis of the relationship between linguistic styles of borrower-supplied texts and quality of loans	Quantitative	Prosper
Greenberg and Mollick (2014)	Analysis of choice homophily and the success of female founders in crowdfunding	Quantitative	Kickstarter

(continued)

Table 2 (continued)

Author(s)	Content	Method	Source
Herzenstein and Andrews (2008)	Influence of demographic characteristics, financial strength and borrowers' efforts on lending probability	Quantitative	Prosper
Herzenstein, Dholakia, and Andrews (2011)	Herding behaviour in P2P lending markets and its economic efficiency	Quantitative	Prosper
Herzenstein, Sonenshein, and Dholakia (2011)	Significance of borrowers' descriptions for the investment decision of lenders and the probability of loan defaults	Quantitative	Prosper
Hildebrand, Puri, and Rocholl (2013)	Importance of incentives in P2P lending markets; significance of recommendations and prior investments for subsequent investors	Quantitative	Prosper
Hulme and Wright (2006)	Relevance of social lending through P2P lending platforms; benefits and future prospects	Qualitative, quantitative	Interviews, online questionnaire
Iyer, Khwaja, Luttmer, and Shue (2009)	Influence of borrowers' credit rating on funding success; relevance of soft facts	Quantitative	Prosper
Kawai, Onishi, and Uetake (2013)	Analysis of how signalling affects the functioning of markets for unsecured loans	Quantitative	Prosper
Kim and Viswanathan (2013)	Analysis of the influence of early investments by experts (quality signals) on subsequent investments	Quantitative	Appbackr
Koning and Model (2013)	Analysis of the relationship between number of donations at the beginning of a funding period and funding success	Quantitative	DonorsChoose
Kuppuswamy and Bayus (2013)	Analysis of social behaviour in crowdfunding transactions; interrelation of investment decisions (herding)	Quantitative	Kickstarter
Lee and Lee (2012)	Analysis of herding behaviour in P2P lending markets	Quantitative	Popfunding
Lin, Boh, and Goh (2014)	Identification of crowdfunder archetypes and their distinct reaction to social influences and signals of quality	Quantitative	Kickstarter
Lin, Prabhala, and Viswanathan (2013)	Importance of social networks for lending outcomes in P2P lending markets	Quantitative	Prosper
Lin, Prabhala, and Viswanathan (2009)	Significance of social networks for lending probability, interest rates and default probability	Quantitative	Prosper
Lin and Viswanathan (2013)	Relevance of geographical proximity in crowdfunding markets; explanation of the home bias	Quantitative	Prosper, quasi-experiment
Liu, Lu, and Brass (2013)	Role of friendships (online and offline) in P2P lending markets	Quantitative	PPDai

(continued)

Table 2 (continued)

Author(s)	Content	Method	Source
Lu, Xie, Kong, and Yu (2014)	Analysis of the correlation between social promotion through social media and fundraising results	Quantitative	Kickstarter
Michels (2012)	Relevance of voluntary, unverifiable information in P2P lending markets	Quantitative	Prosper
Mollick (2013)	Analysis of whether investors in crowdfunding markets have the same quality signals as venture capitalists	Quantitative	Kickstarter
Mollick and Nanda (2014)	Comparison between crowd and expert evaluations of projects relying on taste and judgment (theatre)	Quantitative	Kickstarter, interviews
Moritz, Block, and Lutz (2014)	Role of investor communication to reduce information asymmetries between crowd investors and new ventures	Qualitative	Interviews
Ordanini et al. (2011)	Role of customers and service providers (platforms) in crowdfunding	Qualitative	Interviews, case studies
Parker (2014)	Relationship between informed investors, information cascades and the success of crowdfunding transactions	Model-based approach	–
Pope and Sydnor (2011)	Importance of soft facts (e.g. age, race, gender) and discrimination in P2P lending markets	Quantitative	Prosper
Qiu (2013)	Analysis of public good and informational advertising issues in crowdfunding	Model-based approach, quantitative	Kickstarter, Twitter
Ravina (2012)	Importance of soft facts (e.g. beauty, race, age) for lending probability and interest rates	Quantitative	Prosper
Smith, Windmeijer, and Wright (2013)	Analysis of crowding in and crowding out effects in donation-based crowdfunding	Quantitative	JustGiving, Virgin Money
Ward and Ramachandran (2010)	Relevance of peer effects in reward-based crowdfunding (example: experience goods market)	Model-based approach, quantitative	SellaBand
Wash (2013)	Relationship between probability of donation and target achievement (funding goal)	Quantitative	DonorsChoose
Weiss, Pelger, and Horsch (2010)	Investigation of the relationship between screening of P2P lending platforms and adverse selection	Quantitative	Prosper
Xu et al. (2014)	Development of taxonomy of project updates used in crowdfunding campaigns	Quantitative	Kickstarter
Yang (2014)	Evaluation of the role of photographs in online peer-to-peer lending markets	Qualitative	Experiment
Yum, Lee, and Chae (2012)	Analysis of the significance of the "wisdom of the crowd" in P2P lending markets	Quantitative	Popfunding

(continued)

Table 2 (continued)

Author(s)	Content	Method	Source
Zhang and Liu (2012)	Analysis of herding behaviour in P2P lending markets and the rationality of this behaviour	Quantitative	Prosper
Zheng, Wan, Chen, and Wang (2014)	Investigation of the antecedents of crowdfunding project success	Quantitative	Demohour
Zvilichovsky, Inbar, and Barzilay (2013)	Impact of the activities of capital seekers as capital providers for the success of their own crowdfunding projects (reciprocity)	Quantitative	Kickstarter

confirmed by Gerber et al. (2012) in interviews with capital seekers and capital providers. The latter strive for financial and non-financial rewards, they like to support the project or company and they want to be active in social networks. Hemer et al. (2011) further identify the interest in using the product or service and the attainment of self-affirmation and fun, which is associated with this type of investment.

2.4.2 Importance of Social Networks

The desire to interact in social networks has been identified as a key motive for capital providers to participate in crowdfunding transactions. Several studies examine the effect of social networks on the decision behaviour of capital providers. It has been shown that social networks reduce information asymmetries and thus, increase funding probability (Everett, 2010; Freedman & Jin, 2008, 2014; Lin et al., 2009, 2013; Liu et al., 2013; Zvilichovsky et al., 2013). One possible consequence of this social network effect for capital providers is the mimicking of others' behaviour ("herding") (Herzenstein, Dholakia, et al., 2011; Lee & Lee, 2012; Yum et al., 2012; Zhang & Liu, 2012). Herzenstein, Dholakia, et al. (2011) and Zhang and Liu (2012) found that herding behaviour in P2P lending markets contrasts with findings in online auction markets, such as Ebay. They conclude that herding behaviour in crowdfunding is strategic and rational because it seems to reduce the default rates of loans. Kuppuswamy and Bayus (2013) investigated herding behaviour in reward-based crowdfunding by analysing data from Kickstarter. They discovered that projects typically have a U-shaped pattern of project support. According to Kuppuswamy and Bayus (2013), herding behaviour in reward-based crowdfunding is due to payoff externalities. Backers tend to support projects closer to their funding goals as they are more likely to succeed and thus, backers expect their contribution to have a higher impact. In addition, Kuppuswamy and Bayus (2013) found that investments by family and friends as well as promotional activities have a positive influence on the funding process, particularly at the beginning and end stages of the funding. According to Lu et al. (2014), promotional activities are important when the funding starts but later in the process interaction between participants is the main driver for funding success (Lu et al., 2014). However, Lin et al. (2014) identified different archetypes of crowdfunders which seem to react differently to social influences and signals of quality.

2.4.3 Signals in Crowdfunding Transactions

The importance of the timing of investments has also been studied in donation-based crowdfunding. The results are consistent. The behaviour of peers seems to provide a signal to subsequent capital providers (Burtch et al., 2013a; Koning & Model, 2013; Smith et al., 2013; Wash, 2013). This signalling effect of peer behaviour has also been studied by Ward and Ramachandran (2010) in the reward-based experience goods market. In a theoretical model, they showed the impact of peer behaviour and test their results using archival data from the platform SellaBand. Ward and Ramachandran (2010) identified a positive correlation of an investment decision with the results of similar, already-funded projects, the actions of other capital providers, popularity rankings and blog posts. Qiu (2013) also found that blog posts (word-of-mouth effect measured by tweets), media coverage and, in particular, features of the promoting platform, have a positive effect on crowdfunding transactions. Kim and Viswanathan (2013) studied crowdfunding in the mobile application market and find that early investments by experts send positive signals and increase the likelihood of subsequent funding from the crowd. Furthermore, recommendations from friends and acquaintances can also send positive signals and increase funding probability (Lin et al., 2013; Liu et al., 2013; Moritz et al., 2014). Hildebrand et al. (2013) found that endorsements from peers are only understood as credible signals if the endorsements are linked with investments of the respective person ("skin in the game").

Ahlers et al. (2013) investigated which signals are relevant for investment decisions in crowdfunding markets. The authors analysed archival data from the Australian equity-based crowdfunding platform ASSOB. They found that ventures with more board members, higher levels of education and better networks send out positive signals and are more likely to be funded. The exit strategy, the existence of a financial plan and the age of the capital-seeking venture also play significant roles.

According to Mollick (2013), capital providers in crowdfunding markets and venture capitalists trust similar quality signals (e.g. previous successes of entrepreneurs, external references). This result is rather surprising because crowd investors are usually not professional investors with the same degree of know-how (Agrawal et al., 2013; Fink, 2012; Heminway, 2014; Kim & Viswanathan, 2013; Macht & Weatherston, 2014; Mollick, 2013; Schwienbacher & Larralde, 2012). Distortions in venture capital financing created by the location of companies (Tyebjee & Bruno, 1984) and the gender of the entrepreneurs (Harrison & Mason, 2007) were absent in crowdfunding markets (Barasinska & Schäfer, 2010, 2014; Greenberg & Mollick, 2014; Mollick, 2013).

In P2P lending markets, capital seekers often voluntarily provide personal information, such as marital status, number of children, photos, personal descriptions and descriptions of the project. It has been found that these soft facts have a positive effect on establishing trust and thus influence the likelihood of successful financing, lower interest rates and a decrease in the probability of loan defaults (Allison et al., 2014; Berkovich, 2011; Duarte et al., 2012; Gao & Lin, 2014; Herzenstein, Sonenshein, et al., 2011; Pope & Sydnor, 2011; Ravina, 2012; Yang, 2014). Iyer et al. (2009) found that, similarly to banks, capital providers in P2P lending markets primarily rely on hard facts (i.e. credit ratings) to make investment decisions. But, the poorer the credit ratings, the more soft facts are taken into account (Berkovich, 2011; Iyer et al., 2009; Michels, 2012). However, in light of data protection, potential capital seekers should weigh exactly what and how much personal information they need to disclose to achieve their goals (Böhme & Pötzsch, 2010).

2.5 *Crowdfunding Literature with a Focus on the Intermediary*

The involvement of a crowdfunding platform as an intermediary in crowdfunding transactions offers advantages for both capital seekers and providers. In addition to providing a standardised process, platforms act as an information, communication and execution portal. Accordingly, platforms can reduce information asymmetries and thus the risks involved for the participating parties (Allen & Santomero, 1997; Berger & Gleisner, 2009; Elsner, 2013; Haas, Blohm, & Leimeister, 2014; Leland & Pyle, 1977). Platforms can furthermore enable market participants to build trust (Burtch et al., 2013a; Greiner & Wang, 2010). Up to date, very different business models of crowdfunding platforms exist (Ordanini et al., 2011). There is still very little research into which of these business models is best suited for successful crowdfunding. Table 3 summarises the identified research on the intermediary-based crowdfunding literature.

Wash and Solomon (2014) analysed which funding design should be chosen by crowdfunding platforms: the return rule ("all-or-nothing") or the direct donation model ("keep-what-you-get"). In the case of the return rule, payments to capital seekers are only made if a predefined threshold is achieved. Otherwise, the funds will be returned to the capital providers. The direct donation model implies that all money collected will be paid out to the capital seeker. Wash and Solomon (2014) performed a crowdfunding experiment with a total of 168 participants in 14 experimental sessions. The players showed a tendency to contribute higher amounts in the case of a return rule in comparison to the direct donation model. However, fewer projects achieved the predefined funding threshold because funds were split between more projects. As a result, Wash and Solomon (2014) recommended the return rule for platforms that offer high-risk projects to the crowd. However, in order to avoid heavy distributions and increase the chances of reaching the threshold amounts, few projects should be offered simultaneously. The timing of projects being published was also studied by Doshi (2014). He found that crowdfunding platforms should try

Table 3 Crowdfunding literature with a focus on the intermediary

Author(s)	Content	Method	Source
Ashta and Assadi (2010)	Analysis of business models and regulatory environment of P2P microlending platforms in Europe	Market analysis	Case studies
Chen, Ghosh, and Lambert (2013)	Analysis of the auction model in P2P lending markets	Game theoretical analysis	–
Doshi (2014)	Analysis of the impact of high-performing superstar (highly successful) agents on the other side of the market	Quantitative	Kickstarter, Indiegogo
Giudici et al. (2012)	Important research questions; business models of Italian platforms	Literature, market analysis	Case studies
Gonzalez and McAleer (2011)	Illustration of the similarities and differences of listed loans on Zopa.uk and Prosper.com	Market analysis	300 randomly chosen cases on both platforms
Greiner and Wang (2010)	Analysis of trust-building mechanisms of crowdfunding platforms	Quantitative	Prosper
Haas et al. (2014)	Empirical taxonomy of crowdfunding intermediaries; identification of three archetypes of crowdfunding platforms	Quantitative	127 crowdfunding platforms
Heminway (2013b)	Role of platforms in crowdfunding markets and the requirements of the CROWDFUND Act	Legal analysis	CROWDFUND Act
Hornuf and Klöhn (2013)	Brief comparison of two exit models in equity-based crowdfunding: EBIT or revenue multiples vs. enterprise value	Market analysis	Case studies
Maeschle (2012a)	Analysis of the "first come, first served" model of crowdfunding platforms	Model-based approach	–
Maeschle (2012b)	Impact of platform competition in equity-based crowdfunding markets on disclosure requirements for companies	Model-based approach	–
Wash and Solomon (2014)	Comparison of the models "all-or-nothing" and "keep-what-you-get"	Qualitative	Experiment

to attract superstar sellers because superstars increase the overall transaction volume on the platform relative to other platforms ("halo effect") and the funding volume of other projects that are similar to the superstar ("crowding in effect"). Consequently, platforms should distribute the timing and diversity of superstars evenly in order to achieve an optimal outcome for the platform (Doshi, 2014).

Chen et al. (2013) investigated whether using an auction model in crowdfunding markets leads to an optimal result for market participants. To this end, they analysed the results of the auction model used on Prosper.com until 2010. This model implied that the interest rate for a loan is determined by the number of bids from interested capital providers. Chen et al. (2013) found that the auction process does not generate results in the best interest of capital seekers. In addition, this method is more complicated and less transparent than a fixed-rate model for capital providers (Chen et al., 2013).

Maeschle (2012a) studied the "first come, first served" funding principle often used on crowdfunding platforms. This model implies a "hard end" of the funding as soon as the funding limit[12] is reached. In the case of excess demand[13] to finance a specific project, there are several arguments as to why this method does not lead to an optimal economic result. Quick and well-informed crowd investors can prevent a spread of company shares by investing large sums. Thus, there is a possible risk of the entrepreneur losing control in his/her company. Slower and less informed capital providers are at a disadvantage. Furthermore, early capital providers are treated equally even though they face much higher information costs than subsequent capital providers. The possibility of a "free-rider" strategy could restrain capital providers in taking the role of "first-movers". Consequently, crowdfunding projects may not get funded due to a lack of initial investments.

In a second study, Maeschle (2012b) examines whether the increasing competitive pressure of crowdfunding platforms affects disclosure requirements for companies. Based on prior empirical research on the success factors of start-ups (Harhoff, Stahl, & Woywode, 1998; Prantl, 2003); Maeschle (2012b) derives a list of information that should be provided to reduce information asymmetries of capital providers. According to this study, platforms should publish business information about the company (particularly firm size, legal form, ownership structure, industry and location), the company's finances (especially the balance sheet) and the company's management (particularly team structure, education and age) (Kraus, Schulz, & Halberstadt, 2008).

3 Summary and Open Research Questions

This article provides an overview of the existing research on crowdfunding. The focus of our study lies in start-ups as the capital-seeking party. Academic research on crowdfunding new ventures has recently increased due to various market developments: the necessity of start-ups to find alternative funding possibilities, particularly in the early stages of a company's development (fuelled by the financial crisis), the recent success stories of crowdfunding for new ventures and the adoption of the JOBS Act in 2012 in the United States.

Our review has identified a number of research priorities in academic literature. The motives for participating in crowdfunding markets for capital seekers and capital providers have been of major academic interest. We identified several, mainly

[12] Crowdfunding platforms often determine a maximum funding amount per transaction (funding limit).

[13] The funding is closed the moment it reaches the funding limit, even if more capital providers would be willing to invest.

qualitative, studies to answer this research question. In addition, identifying success factors for crowdfunding transactions and analysing different national legal frameworks were of major interest to the researchers. The crowdfunding market is characterised by strong information asymmetries between market actors. Quality signals and the existence of social networks can reduce these information asymmetries and are the subjects of several research papers. Studies focusing on the role of crowdfunding platforms and their optimal business models remain scarce.

Scientific research on crowdfunding is still in its infancy. Quantitative studies based on empirical market data are still rare. As a result, based on our literature review and the chosen structure focusing on capital seekers, capital providers and intermediaries, a number of research questions can be derived. Similar to our review, we focus on new ventures as the capital-seeking party.

Research Questions Focusing on Capital Seekers

- **For which ventures is crowdfunding a suitable financing alternative?**
  Crowdfunding is a new financing alternative for new ventures. The special characteristics of crowdfunding give reason to assume that this type of financing is not appropriate for all companies. For which ventures crowdfunding is a suitable alternative and what effects it has on a company's success should be investigated.
- **To what extent does crowdfunding help to close the early-stage financing gap?**
  Whether crowdfunding can have the desired effect of closing the early-stage financing gap for new ventures is not yet clear due to the relatively young market. Cause-and-effect relationships have yet to be uncovered to prevent market failure due to inefficiencies or the loss of reputation. The interaction of crowdfunding and traditional sources of finance play an important role in this context (Hornuf & Schwienbacher, 2014a). The circumstances under which professional investors, such as venture capitalists or banks, are willing to finance ventures that have received funding from the crowd should be explored.
- **To what extent should crowdfunding markets be regulated?**
  The growth of crowdfunding markets in the last years and the increasing number of crowdfunding platforms could prompt more companies to choose this type of financing (Klöhn & Hornuf, 2012). Critics emphasise the growing risk of fraud through this development (Hazen, 2012; Hornuf & Klöhn, 2013; Wroldsen, 2013). The extent to which the market can regulate itself (Fink, 2012) or whether external regulation is required (Cumming & Johan, 2013) remains unclear.

Research Questions Focusing on Capital Providers

- **What selection criteria do capital providers in crowdfunding markets use to base their investment decision on?**
  Research on the criteria relevant to the investment decisions of capital providers is thus far in its infancy. Venture capital and business angel research may provide some ideas about the decisive factors. However, whether crowd investors use similar decision criteria as professional investors is still unclear.

The entrepreneurial team, the protection of intellectual property through patents, and the newness of the business model or the product are important for professional investors (Baum & Silverman, 2004; Franke, Gruber, Harhoff, & Henkel, 2008; Jell, Block, & Henkel, 2011). Whether these factors are also crucial for the crowd or whether the investment decision is instead influenced by emotions, herd instinct or altruistic motives (Bretschneider, Knaub, & Wieck, 2014) has yet to be explored.

- **What quality signals can reduce information asymmetries between the participating parties?**

  The maximum default risk for a capital provider is total loss. It is extremely difficult to estimate the default probability in crowdfunding markets because of high information asymmetries between the participating parties. Typical risk reduction strategies of private equity investors, such as in-depth screening processes or individual contract negotiations, are not available to the crowd. The results of venture capital research indicate various alternatives for reducing information asymmetries (Audretsch, Bönte, & Mahagaonkar, 2012; Baum & Silverman, 2004; Block, Vries, Schumann, & Sandner, 2013). The communication of quality signals (e.g. patents, trademarks, alliances and education) by the capital-seeking party can help overcome this hurdle (Agrawal et al., 2013; Moritz et al., 2014). Identifying the relevant quality signals in order to facilitate the investment decision can make an important contribution to the future success of venture financing through the crowd.

- **What is the role of social networks for crowdfunding?**

  Empirical studies of P2P lending have identified social networks as important in the crowd's investment decisions. Social networks help inform and motivate capital providers and thus can facilitate investment decisions (Hekman & Brussee, 2013; Lu et al., 2014; Naroditskiy, Stein, & Tonin, 2014). However, thus far, little is known about the importance of social networks in equity-based crowdfunding.

Research Questions Focusing on Intermediaries

- **What business models of crowdfunding platforms facilitate an optimal result for capital seekers and capital providers?**

  Platforms, as intermediaries, play an important role in reducing information asymmetries (Belleflamme et al., 2013a) and building trust in crowdfunding markets (Agrawal et al., 2013; Heminway, 2013b; Vass, 2013). If high losses and failure rates occur, a loss of confidence in crowdfunding and the respective platform is to be expected. However, thus far, little is known about which platform business models are the most suitable for facilitating these positive results for the market participants.

- **Which disclosure requirements should the platforms demand from capital seekers?**

  Capital seekers should provide information that will allow the platforms and capital providers to assess the risks associated with the investment. In this context, it should be identified if and how crowd investors evaluate information disclosed by new ventures (Heminway, 2014). Furthermore, the disclosure of sensitive information poses risks for the capital-seeking party (i.e. the risk of imitation by competitors) (Agrawal et al., 2013). In the interest of all market participants, the optimal amount of information disclosed by capital seekers should be identified.

Our literature review shows that from a scientific perspective, little is known about crowdfunding. From a practical perspective, it is necessary to fill this gap in order to develop this new form of financing further. From a theoretical and scientific perspective, it would be interesting to research the possibilities of crowdfunding further. Crowdfunding offers several links to other research areas, such as entrepreneurial and innovation financing, and can thus build on existing theories.

References

Agrawal, A., Catalini, C., & Goldfarb, A. (2011). *The geography of crowdfunding* (NBER Working Paper No. 16820). Retrieved March 24, 2013, from http://www.nber.org/papers/w16820*

Agrawal, A., Catalini, C., & Goldfarb, A. (2013). *Some simple economics of crowdfunding* (NBER Working Paper No. w19133). Retrieved August 6, 2013, from http://www.nber.org/papers/w19133*

Agrawal, A., Catalini, C., & Goldfarb, A. (2014). *Crowdfunding: Geography, social networks, and the timing of investment decisions* (Working Paper). Retrieved July 20, 2014, from http://www.catalini.com/s/Crowdfunding_Geography_Social_Networks_2014_05_27.pdf*

Ahlers, G., Cumming, D., Günther, C., & Schweizer, D. (2013). *Equity crowdfunding* (SSRN Working Paper No. 2362340). Retrieved May 15, 2014, from http://papers.ssrn.com/sol3/papers.cfm?abstract_id=2362340*

Aitamurto, T. (2011). The impact of crowdfunding for journalism. *Journalism Practise*, *5*(4), 429–445. doi:10.1080/17512786.2010.551018*

Allen, F., & Santomero, A. (1997). The theory of financial intermediation. *Journal of Banking & Finance*, *21*(11–12), 1461–1485. doi:10.1016/S0378-4266(97)00032-0

Allison, T. H., Davis, B. C., Short, J. C., & Webb, J. W. (2014). Crowdfunding in a prosocial microlending environment: Examining the role of intrinsic versus extrinsic cues. *Entrepreneurship Theory and Practice*. doi:10.1111/etap.12108*

An, J., Quercia, D., & Crowcroft, J. (2014). Recommending investors for crowdfunding projects. In *WWW'14 Proceedings of the 23rd International Conference on World Wide Web. International World Wide Web Conferences Steering Committee* (pp. 261–270). doi:10.1145/2566486.2568005*

Ashta, A., & Assadi, D. (2010). An analysis of European online micro-lending websites. *Innovative Marketing*, *6*(2), 7–17. Retrieved from http://businessperspectives.org/journals_free/im/2010/im_en_2010_2_Ashta.pdf*

Audretsch, D. B., Bönte, W., & Mahagaonkar, P. (2012). Financial signaling by innovative nascent ventures: The relevance of patents and prototypes. *Research Policy*, *41*(8), 1407–1421. doi:10.1016/j.respol.2012.02.003

Bachmann, A., Becker, A., Buerckner, D., Hilker, M., Kock, F., Lehmann, M., & Tiburtius, P. (2011). Online peer-to-peer lending—A literature review. *Journal of Internet Banking and Commerce*, *16*(2). Retrieved from http://www.arraydev.com/commerce/JIBC/2011-08/Alexander Becker.pdf*

BaFin. (2012, September). *BaFinJournal*. Retrieved from http://www.bafin.de/SharedDocs/Downloads/DE/BaFinJournal/2012/bj_1209.html

Barasinska, N., & Schäfer, D. (2010). *Does gender affect funding success at the peer-to-peer credit markets?* (DIW Berlin Discussion Papers No. 1094). Retrieved July 15, 2013, from http://www.diw.de/sixcms/detail.php?id=diw_01.c.366504.de*

Barasinska, N., & Schäfer, D. (2014). Is crowdfunding different? Evidence on the relation between gender and funding success from a german peer-to-peer lending platform. *German Economic Review*. doi:10.1111/geer.12052*

Baum, J. A. C., & Silverman, B. S. (2004). Picking winners or building them? Alliance, intellectual, and human capital as selection criteria in venture financing and performance of biotechnology startups. *Journal of Business Venturing, 19*(3), 411–436. doi:10.1016/S0883-9026(03)00038-7

Beck, R. (2012). *Crowdinvesting: Die Investition der Vielen*. Düsseldorf: Amazon Distribution.

Belleflamme, P., & Lambert, T. (2014). *Crowdfunding: Some empirical findings and microeconomic underpinnings* (SSRN Working Paper No. 2437786). Retrieved June 20, 2014, from http://papers.ssrn.com/sol3/papers.cfm?abstract_id=2437786*

Belleflamme, P., Lambert, T., & Schwienbacher, A. (2010). *Crowdfunding: An industrial organization perspective*. Prepared for the Workshop Digital Business Models: Understanding Strategies, Paris, June 2010. Retrieved from http://economix.fr/pdf/workshops/2010_dbm/Belleflamme_al.pdf*

Belleflamme, P., Lambert, T., & Schwienbacher, A. (2013a). Crowdfunding: Tapping the right crowd. *Journal of Business Venturing, 29*(5), 585–609. doi:10.1016/j.jbusvent.2013.07.003*

Belleflamme, P., Lambert, T., & Schwienbacher, A. (2013b). Individual crowdfunding practices. *Venture Capital, 15*(4), 313–333. doi:10.1080/13691066.2013.785151*

Berger, S., & Gleisner, F. (2009). Emergence of financial intermediaries in electronic markets: The case of online P2P lending. *BuR Business Research Journal, 2*(1), 39–65. doi:10.1007/BF03343528*

Berger, A. N., & Udell, G. F. (1998). The economics of small business finance: The roles of private equity and debt markets in the financial growth cycle. *Journal of Banking & Finance, 22*, 613–673. doi:10.1016/S0378-4266(98)00038-7

Berkovich, E. (2011). Search and herding effects in peer-to-peer lending: Evidence from prosper.com. *Annals of Finance, 7*(3), 389–405. doi:10.1007/s10436-011-0178-6*

Block, J., & Sandner, P. (2009). What is the effect of the financial crisis on venture capital financing? Empirical evidence from US Internet start-ups. *Venture Capital, 11*(4), 295–309. doi:10.1080/13691060903184803

Block, J., Vries, G. D., Schumann, J., & Sandner, P. (2013). Trademarks and venture capital valuation. *Journal of Business Venturing, 29*(4), 525–542. doi:10.1016/j.jbusvent.2013.07.006

Böhme, R., & Pötzsch, S. (2010). *Social lending aus der Perspektive des Datenschutzes*. Retrieved July 15, 2013, from http://is.uni-muenster.de/security/publications/BP2010_SocialLending_Sicherheit2010_LNI.pdf*

Bradford, C. (2012). Crowdfunding and the federal securities laws. *Columbia Business Law Review*. Retrieved from http://digitalcommons.unl.edu/cgi/viewcontent.cgi?article=1118&context=lawfacpub*

Brem, A., & Wassong, N. (2014). Wer investiert warum? Eine Analyse von Investmententscheidungen bei Crowdfunding-Projekten. *ZfKE—Zeitschrift für KMU und Entrepreneurship, 62*(1), 31–56.*

Bretschneider, U., Knaub, K., & Wieck, E. (2014). *Motivations for crowdfunding: What drives the crowd to invest in start-ups?* Paper presented at Twenty Second European Conference on Information Systems, Tel Aviv 2014. Retrieved July 20, 2014, from http://aisel.aisnet.org/ecis2014/proceedings/track05/6/

Burtch, G., Ghose, A., & Wattal, S. (2013a). An empirical examination of the antecedents and consequences of contribution patterns in crowd-funded markets. *Information Systems Research, 24*(3), 499–519. Retrieved from http://pubsonline.informs.org/doi/abs/10.1287/isre.1120.0468*

Burtch, G., Ghose, A., & Wattal, S. (2013b). *Cultural differences and geography as determinants of online pro-social lending* (SSRN Working Paper No. 2271298). Retrieved July 15, 2013, from http://papers.ssrn.com/sol3/papers.cfm?abstract_id=2271298*

Chen, N., Ghosh, A., & Lambert, N. S. (2013). Auctions for social lending: A theoretical analysis. *Games and Economic Behavior, 1*, 1–25. doi:10.1016/j.geb.2013.05.004*

Cohn, S. (2012). *The new crowdfunding registration exemption: Good idea, bad execution* (SSRN Working Paper No. 2066016). Retrieved July 15, 2013, from http://papers.ssrn.com/sol3/papers.cfm?abstract_id=2066016*

Collins, L., & Pierrakis, Y. (2012, July). The venture crowd. *NESTA*. Retrieved from http://www.thesoholoft.com/wp-content/uploads/2012/07/TheVentureCrowd.pdf*

Cumming, D., & Johan, S. (2013). Demand driven securities regulation: Evidence from crowdfunding. *Venture Capital, 15*(4), 361–379. doi:10.1080/13691066.2013.847635*

Cumming, D. J., Leboeuf, G., & Schwienbacher, A. (2014). *Crowdfunding models: Keep-it-all vs. all-or-nothing* (SSRN Working Paper No. 2447567). Retrieved June 20, 2014, from http://papers.ssrn.com/sol3/Papers.cfm?abstract_id=2447567*

De Buysere, K., Gajda, O., Kleverlaan, R., & Marom, D. (2012). *A framework for European crowdfunding*. Retrieved from http://www.europecrowdfunding.org/Resources/Documents/FRAMEWORK_EU_CROWDFUNDING.pdf*

Dorfleitner, G., Kapitz, J., & Wimmer, M. (2014). Crowdinvesting als Finanzierungsalternative für kleine und mittlere Unternehmen. *Die Betriebswirtschaft*. Retrieved from http://epub.uni-regensburg.de/30104/1/preprint.pdf*

Doshi, A. (2014). *Agent heterogeneity in two-sided platforms: Superstar impact on crowdfuding* (SSRN Working Paper No. 2422111). Retrieved May 15, 2014, from http://papers.ssrn.com/sol3/papers.cfm?abstract_id=2422111*

Duarte, J., Siegel, S., & Young, L. (2012). Trust and credit: The role of appearance in peer-to-peer lending. *Review of Financial Studies, 25*(8), 2455–2484. doi:10.1093/rfs/hhs071*

Duygan-Bump, B., Levkov, A., & Montoriol-Garriga, J. (2011). *Financing constraints and unemployment: Evidence from the great recession* (Federal Reserve Bank of Boston, Working Paper No QAU10-6). Retrieved April 10, 2013, from http://www.frbatlanta.org/documents/news/conferences/10smallbusiness_levkov.pdf

Elsner, D. (2013). Corporate crowdfunding. In O. Everling & R. Lempka (Eds.), *Finanzdienstleister der nächsten Generation—Die neue digitale Macht der Kunden* (pp. 401–422). Frankfurt am Main: Frankfurt-School-Verlag.

Everett, C. (2010). *Group membership, relationship banking and loan default risk: The case of online social lending* (SSRN Working Paper No. 1114428). Retrieved April 10, 2013, from http://papers.ssrn.com/sol3/papers.cfm?abstract_id=1114428*

Feller, J., Gleasure, R., & Treacy, S. (2013). *From the wisdom to the wealth of crowds: A metatriangulation of crowdfunding research* (TOTO Working Paper 2013.01 v2). Retrieved July 27, 2013, from http://www.ucc.ie/en/toto/workingpapers/*

Fink, A. (2012). *Protecting the crowd and raising capital through the JOBS Act* (SSRN Working Paper No. 2046051). Retrieved April 10, 2013, from http://papers.ssrn.com/sol3/papers.cfm?abstract_id=2046051*

Franke, N., Gruber, M., Harhoff, D., & Henkel, J. (2008). Venture capitalists' evaluations of start-up teams: Trade-offs, knock-out criteria, and the impact of VC experience. *Entrepreneurship Theory and Practice, 32*(3), 459–483. doi:10.1111/j.1540-6520.2008.00236.x

Freedman, S., & Jin, G. (2008). *Do social networks solve information problems for peer-to-peer lending? Evidence from prosper.com* (NET Institute Working Paper No. 08-4). Retrieved April 10, 2013, from http://www.nsd.edu.cn/cn/userfiles/Other/2010-05/20100507142111516715 81.pdf*

Freedman, S., & Jin, G. (2014). *The signaling value of online social networks: Lessons from peer-to-peer lending* (NBER Working Paper No. 19820). Retrieved May 15, 2014, from http://www.nber.org/papers/w19820*

Frydrych, D., Bock, A., Kinder, T., & Koeck, B. (2014). Exploring entrepreneurial legitimacy in reward-based crowdfunding. *Venture Capital, 16(3),* 247–269. doi:10.1080/13691066.2014.916512*

Gao, Q., & Lin, M. (2014). *Linguistic features and peer-to-peer loan quality: A machine learning approach* (SSRN Working Paper No. 2446114). Retrieved May 15, 2014, from http://papers.ssrn.com/sol3/papers.cfm?abstract_id=2446114*

Gerber, E., Hui, J., & Kuo, P. (2012). Crowdfunding: Why people are motivated to post and fund projects on crowdfunding platforms. *CSCW Workshop.* Retrieved from http://www.juliehui.org/wp-content/uploads/2013/04/CSCW_Crowdfunding_Final.pdf*

Giudici, G., Guerini, M., & Rossi-Lamastra, C. (2013). *Why crowdfunding projects can succeed: The role of proponents' individual and territorial social capital* (SSRN Working Paper No. 2255944). Retrieved April 29, 2013, from http://ssrn.com/abstract=2255944*

Giudici, G., Nava, R., Rossi Lamastra, C., & Verecondo, C. (2012). *Crowdfunding: The new frontier for financing entrepreneurship?* (SSRN Working Paper No. 2157429). Retrieved March 20, 2013, from http://ssrn.com/abstract=2157429*

Gonzalez, L., & McAleer, K. (2011). Online social lending: A peak at US Prosper and UK Zopa. *Journal of Accounting, Finance and Economics, 1*(2), 26–41. Retrieved from http://www.jafepapers.com/uploads/2011/december/3.pdf*

Greenberg, J., & Mollick, E. (2014). *Leaning in or leaning on? Gender, homophily, and activism in crowdfunding* (SSRN Working Paper No. 2462254). Retrieved July 20, 2014, from http://papers.ssrn.com/sol3/papers.cfm?abstract_id=2462254*

Greiner, M. E., & Wang, H. (2010). Building consumer-to-consumer trust in e-finance marketplaces: An empirical analysis. *International Journal of Electronic Commerce, 15*(2), 105–136. doi:10.2753/JEC1086-4415150204*

Griffin, Z. J. (2012). Crowdfunding: Fleecing the American masses. *Case Western Reserve Journal of Law, Technology & the Internet.* Retrieved from http://papers.ssrn.com/sol3/papers.cfm?abstract_id=2030001*

Guzik, S. S. (2014). *SEC Crowdfunding rulemaking under the jobs act—An opportunity lost?* (SSRN Working Paper No. 2393897). Retrieved May 15, 2014, from http://papers.ssrn.com/sol3/papers.cfm?abstract_id=2393897

Haas, P., Blohm, I., & Leimeister, J. (2014). *An empirical taxonomy of crowdfunding intermediaries.* Retrieved July 20, 2014, from http://www.crowdinvesting.jura.uni-muenchen.de/dokumente/crowdfundingintermediaries.pdf*

Harhoff, D., Stahl, K., & Woywode, M. (1998). Legal form, growth and exit of West German firms—Empirical results for manufacturing, construction, trade and service industries. *The Journal of Industrial Economics, XLVI*(4), 453–488. doi:10.1111/1467-6451.00083

Harrison, R., & Mason, C. (2007). Does gender matter? Women business angels and the supply of entrepreneurial finance. *Entrepreneurship Theory and Practice, 31*(3), 445–472. doi:10.1111/j.1540-6520.2007.00182.x

Harzer, A. (2013). Erfolgsfaktoren im Crowdfunding. In: *Menschen—Märkte—Medien—Management: Schriftenreihe, Band 7.* Ilmenau: Universitätsverlag Ilmenau.

Hazen, T. (2012). Crowdfunding or fraudfunding? Social networks and the securities laws—Why the specially tailored exemption must be conditioned on meaningful disclosure. *North Carolina Law Review, 90,* 1735–1769. Retrieved from http://papers.ssrn.com/sol3/papers.cfm?abstract_id=1954040*

Hekman, E., & Brussee, R. (2013). *Crowdfunding and online social networks.* Retrieved May 15, 2014, from http://www2.mmu.ac.uk/media/mmuacuk/content/documents/carpe/2013-conference/papers/entrepreneurship/Erik Hekman, Rogier Brussee.pdf*

Hemer, J. (2011). *A snapshot on crowdfunding* (Working Paper Firms and Region Nr. R2/2011, Fraunhofer ISI). Retrieved April 10, 2013, from http://www.econstor.eu/handle/10419/52302*

Hemer, J., Schneider, U., Dornbusch, F., & Frey, S. (2011). *Crowdfunding und andere Formen informeller Mikrofinanzierung in der Projekt- und Innovationsfinanzierung.* Stuttgart: Fraunhofer Verlag.*

Heminway, J. (2013a). What is a security in the crowdfunding era? *7 Ohio State Entrepreneurial Business Law Journal, 335*(2012). Retrieved from http://papers.ssrn.com/sol3/papers.cfm?abstract_id=2210162*

Heminway, J. (2013b). The new intermediary on the block: Funding portals under the CROWDFUND Act. *UC Davis Business Law Journal, 13*, 177–205. Retrieved from http://papers.ssrn.com/sol3/papers.cfm?abstract_id=2293248*

Heminway, J. (2014). Investor and market protection in the crowdfunding era: Disclosing to and for the 'Crowd'. *Vermont Law Review, 38,* 827–848. Retrieved from http://papers.ssrn.com/sol3/papers.cfm?abstract_id=2435757*

Heminway, J., & Hoffman, S. (2011). Proceed at your peril: Crowdfunding and the securities act of 1933. *Tennessee Law Review, 78*, 879–972. Retrieved from http://papers.ssrn.com/sol3/papers.cfm?abstract_id=1875584*

Herzenstein, M., & Andrews, R. (2008). *The democratization of personal consumer loans? Determinants of success in online peer-to-peer lending communities* (SSRN Working Paper No. 1147856). Retrieved April 5, 2013, from http://ssrn.com/abstract=1147856*

Herzenstein, M., Dholakia, U. M., & Andrews, R. L. (2011). Strategic herding behavior in peer-to-peer loan auctions. *Journal of Interactive Marketing, 25*(1), 27–36. doi:10.1016/j.intmar.2010.07.001*

Herzenstein, M., Sonenshein, S., & Dholakia, U. M. (2011). Tell me a good story and I may lend you my money: The role of narratives in peer-to-peer lending decisions. *Journal of Marketing Research, XLVIII*(Special Issue 2011), 138–149. doi:10.1509/jmkr.48.SPL.S138*

Hienerth, C., & Riar, F. (2013). *The wisdom of the crowd vs. expert evaluation: A conceptualization of evaluation validity.* Paper presented at 35th DRUID Celebration Conference, Barcelona, Spain, June 17–19. Retrieved from http://druid8.sit.aau.dk/acc_papers/im4od175ix421p8l11ry1qg6gko8.pdf*

Hildebrand, T., Puri, M., & Rocholl, J. (2013). *Adverse incentives in crowdfunding* (SSRN Working Paper No. 1615483). Retrieved May 10, 2013, from http://papers.ssrn.com/sol3/papers.cfm?abstract_id=1615483*

Hornuf, L., & Klöhn, L. (2013). Crowdinvesting und Portfoliodiversifizierung—Eine rechtsökonomische Analyse. *Venture Capital Magazin, 2*, 34–35.*

Hornuf, L., & Schwienbacher, A. (2014a). Crowdinvesting—Angel investing for the masses? *Handbook of research on venture capital: Vol. 3. Business Angels.* Retrieved March 1, 2014, from http://papers.ssrn.com/sol3/papers.cfm?abstract_id=2401515

Hornuf, L., & Schwienbacher, A. (2014b). *Which securities regulation promotes crowdinvesting?* (SSRN Working Paper No. 2412124). Retrieved May 15, 2014, from http://papers.ssrn.com/sol3/Papers.cfm?abstract_id=2412124

Hu, M., Li, X., & Shi, M. (2014). *Product and pricing decisions in crowdfunding* (SSRN Working Paper No. 2405552). Retrieved May 15, 2014, from http://papers.ssrn.com/sol3/papers.cfm?abstract_id=2405552*

Hui, J., Gerber, E., & Greenberg, M. (2012). *Easy money? The demands of crowdfunding work.* Northwestern University, Segal Design Institute, Technical Report No. 4, (4). Retrieved March 15, 2013, from http://egerber.mech.northwestern.edu/wp-content/uploads/2012/11/Easy-Money-_The-Demands-of-CrowdfundingWork-_2012.pdf*

Hui, J., Greenberg, M., & Gerber, E. (2013). Understanding crowdfunding work: Implications for support tools. In *CHI'13 extended abstracts on Human Factors in Computing Systems* (pp. 889–894). ACM. Retrieved from http://www.juliehui.org/wp-content/uploads/2013/03/Hui_CHI2013_CrowdfundingWork_130305_v0.pdf*

Hulme, M., & Wright, C. (2006, October). Internet based social lending: Past, present and future. *Social Futures Observatory*. Retrieved from http://www.socialfuturesobservatory.co.uk/pdf_download/internetbasedsociallending.pdf*

Ingram, C., Teigland, R., & Vaast, E. (2014). Solving the puzzle of crowdfunding: Where technology affordances and institutional entrepreneurship collide. In *System Sciences (HICSS), 2014 47th Hawaii International Conference on, IEEE.* (pp. 4556–4567). doi:10.2139/ssrn.2285426*

Iyer, R., Khwaja, A., Luttmer, E., & Shue, K. (2009). *Screening in new credit markets: Can individual lenders infer borrower creditworthiness in peer-to-peer lending?* (NBER Working Paper No. 15242). Retrieved April 10, 2013, from http://www.nber.org/papers/w15242*
Jell, F., Block, J., & Henkel, J. (2011). Innovativität als Kriterium bei Venture-Capital-Investitionsentscheidungen. *Kredit Und Kapital, 44*(4), 509–541.
Kappel, T. (2009). Ex ante crowdfunding and the recording industry: A model for the US. *Loyola of Los Angeles Entertainment Law Review, 29*(3), 375–385. Retrieved from http://digitalcommons.lmu.edu/cgi/viewcontent.cgi?article=1550&context=elr*
Kassinger, T. W., Kaufmann, Z. D., & Traeger, L. (2013). Democratizing entrepreneurship: An overview of the past, present, and future of crowdfunding. *Securities Regulation & Law Report, 45*(5), 208–217. Retrieved from http://papers.ssrn.com/sol3/papers.cfm?abstract_id=2211698*
Kawai, K., Onishi, K., & Uetake, K. (2013). *Signaling in online credit markets* (2013 Meeting Papers No. 516). Society for Economic Dynamics. Retrieved May 15, 2014, from http://www.economicdynamics.org/meetpapers/2013/paper_516.pdf*
Kim, K., & Hann, I.-H. (2013). *Does crowdfunding democratize access to capital? A geographical analysis*. Retrieved May 15, 2014, from http://innovisops.com/papers/cist2013_submission_46.pdf*
Kim, K., & Viswanathan, S. (2013). *The experts in the crowd: The role of reputable investors in a crowdfunding market* (SSRN Working Paper No. 2258243). Retrieved July 15, 2013, from http://ssrn.com/abstract=2258243*
Klaebe, H., & Laycock, R. (2012, July). How to work the crowd: A snapshot of barriers and motivations to crowdfunding. *Artsupport Australia*. Retrieved April 10, 2013, from http://eprints.qut.edu.au/53471*
Klafft, M. (2008). Online peer-to-peer lending: A lenders' perspective. In *International Conference on E-Learning, E-Business, Enterprise Information Systems, and E-Government 2008*. Proceedings: 14–17 July 2008, Las Vegas, NV, USA. CSREA Press, 2008. Retrieved from http://papers.ssrn.com/sol3/papers.cfm?abstract_id=1352352*
Kleemann, F., Voß, G., & Rieder, K. (2008). Un(der)paid innovators: The commercial utilization of consumer work through crowdsourcing. *Science, Technology & Innovation Studies, 4*(1), 5–26. Retrieved from http://www.sti-studies.de/ojs/index.php/sti/article/view/81
Klöhn, L., & Hornuf, L. (2012). Crowdinvesting in Deutschland—Markt, Rechtslage und Regelungsperspektive. *Zeitschrift für Bankrecht und Bankwirtschaft ZBB, 24*(4), 237–266.*
Koning, R., & Model, J. (2013). *Experimental study of crowdfunding cascades: When nothing is better than something* (Working Paper SSRN No. 2308161). Retrieved August 30, 2013, from http://papers.ssrn.com/sol3/papers.cfm?abstract_id=2308161*
Kortleben, H., & Vollmar, B. (2012). *Crowdinvesting—eine Alternative in der Gründungsfinanzierung?* Forschungspapiere PFH No. 2012/06. Retrieved from http://www.goettingen.pfh.de/images/stories/pfh/pdf/crowdinvesting-eine_alternative_in_der_gruendungsfinanzierung.pdf*
Kraus, S., Schulz, A.-C., & Halberstadt, J. (2008). Humankapital als Erfolgsfaktor für Unternehmensgründungen. In T. T. Schwithal, M. Duensing, & D. Tredop (Eds.), *Kapital, Kompetenz, Konflikte* (pp. 111–124). Oldenburg: BIS-Verlag.
Kuppuswamy, V., & Bayus, B. L. (2013). *Crowdfunding creative ideas: The dynamics of project backers in Kickstarter* (UNC Kenan-Flagler Research Paper No. 2013-15). Retrieved June 20, 2014, from 10.2139/ssrn.2234765*
Lee, E., & Lee, B. (2012). Herding behavior in online P2P lending: An empirical investigation. *Electronic Commerce Research and Applications, 11*(5), 495–503. doi:10.1016/j.elerap.2012.02.001*
Lehner, O. M. (2013). Crowdfunding social ventures: A model and research agenda. *Venture Capital, 15*(4), 289–311. doi:10.1080/13691066.2013.782624*
Lehner, O. (2014). The formation and interplay of social capital in crowdfunded social ventures. *Entrepreneurship & Regional Development*. doi:10.1080/08985626.2014.922623*

Leimeister, J. M. (2012). Crowdsourcing: Crowdfunding, Crowdvoting, Crowdcreation. *Zeitschrift für Controlling und Management (ZFCM), 56*, 388–392. doi:10.1365/s12176-012-0662-5

Leland, H., & Pyle, D. (1977). Informational asymmetries, financial structure, and financial intermediation. *The Journal of Finance, 32*(2), 371–387. doi:10.1111/j.1540-6261.1977.tb03277.x

Ley, A., & Weaven, S. (2011). Exploring agency dynamics of crowdfunding in start-up capital financing. *Academy of Entrepreneurship Journal, 17*, 85–110.*

Lin, Y., Boh, W. F., & Goh, K. H. (2014). *How different are crowdfunders?* (SRRN Working Paper No. 2397571). Retrieved July 25, 2014, from http://papers.ssrn.com/sol3/Papers.cfm?abstract_id=2397571*

Lin, M., Prabhala, N. R., & Viswanathan, S. (2009). Social networks as signaling mechanisms: Evidence from online peer-to-peer lending. *WISE 2009*. Retrieved from http://people.stern.nyu.edu/bakos/wise/papers/wise2009-p09_paper.pdf*

Lin, M., Prabhala, N. R., & Viswanathan, S. (2013). Judging borrowers by the company they keep: Friendship networks and information asymmetry in online peer-to-peer lending. *Management Science, 59*(1), 17–35. doi:10.1287/mnsc.1120.1560*

Lin, M., & Viswanathan, S. (2013). *Home bias in online investments: An empirical study of an online crowd funding market* (SSRN Working Paper No. 2219546). Retrieved April 10, 2013, from http://papers.ssrn.com/sol3/Delivery.cfm?abstractid=2219546*

Liu, D., Lu, Y., & Brass, D. (2013). *Friendships in online peer-to-peer lending: Pipes, prisms, and social herding* (SSRN Working Paper No. 2251155). Retrieved July 30, 2013, from http://papers.ssrn.com/sol3/papers.cfm?abstract_id=2251155*

Lu, C., Xie, S., Kong, X., & Yu, P. S. (2014). Inferring the impacts of social media on crowdfunding categories and subject descriptors. In *Proceeding WSDM '14. Proceedings of the 7th ACM international conference on Web Search and Data Mining* (pp. 573–582). Retrieved from http://www.cs.uic.edu/~xkong/wsdm14_lu.pdf*

Mach, T., Carter, C., & Slattery, C. (2013). Peer-to-peer lending to small businesses. *Federal reserve system community development research conference*. Retrieved July 30, 2013, https://frbatlanta.org/documents/news/conferences/13resilience_rebuilding_paper_Mach.pdf*

Macht, S., & Weatherston, J. (2014). The benefits of online crowdfunding for fundseeking business ventures. *Strategic Change, 23*(1–2), 1–14. doi:10.1002/jsc*

Maeschle, O. (2012a). *Rationing of excessive demand on crowdinvesting-platforms* (Thünen-Series of Applied Economic Theory, Working Paper No. 126). Retrieved April 10, 2013, from http://www.econstor.eu/handle/10419/74657*

Maeschle, O. (2012b). *Which information should entrepreneurs on German crowdinvesting-platforms disclose?* (Thünen-Series of Applied Economic Theory, Working Paper No. 127). Retrieved April 10, 2013, from http://www.econstor.eu/handle/10419/74650*

Martin, T. (2012). *The Jobs Act of 2012: Balancing fundamental securities law principals with the demands of the crowd* (SSRN Working Paper No. 2040953). Retrieved April 10, 2013, from http://papers.ssrn.com/sol3/papers.cfm?abstract_id=2040953*

Martínez-cañas, R. (2012). Crowdfunding and social networks in the music industry: Implications. *International Business & Economics Research Journal, 11*(13), 1471–1476. Retrieved from http://www.cluteinstitute.com/journals/international-business-economics-research-journal-iber*

Meinshausen, S., Schiereck, D., & Stimeier, S. (2012). Crowdfunding als Finanzierungsalternative-Innovative Ansätze in der Unternehmensfinanzierung. *WiSt, 11* (November 2012), 583–588. Retrieved from http://ideas.repec.org/p/dar/wpaper/59836.html*

Michels, J. (2012). Do unverifiable disclosures matter? Evidence from peer-to-peer lending. *The Accounting Review, 87*(4), 1385–1413. doi:10.2308/accr-50159*

Mitra, D. (2012). The role of crowdfunding in entrepreneurial finance. *Delhi Business Review, 13* (2), 67–72. Retrieved from http://www.delhibusinessreview.org/v_13n2/v13n2g.pdf*

Mollick, E. (2013). *Swept away by the crowd? Crowdfunding, venture capital, and the selection of entrepreneurs* (SSRN Working Paper No. 2239204). Retrieved April 10, 2013, from http://papers.ssrn.com/sol3/papers.cfm?abstract_id=2239204*

Mollick, E. (2014). The dynamics of crowdfunding: An exploratory study. *Journal of Business Venturing, 29*(1), 1–16.*

Mollick, E., & Kuppuswamy, V. (2014). *After the campaign: Outcomes of crowdfunding* (UNC Kenan-Flagler Research Paper No. 2376997). Retrieved May 15, 2014, from http://papers.ssrn.com/sol3/papers.cfm?abstract_id=2376997*

Mollick, E., & Nanda, R. (2014). *Wisdom or madness? Comparing crowds with expert evaluation in funding the arts* (Harvard Business School Working Paper No. 14-116). Retrieved June 20, 2014, from http://papers.ssrn.com/sol3/papers.cfm?abstract_id=2443114*

Moritz, A., Block, J., & Lutz, E. (2014). *Investor communication in crowdfunding: A qualitative-empirical study* (SSRN Working Paper No. 2462282). Retrieved July 20, 2014, from http://papers.ssrn.com/sol3/papers.cfm?abstract_id=2462282*

Naroditskiy, V., Stein, S., & Tonin, M. (2014). *Referral incentives in crowdfunding*. Bonn: IZA—Institute for the Study of Labor. Retrieved May 15, 2014, from http://ftp.iza.org/dp7995.pdf

Ordanini, A., Miceli, L., Pizzetti, M., & Parasuraman, A. (2011). Crowd-funding: Transforming customers into investors through innovative service platforms. *Journal of Service Management, 22*(4), 443–470. doi:10.1108/09564231111155079*

Parker, S. C. (2014). *Crowdfunding, cascades and informed investors* (IZA Discussion Paper No. 7994). Retrieved May 15, 2014, from https://www.econstor.eu/dspace/bitstream/10419/93354/1/dp7994.pdf*

Pierrakis, Y., & Collins, L. (2013). *Crowdfunding: A new innovative model of providing funding to projects and businesses* (SSRN Working Paper No. 2395226). Retrieved May 15, 2014, from http://papers.ssrn.com/sol3/papers.cfm?abstract_id=2395226*

Pope, N. (2011). Crowdfunding microstartups: It's time for the securities and exchange commission to approve a small offering exemption. *University of Pennsylvania Journal of Business Law, 13*(4), 101–129. Retrieved from http://papers.ssrn.com/sol3/papers.cfm?abstract_id=1916985*

Pope, D., & Sydnor, J. (2011). What's in a picture? Evidence of discrimination from Prosper.com. *Journal of Human Resources, 46*(1), 53–92.*

Prantl, S. (2003). *Bankruptcy and voluntary liquidation: Evidence for new firms in East and West Germany after unification* (ZEW Discussion Papers, No. 03-72). Retrieved April 10, 2013, from http://www.econstor.eu/handle/10419/24022

Qiu, C. (2013). *Issues in crowdfunding: Theoretical and empirical investigation on Kickstarter* (SSRN Working Paper No. 2345872). Retrieved May 15, 2014, from http://papers.ssrn.com/sol3/papers.cfm?abstract_id=2345872*

Ravina, E. (2012). *Love & loans: The effect of beauty and personal characteristics in credit markets* (SSRN Working Paper No. 1107307). Retrieved April 10, 2013, from http://papers.ssrn.com/sol3/papers.cfm?abstract_id=1107307*

Robb, A., & Robinson, D. (2014). The capital structure decisions of new firms. *The Review of Financial Studies, 27*(1), 153–179. doi:10.1093/rfs/hhs072

Röthler, D., & Wenzlaff, K. (2011, September). Crowdfunding schemes in Europe. *EENC Report*. Retrieved from http://tosca.vtlseurope.com:8098/arxius/pdf/E130066.pdf*

Saxton, G. D., & Wang, L. (2013). The social network effect: The determinants of giving through social media. *Nonprofit and Voluntary Sector Quarterly*. doi:10.1177/0899764013485159*

Schwienbacher, A., & Larralde, B. (2012). Crowdfunding of small entrepreneurial ventures. In D. Cumming (Ed.), *The Oxford handbook of entrepreneurial finance* (pp. 369–391). New York: Oxford University Press.*

Smith, S., Windmeijer, F., & Wright, E. (2013). Peer effects in charitable giving: Evidence from the (running) field. *The Economic Journal*. doi:10.1111/ecoj.12114*

Stemler, A. R. (2013). The JOBS Act and crowdfunding: Harnessing the power—and money—of the masses. *Business Horizons, 56*(3), 271–275. doi:10.1016/j.bushor.2013.01.007*

Surowiecki, J. (2004). *The wisdom of crowds*. New York: Anchor Books.

Tomczak, A., & Brem, A. (2013). A conceptualized investment model of crowdfunding. *Venture Capital, 15*(4), 335–359.*

Tyebjee, T., & Bruno, A. (1984). A model of venture capitalist investment activity. *Management Science, 30*(9), 1051–1066.

Vass, T. (2013). *The Nexus of financial and political interests between crowdfunders and regional economic development professionals: The new-new innovation economics* (SSRN Working Paper No. 2291198). Retrieved April 10, 2013, from http://papers.ssrn.com/sol3/papers.cfm?abstract_id=2291198

Vitale, M. (2013). *Crowdfunding: Recent international developments and analysis of its compatibility with Australia's existing regulatory framework* (SSRN Working Paper No. 2324573). Retrieved May 15, 2014, from http://papers.ssrn.com/sol3/papers.cfm?abstract_id=2324573*

Von Krogh, G., Rossi-Lamastra, C., & Haefliger, S. (2012). Phenomenon-based research in management and organisation science: When is it rigorous and does it matter? *Long Range Planning, 45*(4), 277–298. doi:10.1016/j.lrp.2012.05.001

Ward, C., & Ramachandran, V. (2010). Crowdfunding the next hit: Microfunding online experience goods. In *Workshop on Computational Social Science and the Wisdom of Crowds at NIPS2010*. Retrieved from http://people.cs.umass.edu/~wallach/workshops/nips2010css/papers/ward.pdf*

Wash, R. (2013, July). The value of completing crowdfunding projects. In *International Conference on Weblogs and Social Media (ICWSM)*. AAAI Press. Retrieved from http://www.aaai.org/ocs/index.php/ICWSM/ICWSM13/paper/viewFile/6003/6403*

Wash, R., & Solomon, J. (2014). Coordinating donors on crowdfunding websites. In *Proceedings of the 17th ACM conference on Computer Supported Cooperative Work & Social Computing* (pp. 38–48). ACM. Retrieved from http://www.rickwash.com/papers/return-rule.pdf*

Weiss, G., Pelger, K., & Horsch, A. (2010). *Mitigating adverse selection in P2P lending—empirical evidence from Prosper.com* (SSRN Working Paper No. 1650774). Retrieved April 10, 2013, from http://papers.ssrn.com/sol3/papers.cfm?abstract_id=1650774*

Wheat, R. E., Wang, Y., Byrnes, J. E., & Ranganathan, J. (2013). Raising money for scientific research through crowdfunding. *Trends in Ecology & Evolution, 28*(2), 71–72. doi:10.1016/j.tree.2012.11.001*

Wroldsen, J. S. (2013). The social network and the Crowdfund Act: Zuckerberg, Saverin, and venture capitalists dilution of the crowd. *15 Vanderbilt Journal of Entertainment & Technology Law, 583*(2012–2013). Retrieved from http://papers.ssrn.com/sol3/papers.cfm?abstract_id=2141015*

Xu, A., Yang, X., Rao, H., Fu, W., Huang, S., & Bailey, B. P. (2014). Show me the money! An analysis of project updates during crowdfunding campaigns. In *Proceedings of the 32nd annual ACM conference on Human Factors in Computing Systems* (pp. 591–600). ACM. Retrieved from http://web.engr.illinois.edu/~xu26/index_files/crowdfunding-xu.pdf*

Yang, X. (2014). The role of photographs in online peer-to-peer lending behavior. *Social Behavior & Personality, 42*(38), 445–452. doi:10.2224/sbp.2014.42.3.445*

Yum, H., Lee, B., & Chae, M. (2012). From the wisdom of crowds to my own judgment in microfinance through online peer-to-peer lending platforms. *Electronic Commerce Research and Applications, 11*(5), 469–483. doi: 10.1016/j.elerap.2012.05.003*

Zhang, J., & Liu, P. (2012). Rational herding in microloan markets. *Management Science, 58*(5), 892–912. doi:10.1287/mnsc.1110.1459*

Zheng, H., Wan, N., Chen, D., & Wang, T. (2014). Antecedents of project implementation success in crowdfunding. In *PACIS 2014 Proceedings*. Retrieved July 20, 2014, from http://aisel.aisnet.org/pacis2014/318*

Zvilichovsky, D., Inbar, Y., & Barzilay, O. (2013). Playing both sides of the market: Success and reciprocity on crowdfunding platforms. In *International Conference on Information Systems, Milan 2013*. Retrieved from http://aisel.aisnet.org/cgi/viewcontent.cgi?article=1031&context=icis2013*

*included in the review

Crowd and Society: Outlining a Research Programme on the Societal Relevance and the Potential of Crowdfunding

Britta M. Gossel, Dennis Brüntje, and Andreas Will

Abstract In its early stages, research on crowdfunding focused primarily on the inside perspective of the phenomenon. The following article introduces a more comprehensive perspective, exploring the relevance of crowdfunding for society. With respect to the consequences of the financial crisis and societal challenges, the article outlines a research programme that contributes to the potential of crowdfunding on a societal level that can be explored from a media and communication science perspective and theory of financial intermediaries.

Keywords Crowdfunding • Society • Financial crisis • Role of intermediaries

1 Introducing the Topic: Financial Crisis, Societal Challenges—Assignments for Crowdfunding?

The financial crisis of 2007 caused profound changes to and challenges for society. From local to European and worldwide levels, various areas of society are affected and have to deal with the consequences. Even though, according to the government, the peak of the crisis has passed, consequences are still visible and omnipresent in Germany. Trust in financial markets has been affected (Beckert, 2010). There has been a noticeable increase in public debt at a federal and country level (Ministry of Finance, 2013a). Recent political decisions illustrate these consequences, e.g. decreasing investments of governments [e.g. in culture and regional economy (Ministry of Finance, 2013b)], reform of federalism in 2009, and a resulting debt brake (BPB, 2013). Furthermore, inflation and wage increases do not offset the budget items, for example in the fields of science and education (Ministry of Finance, 2013c). Parallel to this, we observe a rapid change of the media landscape caused by digitisation and progressing development of media technology, particularly based on the dynamics of the social web: Today, not only technically but on a level of everyday practice it is possible to bring together and to connect different actors not reliant on time and space but according to their individual interests.

B.M. Gossel (✉) • D. Brüntje • A. Will
Technische Universität Ilmenau, Ilmenau, Germany
e-mail: britta.gossel@tu-ilmenau.de

D. Brüntje, O. Gajda (eds.), *Crowdfunding in Europe*, FGF Studies in Small Business and Entrepreneurship, DOI 10.1007/978-3-319-18017-5_4

Consequences of these phenomena are discussed in the scientific community, for example, under the labels of open innovation (Chesbrough, 2003; Chesbrough & Appleyard, 2007), crowdsourcing (Howe, 2006) and particularly crowdfunding as specific adoption of crowdsourcing (Brabham, 2013).

Existing definitions aside (e.g. Belleflamme, Lambert, & Schwienbacher, 2014; Mollick, 2014; Schwienbacher & Larralde, 2012), we decided to define crowdfunding referring to Müllerleile and Joenssen (2014) as "a process where commercial or non-commercial projects are initiated in a public announcement by organisations or individuals to receive funding, assess the market potential, and build customer relationships. Pledgers may then contribute individual amounts of monetary or non-monetary resources, during a specified timeframe, using offline or online campaign platforms that utilise different payment schemes, in exchange for a product-specific or unspecific, material or immaterial reward".

Research on crowdfunding is at its beginnings, due to the novelty of the phenomenon itself. But in the past 4 years, it increasingly captured the interest of the scientific community. Recent studies are based on approaches from various disciplines such as social sciences, psychology, information technology and economics (e.g. Dolata & Schrape, 2013; Kuppuswamy & Bayus, 2013; Leimeister, 2012). Those works focus primarily on psychological aspects or the inside perspective of the phenomenon, dealing with success factors (e.g. Harzer, 2013; Mollick, 2014; Müllerleile & Joenssen, 2014), capital seeker and provider motivation (e.g. Gerber, Hui, & Kuo, 2012; Helm, 2012), and the (decision) behaviour of capital providers (e.g. Agrawal, Catalini, & Goldfarb, 2011; Beier & Wagner, 2014; Burtch, Ghose, & Wattal, 2013; Kuppuswamy & Bayus, 2013) in the different types of crowdfunding [i.e. equity-, lending-, reward- or donation-based (Massolution, 2012)]. Furthermore, regulatory issues are in scope of recent investigations (e.g. Germany: Klöhn & Hornuf, 2012; USA: Bradford, 2012; EU: De Buysere, Gajda, Kleverlaan, & Marom, 2012). Nevertheless, a lack of theory in the arising scientific discussion has already been observed and criticised (e.g. Dolata & Schrape, 2013). Empirical investigations predominantly focus on industry reports (e.g. Massolution, 2012, 2013), literature investigations (e.g. Moritz & Block, 2014), overview articles (e.g. Hemer, 2011), model-theoretical comparisons (e.g. Belleflamme, Lambert, & Schwienbacher, 2010, 2014), and expert interviews (e.g. Steward & Ramos, 2014). Furthermore, first model-theoretical approaches (e.g. Burtch et al., 2013) and impact studies (e.g. Hulme & Wright, 2006) exist in the field of social lending.

Reflecting this status quo on crowdfunding research, we observe a focus on different crowdfunding subareas. A comprehensive overview on crowdfunding as well as its impact for society is rarely undertaken. Since we observe a lack of examination of crowdfunding's relevance for society and in-depth empirical investigations within this context, this article introduces a more comprehensive perspective, exploring the relevance of crowdfunding for society from a sociological and economic perspective. We lift the focus on crowdfunding from micro- to meso- and macro-level by redirecting the question: To what extent can crowdfunding contribute to specific areas of society and its organisations by breaking off or substituting traditional roles of financial intermediaries?

By the following, we introduce our preliminary thoughts conceptualising a research programme. Based on theoretical assumptions on society, its sub-systems and organisations, we will introduce two perspectives of observation: Media and communication science and financial intermediation. Furthermore, we will highlight the aims and scope of research, and give an outlook on the core questions for the programme.

2 Theoretical Background

Society is described in the contexts of classical sociological theory (Simmel, 1989; Tönnies, 2005; Weber, 2002), structural functionalism (Parsons, 2009), social systems theory (Luhmann, 1987, 1995, 2000) or the theory of power and practice (Bourdieu, 1979). Social systems theory and its enhancements are recently influencing several scientific discourses, e.g. in the field of organisational studies (Cooren, Kuhn, Cornelissen, & Clarke, 2011; Putnam & Nicotera, 2009; Schoeneborn, 2011; Schoeneborn, Blaschke, & Seidl, 2012), in the areas of media and communications research (Theis-Berglmair, 2013; Wendelin, 2008), and sociology (Roth, 2012). Taking these developments seriously, we argue the following based on the structuring framework of social systems theory according to Luhmann (1987, 1995, 2000). By doing so, we will not delve into the complexities of the theory, but we will focus on three core concepts, which provide an appropriate framework to our research programme: Society, sub-systems and organisations.

In social systems theory, Luhmann introduces the concept of social systems based on the core and constitutive process of communication (Seidl, 2004). This concept of social systems provides the basis to his assumption of society: "According to Luhmann we can distinguish three types of social systems: Society, face-to-face interaction and organisation. All three systems are social systems insofar as they reproduce themselves on the basis of communications. They are, however, different types of social systems insofar as they reproduce different types of communications" (Seidl, 2004, p. 13). Society in this context "is the all-encompassing social system that includes everything that is social" (Luhmann, 1995, p. 408). This most complex version of a social system is assumed to be functionally differentiated: "The functionally differentiated society as the present form of differentiation is of most interest to us here. It is characterised by the existence of different functional systems" (Seidl, 2004, p. 13). Those functional systems can be assumed as sub-systems of society, supporting society with specific functions. Examples might be the legal system, the economic system or the political system (Seidl, 2004). How many of these sub-systems might be differentiated is in discussion. For example Roth (2012) analysed the discussion on functional differentiation and suggests ten sub-systems.

Orthogonally to this differentiation, the theory of social systems introduces the concept of organisation, which is assumed on the meso-level of society. This specific type of social systems has decision communication as a core and constitutive element: "Organisations arise and reproduce, if decision communication is processed and the system is operatively closed on this level of operation. Anything else—goals, hierarchy, membership, or whatever else is yet seen as a criterion of organisation, is in contrast derivative and can be assumed as a result of decision operations of the system" (Luhmann, 2000, p. 63, own translation). Even though an orientation of an organisation to primarily one societal sub-system might be assumed (e.g. a school as an organisation in the sub-system of education, a venture as an organisation in the sub-system of economy, a political party as an organisation in the sub-system of politics), the recent debate goes towards a multi-referential orientation (e.g. Gossel & Will, 2012; Lieckweg & Wehrsig, 2001). Within this framework we go one step further and focus on a special type of organisations, which are called intermediating organisations. These can be ascribed a specific role in and for society. Intermediating organisations connect structurally disconnected areas of society. These organisations have the function of coordinating society (Bauer & Grenzdörffer, 1997; Jarren, 2008). Intermediating organisations in a traditional sense are interest groups (Willems & von Winter, 2007), NGOs, registered associations (Braun, 2010) and financial intermediaries (Buhl & Kundisch, 2003; Will, 1999). Financial intermediaries are traditional players in the financial system of Europe, such as banks, insurance companies and other actors (e.g. holdings). Those financial intermediaries enable suitable transaction partners to be found and their quality to be explored. Lastly, they process exchanges (e.g. money) (Will, 1999).

If we now challenge this theoretical background with recent developments, we can open up our research programme on crowd and society. Here, we argue on the basis of two different perspectives of observation: (a) recent developments in media technology, and (b) decreasing trust in financial intermediaries.

(a) Massive and fundamental changes caused by technological advantages have been observed in the context of media and society—one example might be the use of the Internet and its applications. Taking the example of Germany, today 46 % of online users are active in social networks, 60 % have their own profile which they use daily. Activities vary and include specifically the dimension of sharing (Bitkom, 2011; Busemann, 2013; Frees & van Eimeren, 2013; van Eimeren, 2013; van Eimeren & Frees, 2013). A large amount of scientific observation and analysis of this field is made by media and communication scientists. Media and communication science focuses on social contexts and consequences of medial, public and interpersonal communication and is facing challenges recently caused by changing society, digitisation, globalisation, individualisation, mediatisation and economisation (DGPuK, 2013). Based on the above-described developments, media and communication science turns in some respects from traditional mass media orientation to an expanded assumption of media as platforms that allow a mass topic-related connection (peer-to-peer) of singular actors along their interests and needs, bringing together different actors along specific topics. They allow mass communication on a new level and offer a basis for further interactions, such as the financing of projects. Thus, introducing the phenomenon of crowdfunding and connecting it with the above-mentioned changes of media and society, new areas of research arise for media and communication science, following questions such as: What are the implications of these new forms of media platforms for society, social cohesion and participation? Which specific problems of society and its organisations can these media help to solve? Which role do these media play as a novel form of societal intermediaries?

(b) If we examine intermediating organisations, we should also observe fundamental changes and challenges. Since 2007, the financial crisis has resulted in a crisis of financial intermediaries. Society's trust in traditional financial intermediaries has sunk dramatically in the face of business practices as securitisation and selling mortgage loans, high-risk over-the-counter derivative transactions, manipulation of markets by interest agreements or miscounseling with serious financial consequences. We observe an inert commercial and inter-bank credit business. Many ventures were not able to finance planned investments due to the credit crunch, leading to massive retracement of economic activity (Deutsche Bundesbank, 2014). Public authorities have narrowed scope to implement and support societal eligible intentions. On the contrary, monetary assets of private households and private non-profit organisations in Germany have increased between 2007 and 2012 (except 2008) and currently have a level of 3.373 trillion euros (Deutsche Bundesbank, 2013).

Summing up these reflections, we can observe decreasing trust in traditional financial intermediaries, increasing monetary assets of private households, and immense societal and entrepreneurial challenges for society and its organisations. Referring to these observations, questions on how to re-organise financial intermediaries can be reflected. In focus might be questions on new ways of organising the coordination between supply and demand of capital beside traditional financial intermediaries. Specifically referring to crowdfunding, and focusing on societal consequences of the financial crisis, it has to be explored, how and to what extent new actors based on social web technology supplement, e.g. crowdfunding platforms, can expand or substitute the function of financial intermediaries.

3 Objectives, Scope and Core Questions of the Research Programme

Reflecting these perspectives, we suggest crowdfunding to be put on the agenda of research disciplines, focusing on both, the role of media for society and financial intermediaries. We therefore introduce in the following a work-in-progress research

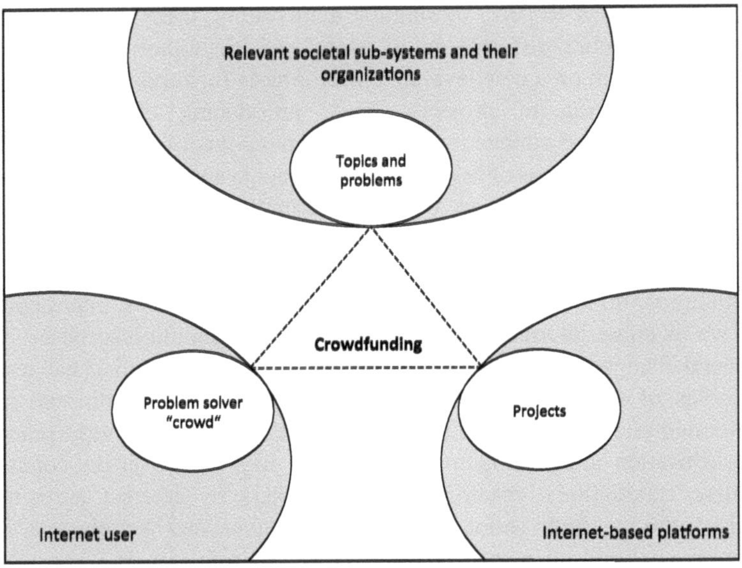

Fig. 1 Research field crowdfunding

programme on crowd and society as a field of research from the perspectives of media and communication science.

Observing crowdfunding, we distinguish *three intertwined areas* (Fig. 1):

a) Societal sub-systems and their organisations appeal to the crowd with specific *topics or problems* aiming at getting these issues solved by the crowd. This might be a movie production company (organisation) from the societal sub-system culture. The company strives for hosting a short film festival (topic), but is lacking some budget (problem). By crowdfunding (project), the company wants to finance the festival through Kickstarter (internet-based crowdfunding platform) by engaged and interested Internet users (crowd).
b) *Projects* are calls for action to the crowd, constrained by time, scope and budget. They are published on internet-based platforms and follow the platforms' structure and conditions. For example, a respective project would be the description and presentation of the film production company's problem by text, pictures, audio and video, of the budget requested and of rewards offered on the Kickstarter platform over a certain period of, for example, 6 weeks.
c) The *crowd* are those Internet users who obtain knowledge about projects (directly from the platforms or indirectly via further communication campaigns) and who share material or immaterial resources to support the objectives of the project. In our example, the crowd are those interested users of the Internet, who find out about the project (on Kickstarter, via Facebook, Twitter, e-mail, word of mouth etc.) and support the festival by contributing to the budget, and receiving, for example, a festival ticket as a reward.

Main objective of the research programme is to understand, describe and explain crowdfunding as a specific phenomenon reflecting its relevance for society. In a first step the programme aims at identifying and describing areas of society that potentially benefit from crowdfunding. This may include the identification and description of relevant organisations in various areas of society (e.g. culture organisations, private foundations, sports organisations), the identification and description of recent challenges and needs of these organisations that can be solved with crowdfunding (e.g. decreasing municipal, country or federal grants, increasing public debts), identification of knowledge, experience and shortcomings of these organisations with respect to crowdfunding.

Secondly, the specific crowds within these contexts should be identified and described. This may include a profile and typology of actors that participate as part of a crowd, such as sociodemographic variables, media usage behaviour and cultural characteristics. It is intended to evaluate personal and contextual characteristics, which influence the motivation and actions of specific crowds. Research should aim to analyse crowd clusters and their connection to topics relevant to identified organisations/societal areas as well as success factors of crowdfunding.

Finally, it should be intended to analyse and explain crowdfunding along its processes and deduce success factors. This includes a detailed description and analysis of relevant crowdfunding platforms and its operating companies, identification and description of projects comprising initiating persons/teams/organisations. Furthermore, project topics, project implementation on crowdfunding platforms, surrounding media campaign activities and success factors will be examined.

To reduce complexity, the analysis of a national crowdfunding market might be a good starting point. Accordingly, the national results and processes will be reflected and analysed with respect to specific cultural and societal characteristics. But as we expect extensive national differences, caused, for example, by different federal system or systems of public funding, an international comparative study seems to promise fruitful results.

Summing up, the research programme focuses on four research questions:

(a) For which organisations and topics is crowdfunding a potential solution for recent financial challenges?
(b) What types of Internet users make up a crowd and which dimensions describe these actors?
(c) Which success factors characterise successful crowdfunding projects in this context?
(d) To what extent can crowdfunding substitute roles and assignments of traditional societal financial intermediaries?

4 Method

To answer these questions, the research programme will be conducted from the perspective of media and communication science working with a well-grounded theoretical and empirical approach based on social sciences. Following a reality-oriented approach (Kubicek, 1977; Tomczak, 1992), crowdfunding is described and explained in terms of a theory-driven empiricism. A mix of qualitative and quantitative empirical methods in terms of a triangulation will generate maximum scientific knowledge. Here we consider both a parallel and sequential combination of qualitative and quantitative research methods (Flick, 2011).

To gain a more thorough understanding, we first suggest conducting three consecutive studies in order to prepare the main one. The objective of the first study is to conduct a situation analysis on crowdfunding carrying out literature work, collecting data about relevant platforms, tools, widgets and different investor types in one database as well as adapting and concretising the analysis units of the aforementioned intertwined areas (see again Fig. 1). Furthermore, the necessary project infrastructure has to be established, the industry network has to be expanded, and theoretical, methodological and technological preparations have to be undertaken. Building on this ground work, the second study aims at obtaining expert knowledge by conducting expert interviews about topics and problems of societal sub-systems as well as crowdfunding in order to develop the research tools. The objective of the third study is to develop these tools for the empirical investigations in the main study. This includes the development of instruments for the analysis of (1) organisations, topics and problem areas concerning crowdfunding, (2) the crowd, (3) platforms, and (4) campaigns. Furthermore, the technological infrastructure for holistic data collection and analysis will be prepared.

Based on this preliminary work the main study will focus on field work as well as data analysis and evaluation. The field work includes four partial surveys:

(1) **Organisations, topics and problem areas:** Qualitative interviews and quantitative surveys will be conducted with all relevant organisations in different national and regional societal sub-systems. The objective is to identify and characterise topics and problem areas in these organisations which are solvable by crowdfunding, and the existing knowledge about these phenomena.
(2) **Crowd analysis:** To develop a crowd typology, Internet users being active on crowdfunding platforms will be questioned in a comprehensive quantitative online survey about their sociodemography, media usage, cultural traits, personality traits, context traits and motivation.
(3) **Platform analysis:** By a quantitative content analysis of crowdfunding project processes and by qualitative interviews with platform operators, success factors will be determined. For the automated collection of data in the content analysis a technological solution will be developed and implemented.
(4) **Campaign analysis:** All running projects and their accompanying campaigns will be analysed through content analysis and a quantitative survey with project

starters focusing on communicative activities beyond the platforms. Partially, the data collection will be automated again.

All data will be digitised (qualitative methods) or will be collected digitally (technological extraction of data, online survey tools) and aggregated in one infrastructure to ease the data analysis. After the field work the large data set will be analysed and evaluated, the results will be formulated and interpreted. For that purpose explorative statistic methods as well as methods of qualitative content analysis will be used. The results and interpretation will refer to theoretical work, the programme's starting situation and will be in accordance with the objectives.

5 Outlook

The results shall deduce consequences, chances and change capabilities of crowdfunding for specific areas of society and its organisations. Topics and challenges of organisations from diverse areas of society that have the potential to be solved by crowdfunding shall be identified and described. By focusing on a changed role of financial intermediaries, conclusions on the potential financial volume of crowdfunding shall be deducted.

The results will enrich the discourse in media and communication science, especially concerning current challenges of the changing digital media society and the changing media usage behaviour. The proposed research agenda will contribute to the debate on the "digital dawn" by explaining the changing role of societal intermediaries and the consequences for society and its sub-systems. Furthermore, the results provide insights to better understand the role of new intermediaries, their role in the financial sub-system and the societal perception of intermediary functions. Finally, the results can be used to deduce and actively communicate individual recommendations of action to the stakeholders involved. They enable policy-makers on a European as well as on a national and regional level to obtain a broad picture of crowdfunding and an enhanced information basis for decision-making in this important field of policy. Therefore, all results as well as preliminary insights and findings (design of the studies, theory etc.) should be brought to the scientific, political and public arena to foster the cooperation and information exchange of European researchers on crowdfunding, of policy-makers and the interested public. The authors of this article, having completed all preliminaries to this research agenda, are looking forward to soon beginning this project on a national level in Germany. We cordially invite fellow scholars from other European countries to cooperate and to follow and further develop this agenda to a true pan-European project on crowdfunding and society.

References

Agrawal, A., Catalini, C., & Goldfarb, A. (2011). *Friends, family, and the flat world: The geography of crowdfunding* (NET Institute Working Paper No. 10-08). Retrieved from http://ssrn.com/abstract=1692661

Bauer, R., & Grenzdörffer, K. (1997). Jenseits der egoistischen Ökonomie und des methodologischen Individualismus. Die Potentiale des intermediären Bereichs. *Leviathan, 25*(3), 38–61.

Beckert, J. (2010). Die Finanzkrise ist auch eine Vertrauenskrise. In Max-Planck-Gesellschaft (Ed.), *Jahresbericht 2009 der Max-Planck-Gesellschaft zur Förderung der Wissenschaften e.V.* (pp. 14–23). Retrieved from http://www.mpg.de/7301104/Jahresbericht_2009.pdf

Beier, M., & Wagner, K. (2014, February). *Getting money from the crowd: Drivers of fundraising success.* Paper presented at 12th Interdisciplinary European Conference on Entrepreneurship Research (IECER), Chur.

Belleflamme, P., Lambert, T., & Schwienbacher, A. (2010). *Crowdfunding: An industrial organization perspective* (SSRN Working Paper No. 2151179). Retrieved from http://ssrn.com/abstract=2151179

Belleflamme, P., Lambert, T., & Schwienbacher, A. (2014). Crowdfunding: Tapping the right crowd. *Journal of Business Venturing, 29*(5), 585–609. Retrieved from http://ssrn.com/abstract=1836873

Bitkom. (2011). *Studie Soziale Netzwerke.* Retrieved from http://www.bitkom.org/de/publikationen/38338_69029.aspx

Bourdieu, P. (1979). *Entwurf einer Theorie der Praxis: auf der ethnologischen Grundlage der kabylischen Gesellschaft* (3rd ed.). Frankfurt a.M.: Suhrkamp Verlag.

BPB (Bundeszentrale für Politische Bildung). (2013). *Finanzförderalismus.* Retrieved from http://www.bpb.de/izpb/159356/finanzfoederalismus?p=all

Brabham, D. C. (2013). *Crowdsourcing.* Cambridge, MA: MIT Press.

Bradford, C. (2012). Crowdfunding and the federal securities laws. *Columbia Business Law Review, 2012*(1), 1–150.

Braun, S. (2010). Struktur- und Funktionswandel intermediärer Großorganisationen als demokratie- und sozialpolitische Herausforderung—zu Kernanliegen des ersten Engagementberichts "Für eine Kultur der Mitverantwortung". *BBE-Newsletter* 20/2012.

Buhl, H. U., & Kundisch, D. (2003). Transformation von Finanzintermediären durch Informationstechnologie. *Wirtschaftsinformatik, 45*(5), 503–508.

Burtch, G., Ghose, A., & Wattal, S. (2013). *Cultural differences and geography as determinants of online pro-social lending* (SSRN Working Paper No. 2271298). Retrieved from http://papers.ssrn.com/sol3/papers.cfm?abstract_id=2271298

Busemann, K. (2013). Wer nutzt was im Social Web? Ergebnisse der ARD/ZDF-Onlinestudie 2013. *Media Perspektiven, 7–8*, 391–399.

Chesbrough, H. W. (2003). *Open innovation. The new imperative for creating and profiting from technology.* Boston: Harvard Business School Publishing.

Chesbrough, H. W., & Appleyard, M. M. (2007). Open innovation and strategy. *California Management Review, 50*(1), 57–76.

Cooren, F., Kuhn, T., Cornelissen, J., & Clarke, T. (2011). Communication, organizing and organization: An overview and introduction to the special issue. *Organization Studies, 32*(9), 1149–1170.

De Buysere, K., Gajda, O., Kleverlaan, R., & Marom, D. (2012). *A framework for European crowdfunding.* Retrieved from http://www.eurocrowd.org/files/2013/06/FRAMEWORK_EU_CROWDFUNDING.pdf

Deutsche Bundesbank. (2013). *Geldvermögen und Verbindlichkeiten.* Retrieved from http://www.bundesbank.de/Redaktion/DE/Pressemitteilungen/BBK/2013/2013_05_03_geldvermoegen_verbindlichkeiten.pdf?__blob=publicationFile

Deutsche Bundesbank. (2014). *Geld und Geldpolitik*. Retrieved from http://www.bundesbank.de/Redaktion/DE/Downloads/Veroeffentlichungen/Buch_Broschuere_Flyer/geld_und_geldpolitik.pdf?__blob=publicationFile

DGPuK (Deutsche Gesellschaft für Publizistik und Kommunikationswissenschaft). (2013). *Selbstverständnis*. Retrieved from www.dgpuk.de

Dolata, U., & Schrape, J.-F. (2013). *Zwischen Individuum und Organisation. Neue kollektive Akteure und Handlungskonstellationen im Internet* (SOI Discussion Paper No. 2013-02).

Flick, U. (2011). *Triangulation. Eine Einführung* (3rd rev. ed.). Wiesbaden: VS-Verlag.

Frees, B., & van Eimeren, B. (2013). Multioptionales Fernsehen in digitalen Medienumgebungen. Ergebnisse der ARD/ZDF-Onlinestudie 2013. *Media Perspektiven, 7–8*, 373–385.

Gerber, E. M., Hui, J. S., & Kuo, P. (2012). *Crowdfunding: Why people are motivated to post and fund projects on crowdfunding platforms*. Creative Action Lab, Northwestern University.

Gossel, B. M., & Will, A. (2012). *The communicative side of strategy. Introducing the strategy as practice approach to media management research*. Paper presented at JIBS|MMTC Strategy Workshop, Jönköping, Sweden.

Harzer, A. (2013). Erfolgsfaktoren im Crowdfunding. In A. Will & D. Brüntje (Eds.), *Menschen—Märkte—Medien—Management* (Vol. 7). Ilmenau: Univ.-Verl. Ilmenau.

Helm, M. (2012). *Träume finanzieren 2.0. Eine quantitative Befragung zu den Motivationen der finanziellen Projektunterstützung auf deutschsprachigen Crowdfunding-Plattformen*. Unpublished master's thesis, Technische Universität Ilmenau, Ilmenau.

Hemer, J. (2011). *A snapshot on crowdfunding* (Working Papers Firms and Region No. R2/2011), Fraunhofer ISI.

Howe, J. (2006, June 14). *The rise of crowdsourcing*. Retrieved from http://www.wired.com/wired/archive/14.06/crowds.html

Hulme, M. K., & Wright, C. (2006, October). *Internet based social lending: Past, present and future*. Retrieved from http://www.socialfuturesobservatory.co.uk/pdf_download/internetbasedsociallending.pdf

Jarren, O. (2008). Massenmedien als Intermediäre. Zur anhaltenden Relevanz der Massenmedien für die öffentliche Kommunikation. *M & K—Medien und Kommunikationswissenschaft, 56*(3/4), 329–346.

Klöhn, L., & Hornuf, L. (2012). Crowdinvesting in Deutschland—Markt, Rechtslage und Regelungsperspektive. *Zeitschrift für Bankrecht und Bankwirtschaft ZBB, 24*(4), 237–266.

Kubicek, H. (1977). Heuristische Bezugsrahmen und heuristisch angelegte Forschungsdesigns als Elemente einer Konstruktionsstrategie empirischer Forschung. In R. Köhler (Ed.), *Empirische und handlungstheoretische Forschungskonzeptionen in der Betriebswirtschaftslehre* (pp. 3–36). Stuttgart: Poeschl.

Kuppuswamy, V., & Bayus, B. L. (2013). *Crowdfunding creative ideas: The dynamics of project backers in Kickstarter* (SSRN Working Paper No. 2234765). Retrieved from http://papers.ssrn.com/sol3/papers.cfm?abstract_id=2234765

Leimeister, J. M. (2012). Crowdsourcing: Crowdfunding, Crowdvoting, Crowdcreation. *Zeitschrift für Controlling und Management (ZFCM), 56*, 388–392.

Lieckweg, T., & Wehrsig, C. (2001). Ausdifferenzierung von Organisationen und Funktionssystemen. In V. Tacke (Ed.), *Organisation und gesellschaftliche Differenzierung* (pp. 39–60). Wiesbaden: Westdeutscher Verlag.

Luhmann, N. (1987). Soziale Systeme: Grundriß einer allgemeinen Theorie. Frankfurt a.M.: Suhrkamp Verlag.

Luhmann, N. (1995). *Social systems*. Stanford: Stanford University Press.

Luhmann, N. (2000). *Organisation und Entscheidung*. Wiesbaden: Opladen.

Massolution. (2012). *Crowdfunding industry report 2012*. Retrieved from http://www.crowdsourcing.org/document/crowdfunding-industry-report-abridged-version-market-trends-composition-and-crowdfunding-platforms/14277

Massolution. (2013). *Crowdfunding industry report 2013*. Retrieved from http://research.crowdsourcing.org/2013cf-crowdfunding-industry-report

Ministry of Finance. (2013a). *24. Subventionsbericht. Punkt 36*. Retrieved from http://www.bundesfinanzministerium.de/Content/DE/Downloads/Broschueren_Bestellservice/2013-09-10--24_Subventionsbericht_Langfassung.pdf?__blob=publicationFile&v=4

Ministry of Finance. (2013b). *Finanzbericht 2014*. Retrieved from http://www.bundesfinanzministerium.de/Content/DE/Standardartikel/Themen/Oeffentliche_Finanzen/Wirtschafts_und_Finanzdaten/Finanzbericht-2014-anl.pdf?__blob=publicationFile&v=2

Ministry of Finance. (2013c). *Finanzplan 2013–2017*. Retrieved from http://www.bundesfinanzministerium.de/Content/DE/Standardartikel/Themen/Oeffentliche_Finanzen/Bundeshaushalt/Bundeshaushalt_2013/2013-08-13-finanzplan-2013-2017.pdf?__blob=publicationFile&v=2

Mollick, E. (2014). The dynamics of crowdfunding: An exploratory study. *Journal of Business Venturing, 29*(1), 1–16.

Moritz, A., & Block, J. (2014). Crowdfunding und Crowdinvesting: State-of-the-Art der wissenschaftlichen Literatur. *Zeitschrift für KMU und Entrepreneurship, 62*(1), 57–89.

Müllerleile, T., & Joenssen, D. W. (2014). Key success-determinants of crowdfunded projects: An exploratory analysis. In B. Lausen, S. Krolak-Schwerdt, & M. Boehmer (Eds.), *Data analysis, learning by latent structures and knowledge discovery. Studies in classification, data analysis and knowledge organization*. Berlin: Springer.

Parsons, T. (2009). *Das System moderner Gesellschaften* (7th ed.). Weinheim: Juventa.

Putnam, L., & Nicotera, A. M. (2009). Communicative constitution of organization is a question: Critical issues for addressing it. *Management Communication Quarterly, 24*(1), 158–165.

Roth, S. (2012). Die zehn Systeme. Ein Beitrag zur Kanonisierung der Funktionssysteme. *Social & Political Philosophy eJournal, 12*(6).

Schoeneborn, D. (2011). Organization as communication: A Luhmannian perspective. *Management Communication Quarterly, 25*(4), 663–689.

Schoeneborn, D., Blaschke, S., & Seidl, D. (2012). Organizations as networks of communication episodes: Turning the network perspective inside out. *Organization Studies, 33*(7), 879–906.

Schwienbacher, A., & Larralde, B. (2012). Crowdfunding of small entrepreneurial ventures. In D. Cumming (Ed.), *The Oxford handbook. Entrepreneurial finance*. New York: Oxford University Press.

Seidl, D. (2004). *Luhmann's theory of autopoietic social systems* (Munich Business Research No. 2004-2). Retrieved from http://www.zfog.bwl.unimuenchen.de/files/mitarbeiter/paper2004_2.pdf

Simmel, G. (1989). *Aufsätze 1887–1890. Über sociale Differenzierung. Die Probleme der Geschichtsphilosophie (1892)* (2nd ed.). Frankfurt a.M.: Suhrkamp Verlag.

Steward, J., & Ramos, J. (2014). *Crowdfunding and the role of managers in ensuring the sustainability of crowdfunding platforms* (JRC Scientific and Policy reports No. EUR 26596 EN). European Commission.

Theis-Berglmair, A.-M. (2013). Why "public relations", why not "organizational communication"? Some comments on the dynamic potential of a research area. In A. Zerfaß, L. Rademacher, & S. Wehmeier (Eds.), *Organisationskommunikation und Public Relations. Forschungsparadigmen und neue Perspektiven* (pp. 26–42). Berlin: Springer.

Tomczak, T. (1992). Forschungsmethoden in der Marketingwissenschaft. Ein Plädoyer für den qualitativen Forschungsansatz. *Marketing ZfP, 2*, 77–87.

Tönnies, F. (2005). *Gemeinschaft und Gesellschaft: Grundbegriffe der reinen Soziologie* (4th ed.). Darmstadt: Wissenschaftliche Buchgesellschaft (WBG).

van Eimeren, B. (2013). "Always on"—Smartphone, Tablet & Co. als neue Taktgeber im Netz. Ergebnisse der ARD/ZDF-Onlinestudie 2013. *Media Perspektiven, 7–8*, 386–390.

van Eimeren, B., & Frees, B. (2013). Rasanter Anstieg des Internetkonsums—Onliner fast drei Stunden täglich im Netz. Ergebnisse der ARD/ZDF-Onlinestudie 2013. *Media Perspektiven, 7–8*, 358–371.

Weber, M. (2002). *Wirtschaft und Gesellschaft* (5th ed.). Tübingen: Mohr.

Wendelin, M. (2008). Systemtheorie als Innovation in der Kommunikationswissenschaft. Inhaltliche Hemmnisse und institutionelle Erfolgsfaktoren im Diffusionsprozess. *Communicatio Socialis, 41*(4), 341–359.

Will, A. (1999). *Individuelle Finanzdienstleistungen auf Netzmärkten. Ökonomische Analyse und Angebotsgestaltung*. Habilitation thesis, University of Augsburg, Augsburg. Retrieved from http://www.db-thueringen.de/servlets/DerivateServlet/Derivate-8233/Individuelle%20Finanzdienstleistungen%20auf%20Netzm%C3%A4rkten.pdf

Willems, U., & von Winter, T. (2007). Interessenverbände als intermediäre Organisationen. Zum Wandel ihrer Strukturen, Funktionen, Strategien und Effekte in einer veränderten Umwelt. In T. von Winter & U. Willems (Eds.), *Interessenverbände in Deutschland* (pp. 13–50). Wiesbaden: VS Verlag für Sozialwissenschaften.

Part II
Regional Examinations on Crowdfunding

The Financing Process of Equity-Based Crowdfunding: An Empirical Analysis

Anja Hagedorn and Andreas Pinkwart

Abstract Equity-based crowdfunding is a relatively new method to obtain capital for start-ups. Hereby ventures use special Internet platforms to issue shares of different sorts to the public. However, a great variety of platforms exist, which leads us to the question of whether there is a general crowdfunding process enabling founders to finance their business or not. If we knew of a general model, we could give recommendations to founders, service providers and investors. Therefore, in this article, we analyse the process of equity-based crowdfunding from the perspective of a capital seeker and ask how the process of equity-based crowdfunding is structured in practice. We answer this question by conducting an explorative analysis consisting of an iterative examination of the 16 different platforms existing in Germany. By doing so, we aim to identify commonalities and differences and derive a general model. The findings will be used for further discussion and provide information for stakeholders in order to optimize the process.

Keywords Entrepreneurial finance • Crowdfunding • Crowdinvesting

1 Introduction

Equity-based crowdfunding (also called crowdinvesting) became a promising instrument to overcome a start-up's liquidity problems, known as the early-stage equity gap (Veugelers, 2011). The equity gap reduces the success of new start-ups or prevents them from fully concentrating on its core activities of their business model (Geyer, Heimer, Hölscher, & Schalast, 2010). In 2011, around 16 % of start-ups faced this lack of financial resources (Hagen, Metzger, & Ullrich, 2012). Thus, equity-based crowdfunding is a potential solution for reducing this gap, because it removes barriers to equity.

Crowdinvesting is a subset of crowdfunding, providing a framework with which shares of young companies or projects can be offered to the public. The innovative idea behind it is that anyone can offer investment possibilities if minimum standards are fulfilled and, equally, anyone can invest. Therefore, we define

A. Hagedorn (✉) • A. Pinkwart
HHL Leipzig Graduate School of Management, Leipzig, Germany
e-mail: anja.hagedorn@hhl.de

D. Brüntje, O. Gajda (eds.), *Crowdfunding in Europe*, FGF Studies in Small Business and Entrepreneurship, DOI 10.1007/978-3-319-18017-5_5

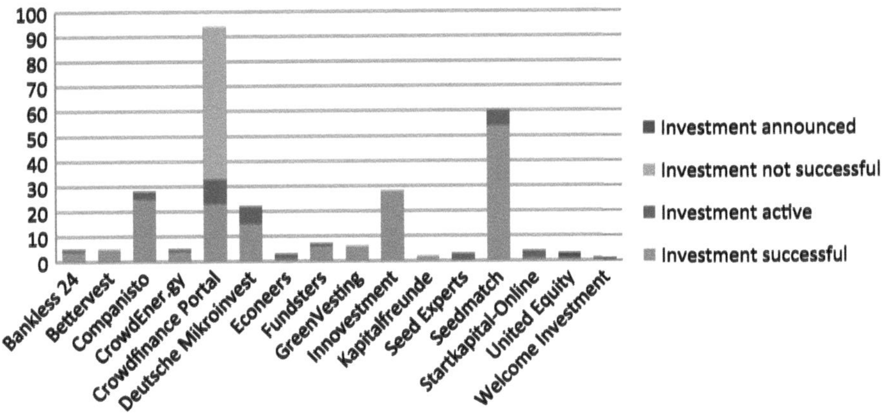

Fig. 1 Platforms that provide equity-based crowdfunding projects, updated in April 2014

crowdinvesting as: "*a financing method for young ventures and other commercial projects that supports the acquisition of equity by coordinating the submission of different forms of shares to an undefined group of possible investors through social virtual communities.*" Unlike crowdfunding, it concentrates mainly on financing young ventures or commercial projects by equity or mezzanine capital through the issue of shares and thereby requires a legal body. Compared to crowdfunding, participation is generally not rewarded by gifts or material incentives, but by return on investment.

However, equity-based crowdfunding is not regulated explicitly in Germany, which leads to a great variety of designs and applications. This is why we have conducted an analysis on the 16 most active crowdinvesting platform providers, shown in Fig. 1. We examined the processes and operating conditions in order to create a general framework, in order to find commonalities and differences and provide information for founders. In the following, we discuss our findings regarding the equity-based crowdfunding platform analysis and combine it with some essential theoretical aspects.

2 Current Literature

Equity-based crowdfunding is a new research area for academia with a rising number of authors concentrating on that field (e.g. Moritz & Block, 2014; Klöhn & Hornuf, 2012; Brem & Wassong, 2014). Until today few researchers have mentioned it in papers about crowdfunding and crowdsourcing (e.g. Gassmann (2012), Wolfson (2012), Schwienbacher and Larralde (2010) or Hemer, Schneider, Dornbusch, and Frey (2011)), most authors focus on the less explored field of crowdsourcing or crowdfunding in general (e.g. Kappel, 2009; Hemer, 2011). Research has also been carried out on motivational aspects in crowdsourcing (e.g. Carpenter, 2011; Reichwald, Ihl, & Seifert, 2004; Reichwald & Piller, 2005) as well as in crowdfunding (e.g. Harms, 2007; Hemer et al., 2011; Kleemann, Voß, & Rieder, 2008), although the special circumstances of crowdinvesting have been neglected.

Very fundamental research in this field has been conducted by Howe (2006), who argues that crowds can be more efficient than individuals. Their advantage is the ability to accumulate wisdom, which is the result of solutions aggregating to each other, ending up with having better overall solutions (Surowiecki, 2005). In the case of crowdinvesting, it is not discussed with any finality whether the "wisdom of the crowds" applies or not, because it is questionable whether the decision of an individual in the crowd is really independent (Klöhn & Hornuf, 2012). On the contrary, Shiller (2000) teaches us that crowds can lead to "irrational exuberance" with huge macroeconomic effects, as we have seen during the last financial crisis. Hence, Kortleben and Vollmar (2012) draw theoretic considerations regarding possible agency-constellations between the investor, the start-up and the crowdinvesting platform.

Also the work of Hemer et al. (2011) can be mentioned as fundamental to crowdfunding research. Hemer et al. (2011) provide a general overview of the German crowdfunding market. Their work contains basic principles, which can also be relevant for equity-based crowdfunding. The great variety of the examined study objects so far inhibits generalisation; while a few patterns can be identified that correlate with equity-based crowdfunding (for instance functions, like the threshold-pledge system). Furthermore, crowdinvesting uses a different approach compared to crowdfunding regarding the financing method. This difference implies different motivations of the money provider (we are already speaking of investors here), increasing possibilities for start-ups in terms of the amount of acquirable capital.

As a starting point for equity-based crowdfunding research, the work of Schwienbacher and Larralde (2010) can be mentioned. He and his colleagues were the first European scholars to discuss crowdfunding focusing mainly on venture financing (see also Belleflamme, Lambert, & Schwienbacher, 2010; Lambert & Schwienbacher, 2010). While we found few works in academia solely discussing equity-based crowdfunding, the daily media, digital media and fact books paid a lot of attention to it. For example, the private institute ikosom (Institut für Kommunikation in den sozialen Medien) carried out a survey among all six crowdfunding and equity-based crowdfunding websites between May 2010 and April 2011. The result was the first comprehensive study on German equity-based crowdfunding and crowdfunding platforms (Eisfeld-Reschke & Wenzlaff, 2011).

During our literature research we also identified one recent study by Klöhn and Hornuf (2012), who examined all five of the then existing equity-based crowdfunding platforms from a legal perspective. This very detailed work gave us an impression of the complexity and disorder of the market and motivated us for further investigation, the result of which is this article. There has also been general research into the functioning of social media platforms. In his model of social contagion, Russ (2007) describes the phases of contagion a social media platform needs to establish in order to be successful. Since social media plays a crucial role in crowdinvesting, we presume this to be also valid for its service providers.

3 Methodology

The aim of this paper is to provide a deeper insight into the process of equity-based crowdfunding. To this end, we conducted a platform analysis. In the first step, we made an explorative analysis to obtain an overview of crowdfunding and crowdinvesting. Thereby we started with a literature review to gain first knowledge and then expanded our research by interviewing experts, visiting conferences and participating in workshops.

To identify equity-based crowdfunding platforms, we also used a collection of 139 worldwide listed crowdfunding and equity-based crowdfunding platforms, which had been collected in a crowdsourced project (Wattig, 2010). Out of this set we identified 20 equity-based crowdfunding platforms in total in Germany, of which 16 are currently active. In the second step we analysed, categorized and compared the different platforms in Germany in an iterative process by using the categories presented in Table 1. The result is a general crowdinvesting process, discussed in Sect. 4.

4 Functionality of Equity-Based Crowdfunding

From our empirical analysis we derived an equity-based crowdfunding process, which is presented in the following, Fig. 2. It consists of an application phase, where a founder makes an application with a business plan and other data on an equity-based crowdfunding platform. In the screening and selection phase, the platform evaluates the applications and prepares a negotiation strategy calculating the business value and evaluating the possible conditions. Sometimes the evaluation of the crowd is also taken into account. After a positive evaluation, the founder agrees on a contract in the contracting phase. After this phase, the investment offer will be announced in the roadshow phase to the crowd, including a fixed starting date of the subscription period. The following subscription phase is essential for the success of the funding. If the investment threshold is not reached, the submission of shares will be cancelled and neither the equity-based crowdfunding platform nor the emitter would get any money. Therefore, both parties have a strong interest in the success of this phase, which is expressed in a high marketing activity. Also in

Table 1 Categories of the empirical analysis

Funding system	Funding instrument	The branch	Financing phase	Costs for issuers
Minimum investment amount	Type of platform service	Evaluation of the business idea	Evaluation of the business value	Number of projects conducted
Holding period	Used additional service providers	Community building		

Fig. 2 Phases of the equity-based crowdfunding process, own presentation

this phase, the issuer agrees on contracts regarding the conditions of the holding of the shares, for instance the holding period or the dilution of the same. After the positive subscription of shares (which means the reach of the investment threshold) the holding phase follows. Depending on the individual contracts, the investor must hold the shares for some determined time period. After this time period, the investor is free to sell the shares, give them back to the issuer or to prolong the contract. This is called the exit-phase. In the following, each step of this process will be discussed, based on empirical and theoretical data.

4.1 *Application, Screening and Selection Phase*

First the founders make an application to the platform, because they benefit from using its infrastructure to get in contact with the investors-community for marketing and financial purposes. The platform provider selects the best applications by performing a very simplified due diligence (Klöhn & Hornuf, 2012), done in personal talks or online in template questionnaires. This due diligence can contain credit-ratings, the business plan evaluations or even personality tests. Hereby the innovativeness, uniqueness of the idea, scalability, usefulness and explicability are the most used selection criteria (Sauer, 2012).

Apart from that, the company value is calculated. Basis is often a reliable financial plan from which a possible exit-revenue at the end of the holding period is calculated. From this specific value the platform discounts the yield expectations to calculate the current company value. In one case a pre-auction system is used as a method to indicate the company value. Here the pitfall might be that the investors may not have all information at this time to evaluate the company information correctly, which may cause a winner's curse.

4.2 *Contracting Phase*

After a positive evaluation of the business plan and further information, the platform provider settles with the founder on financial and managerial conditions. Besides the settlement on the acquired amount of capital, which influences the percentage of service fee, it is important for the founder to choose an appropriate form of submission. In our analysis we identified four main funding instruments with varying characteristics. As shown in Fig. 3, the platforms make use of typical and atypical silent partnerships, subordinated participating profit loans,

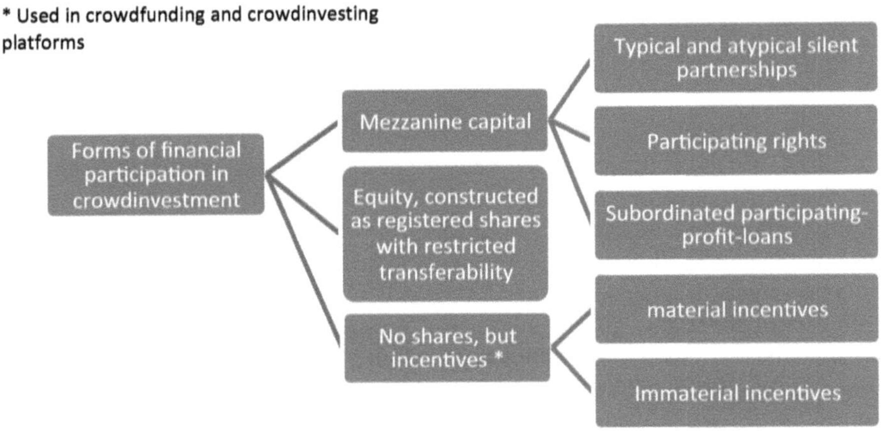

Fig. 3 Forms of participation used in equity-based crowdfunding own presentation

participation rights and registered shares with restricted transferability to finance a business. Moreover, we found a platform which cooperated with a bank. By doing so, it can offer investment possibilities above the legal investment threshold of 100,000 euros without bearing the costs of owning a banking license. For institutional investors, a new costumer segment is made accessible by the equity-based crowdfunding platform. In contrast, due to the partnership the platform can offer a reliable and credible professionalized service that signals trustworthiness.

All funding instruments except stock shares[1] are issued with a revenue and loss share amounting individually to each campaign and deposit and controlling rights (which cannot be removed due to the German law), but without participation rights. This is advantageous for the entrepreneur because it is essential that he/she does not fear investors either enforcing a new management against his/her will or taking over the whole company. On the contrary, this disadvantage lowers the attractiveness of shares and thus also the price of non-voting shares (Zingales, 1994), which could make some investors abstain from the investment (Brennan & Franks, 1997; Mäschle, 2012a). In order to attract investors the emitter should use an underprizing strategy, which is not trivial for the investor to observe since the evaluation of the firm value is only rudimentarily done (Mäschle, 2012b).

While the German law restricts the funding amount by using silent partnerships to 100,000 euros, subordinated participating profit loans and participation rights are unrestricted. Most of the platforms, who use this kind of financing instrument already, included the possibility to enlarge the financing limit above 100,000

[1] Regarding the issuing of stock shares we found only one platform. Since for the submission and trading of stock shares a license by the German financial service authority "Bundesamt für Finanzdienstleistungsaufsicht" is required, the platform might easily obtain a competitive advantage due to high entry barriers and a high credibility. Compared to other platforms, the ownership of the license signals the trustworthiness of the platform.

euros. Especially for high-technology-based ventures, which often need a high financing budget, this could be an alternative method to obtain capital.

Besides the settlement on financial conditions, the usage of additional marketing and legal services would also be arranged in this phase, such as the creation of a public-relations concept including a pitching video and photo-shoots, the maintenance of investors relations, the procurement of management experts or lawyers, substantial support in preparing a prospectus as well as the provision of co-working spaces. Besides that mentoring services can also be offered. The extent of additional services differs between crowdinvestment providers, and often must be paid in addition, which is why users should carefully examine the platforms in order to avoid unnecessary costs. Besides that, all equity-based crowdfunding providers have in common that they support the issuer with the shareholder-management by providing standardised contracts. The contracts, which we found are individual for each platform, leave little space for individual agreements. Mostly, they are written out in full regarding participation, information and controlling rights as well as administrative issues and termination agreements (see also Klöhn & Hornuf, 2012).

4.3 Roadshow Phase

Here the platform provider announces the new investment opportunity and the potential investors are given time to evaluate the new venture and the business model itself. Therefore, the platform provides the crowd with the business plan of the venture, business descriptions, image videos and other additional material. Every investor is responsible for the evaluation of the investment. Platforms do not provide any investment advisory services and are not investment brokers in terms of customer-related order fulfilment (Klöhn & Hornuf, 2012), but sometimes give investors the chance to interact with each other and the issuers.

In this context, the risk of copying the business idea is given by the fact, that with equity-based crowdfunding, confidential business information is transfered to an unknown group of people. For knowledge-based business models especially, the risk of reproduction by competitors could appear as a threat to young founders, potentially violating their first-mover advantage. Surprisingly, the expert interview with Neuronation, a founder team, which used equity-based crowdfunding, leaves an ambivalent opinion: on the one hand, the problem could be solved by reducing the detailedness of the provided information, while issuers risk the possibility of lawsuits in the case of loss. On the other hand, some founders do not regard this as a problem. They went public with their offering, when their core product or service should be ready for the market and thus the business model should be already developed (Neuronation, 2011). Hereby the founders could even use the first-mover advantage offered by the timespan between starting their business activity and the appearance of first competitors.

The fact that every investor must analyse the business plan by him/herself leads to a discrimination problem for the investor: In a setting with informed and uninformed investors, the informed investors can discriminate against the uninformed ones by buying the underprized shares, while leaving the overprized shares to the uninformed investors (Mäschle, 2012b). In contrast, the uninformed investors can overcome the discrimination if they have the chance to follow herding behaviour. Mäschle (2012b) notes that investors are likely to use a free-rider strategy in order to avoid time-costing searching and evaluation activities, which would reduce individual costs of information production but raises the risk of irrational exuberance. That is why an equity-based crowdfunding platform should install a mechanism to either inform every investor properly, or to make sure that every investor who is interested in the venture can do so. Until now, no analysed platform has installed such a mechanism in their funding system, although the time span with which the shares are sold out depends on the platform and the investment offer.[2]

Considering the possibility of small investment amounts, it is doubtful that investors take enough time to evaluate the business idea. Also, the range of possible types of investors is greater by using smaller minimum investment amounts, so that the knowledge and expertise of the investors regarding the ability to evaluate the investment decision can be questioned. Besides that Klöhn and Hornuf (2012) found in their study among five equity-based crowdfunding platforms, that the smaller the investment amount the higher the number of investors. This could also be verified in our study. That means that a smaller investment limit would also increase the transaction costs for shareholder management. Two of the examined platforms were supporting small investment amounts and also carried the shareholder management. Those platforms directly buy the shares from the issuer under the suspensive condition that the re-funding reaches the funding limit at minimum, and refund this transaction at the same time by offering the shares to private investors. The advantage is the reduced transactional costs for issuers, who do not have to deal with a crowd but only with the crowdfunding platform.

For higher investments per share, a self-selection mechanism regarding socio-economic characteristics of the investor could occur. However, whether an investor is able to assess the risks and benefits from the business model, especially because everybody can be a potential investor despite one's ability or knowledge, could not be finally examined in our study.

Hence, most platforms therefore use the *first-come-first-serve model* in combination with the *threshold-pledge system* for their funding process (Hemer et al., 2011). The threshold-pledge system is using a minimum funding threshold (Hemer et al., 2011) that must be reached within a period. The period is normally 60 days; most platforms provide the possibility of an extension for an additional 60 days. In this time the issuer has the possibility to activate lead users and start the social

---

[2] In the case "easy card" some investors were complaining that they were not able to participate in the investment due to the fast submission (expert interview with Jens-Uwe Sauer, 2012). The investment limit of a 100,000 euros was reached after 87 min (Seedmatch GmbH, 2012). This raises the question whether investors are really evaluating the business or just following the herd.

contagion process. If the funding threshold is not reached within the agreed period, the project fails and the money is transferred back to the investors. The days before the deadline are especially critical if the venture just reaches the limit. German consumer protection allows the cancellation of contracts agreed on the Internet within 2 weeks of the day the contract was concluded (§321d (1) BGB, §355 BGB). To support this critical phase, platforms sometimes agree to allow a cancellation rate of, for instance, 10 %. That means that 10 % of the investors can cancel their contract without declaring the project as failed.

4.4 Subscription Phase

If an investor is positive about supporting the business, he is free to subscribe shares in a determined time span, the subscription phase. The minimum investment limit per share varies between websites and depending on the type of financing instrument. It differs between 5 and 1,000 euros at minimum for the platform using the auctioning system. This starts with 1,000 euros in the first round and might be raised during the following auction rounds.

There are two main, distinguishable investment methods: the simple subscription method and a pre-auction method. In the *pre-auction method* the value of the shares is determined by the demand of investors. The advantage is a realistic market estimation of the company value. On the contrary, irrational exuberance might be a result through rising share-prices. The *simple subscription method* works after the first come-first serve principle. In this case the investment contract is made directly between the company and the founder, while the platform provides the infrastructure and support. In the other case the investor contracts with the platform in the first step, which itself participated in the start-up and refinanced the participation through a following submission of shares in a second step. The advantage is a reduction of complexity for the start-up, which has only one investor and not many small ones.

Our research also identified different legal settings regarding the submission of shares: a *trust model* (direct submission of shares with platform as issuer), a *peer-to-peer model* with a direct submission with platform as intermediary or a *stock model* as funding systems. In the trust model, which has been identified two times, the investor is, like in a trust investment, not directly investing in a company but contracting with the platform. The financing instruments generally used on equity-based crowdfunding platforms are either silent partnerships or participating loans. In the peer-to-peer model, which has been recorded in the majority of cases, one can subscribe any desired amount of shares with a constant value directly from the venture until the budget target is reached. Here the first come-first serve principle is applied. The value of the shares is either set by the issuer or it is calculated by an *auction mechanism* (identified one time during the analysis). On the contrary the *stock-model* is used by one equity-based crowdfunding platform. Here it offers

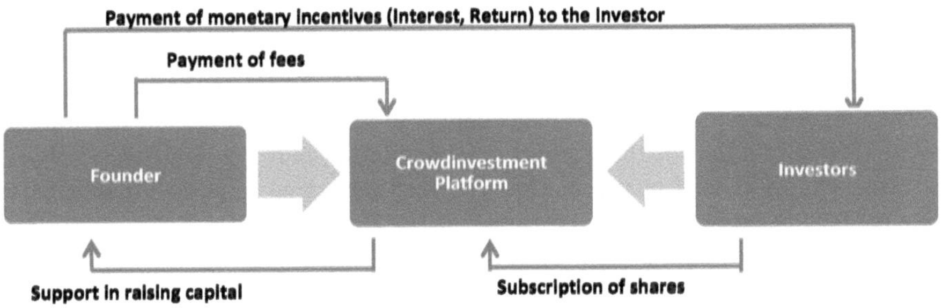

Fig. 4 Equity-based crowdfunding process, own presentation

stock shares as a way to finance a business, but is also providing the possibility to trade them using the *company-own trading system.*

By clicking on a virtual button the investor accepts the investment offer. For the conclusion of the contract we experienced two main systems: the "offer acceptance" or "invitation to treat". With the *"offer-acceptance"-model*, the offer made by the issuer is directly confirmed by clicking on the button on the website. Mostly an automatic payment procedure follows for the investor, supported by a trustee bank. Hereby we identified one bank, which seems to have specialized among others in equity-based crowdfunding transactions. In some cases the investor can pay via bank transfer or other transfer services. When the money has been transferred, the investor usually gets the signed contract via e-mail or post. The advantage is a fast handling of payments, although it would not be controllable who is investing.

This is different to the *"invitation to treat"-model*, where the investor signals interest in investing in this offer by clicking on the button on the project-website. The emitter now can decide whether to accept the investor or not, which would be positively confirmed by the submission of the contract to the investor. The money has to be transferred afterwards individually by the investor. Hereby the advantage is that the issuer can control who is investing. On the contrary, this system implies high transactional costs for the issuer. If the funding limit is reached, the capital seeker transfers the service fees to the equity-based crowdfunding platform. The process is sketched in Fig. 4.

4.5 Holding Phase

During the holding period the investor is frequently provided with information by the issuer, for instance about the annual and quarterly business development, or gets informed if something unplanned happens. After the ending of the holding period, the investor can decide whether to prolong or cancel the investment. Hereby, the exit strategy depends on the individual investor and remains unclear, because it is too early to consider any empirical data.

The holding period varies between platforms and projects. In general it would be very hard for start-ups to calculate on a short-term holding period for re-funding of sold shares. Therefore, the most platforms offer medium-term holding periods (between 5 and 10 years). Hereby the platforms using the trust model and the stock model have the advantage of providing a higher flexibility in terms of offering a variable holding period resulting from their special business model.

The costs for issuers also vary widely between platforms and depend on the type of investment of the additional services. Generally, it is an amount of 5–10 % of the funding in total. All platforms only charge the fee if the funding is successful. Attention should be paid to the detailed service arrangements: sometimes additional costs for the trustee service, managerial and lawing service as well as certifications, like a prospectus, occur. One platform has been identified that uses a rating service ("Crefo-Auskunft") to signal the liquidity to investors on the project page, which must be paid for as an extra cost. In the case of another equity-based crowdfunding provider, ventures have to prepare a prospectus if they would like to obtain more than a 100,000 euros. This is necessary because of legal issues but would cause an additional cost of around 20,000 euros. Also most platforms want to install a project video or photos, which must also be paid for individually.

For the shareholder, the service is mostly free. One platform is charging an ordering fee of 5 euros, which is due to the special stock model. Another equity-based crowdfunding platform with a trust model charges for services at 10 % of the owned shares, which is charged related to the performance, like preparing performance and tax reporting. In the case where there is a negative performance, no fee would be charged as well.

4.6 Exit Phase

For this phase we have almost no information regarding the processes and possibilities, because there was no empirical data about the exit of an investment made by equity-based crowdfunding. This is due to the fact that the holding period of the first investments will only end in 2014. The exit of an equity-based crowdfunding is due with the expiration of the holding period if no automatic prolongation mechanism was agreed in the contract. Otherwise, the investor or the company could cancel the contract after the expiration of the holding period. If the venture has submitted shares with different holding periods and is thus planning an incremental exit, the dilution of shares could be possible. The higher the difference between the costs for the new capital and the current equity-based crowdfunding, the higher the likelihood of this.

For a sharp exit, it depends on the individual development of a financed company how it would be processed. From this point of view, there are two main ways of pursuing the exit: (a) if the issuer has a weak financial basis or is even insolvent, it is likely that only a small part of the shares or less can be repaid, which means that the investment has failed, and (b) if the venture is performing well or even better than before the equity-based crowdfunding, it is likely that the shares including the return would be repaid and the venture could once more do equity-based crowdfunding if the costs for it are lower than for using another financing instrument, like obtaining venture capital, etc.

Empirical data show that the market is still supplying equity-based crowdfunding capital, which allows capital seekers to open new financial rounds on it, even if the first equity-based crowdfunding round would be on-going.[3] Here also the investor faces the possibility of the dilution of shares. Thereby it depends on the individual contract with the issuer and the platform if an anti-dilution agreement is arranged. During our analysis we found only a few contracts where this was the case (Klooß, 2013).

5 Implications for Entrepreneurship Research

The entrepreneurship research is facing a new, very creative market development, which is investigated in a growing number of studies. Equity-based crowdfunding is only one example. At this juncture the advantages for founders and investors predominates the usage, because a fast capital acquirement and capital investment for small amounts is provided, while the revenue for the investor remains uncertain, since no past experience can help to build expectations.

In the presented paper we investigated the current equity-based crowdfunding websites by analysing 16 active crowdinvesting platforms. Through this, we contributed to recent research by providing a general overview over the functioning of equity-based crowdfunding. However, the total number of 16 active platforms (and the 7 additional platforms that have not started yet) compared to the number of projects executed on each one leave the impression that the market is already saturated and is now slowly downsizing. Nevertheless, many new equity-based crowdfunding platforms are starting the business activity, while investors are demanding more new investment opportunities. This reflects the need of the founders for new ways to obtain small amounts of money but also the need for investors to invest in times of low credit rates and high economic uncertainty. It is characteristically of a systemical weakness of the German market; the missing financial support especially for small and medium sized start-ups. In conclusion, equity-based crowdfunding cannot be the universal remedy for closing the equity gap, but a good alternative for financing small businesses.

On the contrary, the market is still young but still developing in terms of the platforms' business models and fast-growing in terms of the number of financed projects. How the subscribed shares will develop, which must be held at least 3 years, if they are losing or winning value, will be shown by the end of 2014,

[3] Examples are funding projects like Cloud&Heat, Secucloud, Laserad, Front Row Society, Honestly, Protonet, Refined Investments (Seedmatch GmbH, 2015).

when the first shares are liquidated. Therefore, further research should concentrate on the aspects that will come up with the first investments that have reached their due date: Are the ventures able to pay back the investment? What happens if the company becomes insolvent in the meantime? How could replacements or connected investment be designed? Hereby the research should pay more attention to investor behaviour, regarding the attraction of them to the platform and new investments. We must learn more about the investor in order to find a good way to support founders and investors in serving their interests. Moreover, studies should focus more on the legal and economic framework. It is still unclear how the legal framework could support the investor and founders and build more certainty for equity-based crowdfunding. It is also questionable if crowdinvesting is able to fulfil the high expectations, if the market had a legal framework like in the U.S. Which implication has a higher investment limit, such as we face in the U.S., for start-ups, investors, general economic development and other financing methods like venture capital? Last but not least, the research could pay more attention to the development of equity-based crowdfunding in Europe to provide ways to foster the entrepreneurial development of our neighbours. How could the overall economic impact of crowdinvesting, especially for countries with less developed financial markets, be estimated? Later research therefore should question again the utility of the instrument, the promotion of innovation as well as the sustainability of equity-based crowdfunding.

References

Belleflamme, P., Lambert, T., & Schwienbacher, A. (2010). *Crowdfunding: An industrial organization perspective*. Retrieved from http://economix.fr/pdf/workshops/2010_dbm/Belleflamme_al.pdf

Brem, A., & Wassong, N. (2014). Wer investiert warum? Eine Analyse von Investmententscheidungen bei Crowdfunding-Projekten. *ZfKE—Zeitschrift für KMU und Entrepreneurship, 62*, 31–55.

Brennan, M., & Franks, J. (1997). Underpricing, ownership and control in initial public offerings of equity securities in the UK. *Journal of Financial Economics, 45*(3), 391–413.

Carpenter, H. (2011). Motivating the crowd to participate in your innovation initiative. In P. Sloane (Ed.), *A guide to open innovation and crowdsourcing* (pp. 76–84). London: KoganPage.

Eisfeld-Reschke, J., & Wenzlaff, K. (2011). *Crowdfunding Studie 2010/2011—Untersuchung des plattformgestützten Crowdfundings im deutschsprachigen Raum, Juni 2010 bis Mai 2011*. Retrieved from http://www.ikosom.de/2011/06/13/crowdfunding-studie-2011/

Gassmann, O. (2012). *Crowdsourcing*. München: Hanser.

Geyer, A., Heimer, T., Hölscher, L., & Schalast, C. (2010). *Evaluierung des High-Tech Gründerfonds* (Endbericht). Retrieved from Bundesministerium für Wirtschaft und Technologie website: http://www.bmwi.de/BMWi/Redaktion/PDF/Publikationen/Studien/evalueirung-des-high-tech-gruenderfonds-endbericht.pdf

Hagen, T., Metzger, G., & Ullrich, K. (2012). *KfW-Gründungsmonitor 2012*. Retrieved from https://www.kfw.de/Download-Center/Konzernthemen/Research/PDF-Dokumente-Gr%C3%BCndungsmonitor/Gr%C3%BCndungsmonitor-2012-lang.pdf

Harms, M. (2007). *What drives motivation to participate financially in a crowdfunding community?* (SSRN Working Paper). Retrieved from http://ssrn.com/abstract=2269242

Hemer, J. (2011). *A snapshot on crowdfunding*. Retrieved from http://isi.fraunhofer.de/isi-media/docs/p/de/arbpap_unternehmen_region/ap_r2_2011.pdf?WSESSIONID=ywharkir

Hemer, J., Schneider, U., Dornbusch, F., & Frey, S. (Eds.). (2011). *Crowdfunding und andere Formen informeller Mikrofinanzierung in der Projekt- und Innovationsfinanzierung*. Stuttgart: Fraunhofer-Verl.

Howe, J. (2006, July). The rise of crowdsourcing. WIRED 14.06. Retrieved from http://archive.wired.com/wired/archive/14.06/crowds.html

Kappel, T. (2009). Ex ante crowdfunding and the recording industry: A model for the U.S.? *Loyola of Los Angeles Entertainment Law Review, 29*(3), 375–385.

Kleemann, F., Voß, G. G., & Rieder, K. (2008). Un(der)paid innovators: The commercial utilization of consumer work through crowdsourcing. *Science, Technology & Innovation Studies, 4*(1), 5–26.

Klöhn, L., & Hornuf, L. (2012). Equity-based Crowdfunding in Deutschland. *Zeitschrift für Bankrecht und Bankwirtschaft: ZBB, 24*(4), 237–266.

Klooß, K. (2013, March). Risiken bei Crowdinvestments—Die dunkle Seite der Macht der Masse. *Manager Magazin*. Retrieved from http://www.manager-magazin.de/unternehmen/artikel/a-891280.html

Kortleben, H., & Vollmar, B. H. (2012). *Crowdinvesting. Eine Alternative in der Gründungsfinanzierung?* Retrieved from http://www.pfh.de/images/stories/pfh/pdf/crowdinvestingeine_alternative_in_der_gruendungsfinanzierung.pdf

Lambert, T., & Schwienbacher, A. (2010). *An empirical analysis of crowdfunding*. Retrieved from http://www.crowdsourcing.org/document/an-empirical-analysis-of-crowdfunding-/2458

Mäschle, O. (2012a). *Rationing of excessive demand on equity-based crowdfunding-platforms*. Retrieved from http://econpapers.repec.org/paper/roswpaper/126.htm

Mäschle, O. (2012b). *Which information should entrepreneurs on German equity-based crowdfunding-platforms disclose?* Retrieved from http://www.wiwi.uni-rostock.de/fileadmin/Institute/VWL/VWL-Institut/RePEc/pdf/wp127thuenen.pdf

Moritz, A., & Block, J. (2014). Crowdfunding und Crowdinvesting: State of the Art der wirtschaftswissenschaftlichen Literatur. *ZfKE—Zeitschrift für KMU und Entrepreneurship, 62*(1), 57–89.

Neuronation. (2011). *Expert interview with Neuronation at a funding pitch on Seedmatch*, November 29, 2011.

Reichwald, R., Ihl, C., & Seifert, S. (2004). *Kundenbeteiligung an unternehmerischen Innovationsvorhaben*. München: Technische Universität.

Reichwald, R., & Piller, F. (2005). *Open Innovation: Kunden als Partner im Innovationsprozess*. Retrieved from https://www.impulse.de/downloads/open_innovation.pdf

Russ, C. (2007). Online crowds—Extraordinary Mass Behavior on the Internet. *Proceedings of the International Conferences on New Media Technology and Semantic Systems* (pp. 65–76).

Sauer, J.-U. (2012). *Offener Brief vom 29.03.2012*. Retrieved from http://blog.seedmatch.de/2012/03/29/offener-brief-erleichterung-fur-grunder-bei-crowdfunding-uber-100-000-euro/

Schwienbacher, A., & Larralde, B. (2010). Crowdfunding of small entrepreneurial ventures. In D. Cumming (Ed.), *The Oxford handbook of entrepreneurial finance (2012)*. New York: Oxford University Press.

Seedmatch GmbH. (2012, March 20). easyCARD: "Das Crowdfunding war ein 'social proof of concept'" (Web log post). Retrieved from http://blog.seedmatch.de/2012/03/20/easycard-das-crowdfunding-war-einsocial-proof-of-concept

Seedmatch GmbH. (2015). *Abgeschlossene Fundings*. Retrieved from https://www.seedmatch.de/startups

Shiller, R. J. (2000). *Irrational exuberance*. Princeton, NJ: Princeton University Press.

Surowiecki, J. (2005). *The wisdom of crowds*. London: Anchor Books.

Veugelers, R. (2011). *Mind Europe's early-stage equity gap*. Brussels: Bruegel.

Wattig, L. (2010). *Liste mit Crowdfunding-Plattformen—wer kennt noch andere?* Retrieved from http://leanderwattig.com/2010/10/22/liste-mit-crowdfunding-plattformen-wer-kennt-noch-andere/

Wolfson, S. M. (2012). *Crowdsourcing and the law*. Austin, TX: University of Texas.

Zingales, L. (1994). The value of the voting right: A study of the Milan Stock Exchange experience. *Review of Financial Studies*, *7*(1), 125–148.

The Emerging Crowdfunding Market in Italy: Are "the Crowd" Friends of Mine?

Marco Guerzoni, Dario Peirone, Ivana Pais, and Angelo Miglietta

Abstract Emerging literature on crowdfunding, until now, is missing detailed empirical analyses on profiles of "crowdfunders". Our paper aims to address this shortage, analyzing geographical and socio-economic characteristics of crowdfunders, looking at how crowdfunding influences the nature of geography and social contacts in new ventures. Our analysis concentrates on Italy, a country suffering for a huge economic crisis but that, at the same time, is showing a strong dynamism in crowdfunding. We collect data on donors of about 350 projects, estimating with a micro-econometric model not only which donors' characteristics increase the likelihood of an investment, but also the role played by social media in the crowdfunding process. Our results give some remarkable indications about crowdfunding in different countries and cultural contexts.

Keywords Crowdfunding • Social network • Non-monetary rewards

1 Introduction

Crowdfunding platforms can be considered as "intentional organisations" (Coleman, 1990, p. 312): the use of online platforms facilitates the transformation of social networks into financial capital available for realising ideas, projects and new ventures. Whereas social media removes barriers to the access (and production) of information, crowdfunding removes barriers to the access (and sharing) of capital, usually involving people who are not finance or technology experts. The interesting feature of crowdfunding is thus the possibility of involving a potentially enormous number of backers in the process of financing ideas, eliminating the need for a financial intermediary.

M. Guerzoni • D. Peirone (✉)
University of Turin, Turin, Italy
e-mail: dario.peirone@unito.it

I. Pais
Università Cattolica del Sacro Cuore, Milan, Italy

A. Miglietta
IULM University, Milan, Italy

D. Brüntje, O. Gajda (eds.), *Crowdfunding in Europe*, FGF Studies in Small Business and Entrepreneurship, DOI 10.1007/978-3-319-18017-5_6

The removal of barriers to investment that characterises crowdfunding constitutes the possibility of overcoming the well-known difficulties that new initiatives face in attracting external finance during their start-up phase (see, among others, Aghion & Bolton, 1992; Agrawal, Catalini, & Goldfarb, 2013; Berger & Udell, 2002; Lerner, 1995). Literature on crowdfunding is an emerging field of study that, until now, has investigated structures and profiles of projects and platforms, concentrating on the problem of information asymmetry, trying to understand the signals given off by project-owners to donors/investors (the *backers*) through the platforms, and whether these signals are somewhat different to the ones already analysed in financial literature.

Still missing from crowdfunding literature are detailed empirical analyses on the profiles of "crowdfunders". This paper aims to address this lacuna, analysing the geographical and socio-economic characteristics of crowdfunders and their relations with the project-owner. The main focus of the paper will be to highlight the role of geographical distance and of personal contact, looking at their possible interaction.

Our analysis will concentrate on Italy, one of the countries suffering the most from the global economic crisis and one that presents the most critical levels of access to credit. However, at the same time, Italy shows a strong dynamism in the crowdfunding sector: there are 52 crowdfunding platforms (43 that are active and 9 being launched), as of May 2014, with strong growth in recent months (there were only 16 in November 2012) and some interesting processes of institutional innovation, with the introduction of equity crowdfunding regulation.

2 The Literature on "Crowdfunders"

Only a few works in management and economic theory have empirically addressed the increasing role of crowdfunding with a clear focus on crowdfunders. Some contributions have investigated the role of geographical distance, to test the irrelevance hypothesis, due to the technological characteristics of Internet crowdfunding platforms. The findings confirm the irrelevance of geographical distance, but show an important role for family and friends as the first backers of projects, as well as for the characteristics of the place in which a project is located.

Research carried out by Mollick (2014) on Kickstarter shows direct proportionality between the number of Facebook friends the project-owner has and the project's probability of success. He also tested the effect of the proportion of creative individuals in a project-owner's city on the success of a crowdfunding effort. Economic geographers argue that the underlying success of creative endeavours is dependent on the characteristics of the project-owners' location (Knudsen, Florida, Stolarick, & Gates, 2008; Saxenian, 1996). One geographic effect theorised by researchers, in particular Florida (2002, 2004), is that the underlying talent of an area's population can affect its relative creative productivity. The results of Mollick (2014) show that a proportionally greater creative population was associated with a greater likelihood of success for project-owners, examining the size of the city, the network of the project-owner, and the number of other Kickstarter project-owners in that city.

Agrawal, Catalini, and Goldfarb (2011) show that a significant distinction can be made between local and distant investors on investment patterns over time within a single round of financing. They employed a difference-in-differences-like approach to compare first the difference between local and distant investors in terms of their propensity to invest during a given period, and then how this difference changes with the publicly visible investment decisions of others. They have found that the timing of distant, but not local, investments is very responsive to the investment decisions of others. In addition, "family and friends" investors seem to be disproportionately co-located with the project-owner, and the distance effect disappears when comparing the effect of other investors' investment decisions on the propensity to invest during a given period, mediated by distance after testing for family and friends. Agrawal et al. (2011) interpret this result as implying that the crowdfunding platform eliminates most distance-related economic frictions normally associated with financing early-stage projects, such as acquiring information (e.g. local reputation, stage presence), monitoring progress, and providing input.

Although distant investors are common for publicly traded companies, theory suggests that investors in early-stage entrepreneurial ventures will tend to be local. The characteristics of crowdfunding are consistent with the view that the online setting allows people to overcome offline barriers to market transactions (Goldfarb & Tucker, 2011), because Internet platforms can help reduce market frictions associated with geographical distance.

When the relationship is not based on direct knowledge, social ties can signal to the public that a project is worthy. This is known as social proof (Masum & Tovey, 2011; Rainie, Rainie, & Wellman, 2012). The first people to help out a project, building trust and providing proof of legitimacy, validate it for later supporters. Research carried out on Prosper, a social-lending platform (Lin, Prabhala, & Viswanathan, 2009) shows that if friends are among the lenders the probability of the debt being repaid more than doubles. Moreover, social capital becomes even more influential in the case of weak financial profiles.

On the one hand, the literature on this issue shows a research gap in addressing crowdfunders' characteristics and, on the other hand, suggests that geographical distance, as well as the relational distance between the project-owner and the crowdfunders, should be taken into careful consideration. Based on these perceptions, our paper examines a dataset of crowdfunders and places a particular emphasis on how crowdfunding influences the nature of geography and social contacts in new ventures.

3 Data and Empirical Strategy

We aim to describe some determinants of a crowdfunder's investment choices as dependent on his/her own characteristics (such as demographic and socio-economic characteristics, personal beliefs, etc.) and the characteristics of the financed project (type, size, rewards mechanism, etc.). In particular, in this contribution, both geographical and relational distance from the crowdfunder to the project merits specific attention.

For this purpose we collect data via a survey of crowdfunders' characteristics and motivations, using the crowdfunding platforms' mailing list of crowdfunders.[1] Contextually, from the same platforms we gather data on the projects financed by each crowdfunder and we match the two datasets. For reasons of the platforms' privacy preferences, we could only contact the crowdfunders directly in one case. Five platforms agreed instead to send a request to respond to the survey to their mailing list of people who had financed at least one project.

The unit of the analysis is the investment of a crowdfunder i in the project j via a crowdfunding platform and we examine why a given project is preferred to others as the result of the interaction of the characteristics of crowdfunders and projects.

In the survey we asked three sets of questions. The first set generated demographic variables such as gender, income, and level of studies. The second set attempts to elicit the motivation behind the funding of a project. We ask them what kind of projects they have funded, whether they expect a reward and, if so, what kind of reward. Finally, the last part aims to understand the connection of the respondent to specific projects. Specifically, we map both the geographical and relational distance of the crowdfunder from the project in terms of family relations and social acquaintances and assess whether any interaction on social media took place.

So far we have obtained 351 responses. Table 1 shows descriptive statistics for the variables we use. For dummy variables, the mean can be interpreted as the percentage of positive cases. For two categorical variables (*social acquaintance* and *geocontact*), Figs. 1 and 2 depict the distribution across levels. *Education* is also a categorical variable ranging from 1, primary school education, to 5 for postgraduate education. The variable *social media source* elicits whether an individual is connected on social media with the project leader or a project member. The variables *generosity, innovation*, *award* and *connection* describe the motives for financing the project: respectively an individual can finance the project for generosity, for supporting an innovative venture, for an expected profit, or because he/she knows the project leader and would like to help him/her. The variable *social source* takes the value 1 when the information about the project originates on social media and 0 otherwise. *Gender* is well balanced and, as expected, people with a good educational background are overrepresented in comparison to the Italian population as a whole. Surprisingly, the distribution of respondents over income

[1] Only Italian crowdfunding platforms active for at least 1 year.

Table 1 Descriptive statistics

Variable	Obs	Mean	Min	Max
Gender	177	0.519774	0	1
Education	177	3.711864	1	5
Income	173	4.052023	1	7
Social acquaintance	178	3.016854	1	7
Social media contact	178	0.5786517	0	1
Geocontact	178	2.724719	1	7
Generosity	178	0.6404494	0	1
Innovation	178	0.1629213	0	1
Award	178	0.1966292	0	1
Connection	178	0.488764	0	1
Social source	178	0.3146067	0	1

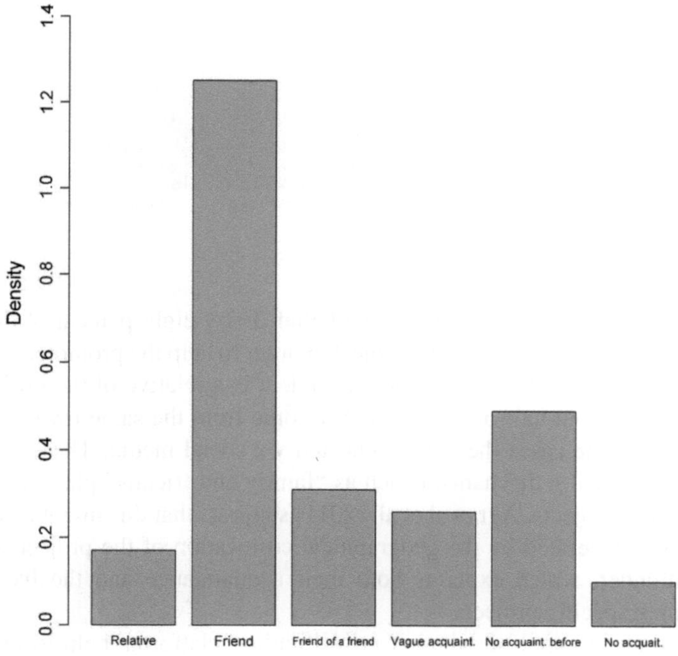

Fig. 1 Social acquaintance

classes is rather homogeneous (see Table 1). This might be well explained by the poor economic performance of the Italian younger generations, but is still an issue to be considered in further analysis.

If we look at the motivation of the crowdfunders, we see that most of them do not finance a project because they expect a reward. About a third of the respondents base their decision to finance a project on whether they like the idea behind it or not. It is evident from the data that knowing the promoter of projects has a significant

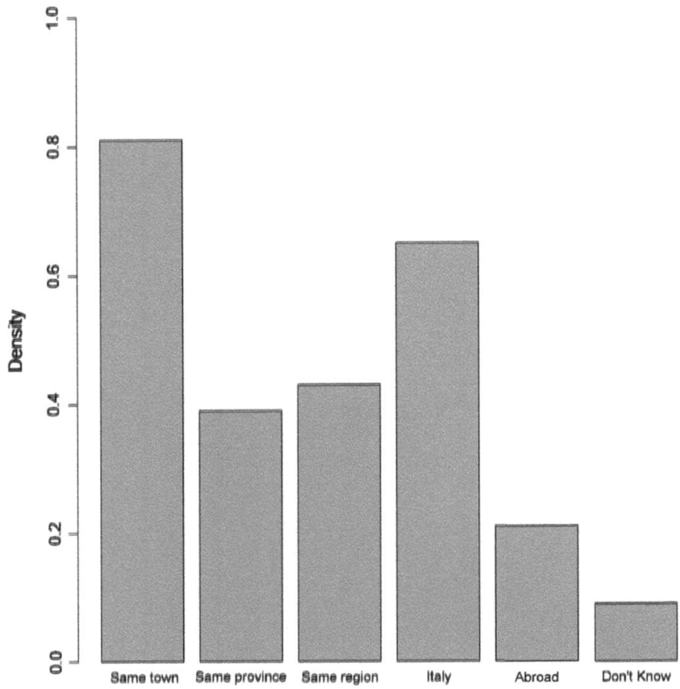

Fig. 2 Geographical distance

impact. This confirms a well-established belief. Forty-eight percent of the respondents answer that they financed the project in order to help the promoters. It is worth noting that in a third of the cases the respondent is a relative of the project-owner (see Fig. 1), in about half of the cases they come from the same town (see Fig. 2) and in 57 % of the cases they are connected via social media. These preliminary results indicate that a mechanism such as "family and friends" plays an important role in funding projects. Agrawal et al. (2011) suggests that this might be a spurious effect mainly generated by the geographical co-location of the project-owner and the crowdfunder, which explains both their acquaintance and the likelihood of discovering a specific project.

Here we aim to analyse whether crowdfunding platforms help in overcoming geographical distance. Ideally, we should expect that crowdfunding platforms, by leveraging on social media connections rather than connections in person and social acquaintances, should allow the project-owner to raise funds from elsewhere other than his close proximity (see Fig. 2).

In order to verify this mechanism, we investigate whether the source of information about a project comes from social media or not. We thus asked crowdfunders if they are connected to project leaders through social media alone, or also in person, and if they are located geographically near to the project leader. We also asked them whether information on the project originated from social media or not. These questions were useful to investigate the following three main research issues:

I1 Geographical co-location between project-owner and crowdfunder.

I2 Social acquaintance and social media contact of project-owner and crowdfunder.

I3 Social media contact with the project-owner as a source of information about the project.

In order to investigate the three issues we run a set of different logit regressions to estimate which factors affect the probability that the donor had a previous contact with the project leader on social media.

Concerning I1 and I2, we observe that most crowdfunders are located in the same town as the funder, that they are connected on social media and that they have strong ties in person (see Table 2).

However, multivariate analysis shows that co-location and friendship on social media seem to be a reflection of social acquaintance, defined along different levels, from the strongest (family) to the weakest: we found that the stronger the social acquaintance between crowdfunder and project-owner, the stronger the probability that they are connected on social media. If we omit the variable social acquaintance (Model 1), there is also a significant and positive correlation between geographical distance and the probability of being connected on social media. However, as expected, we find that this is a spurious relation since when in Model 2 we add also social acquaintance, geographical distance is not significant any longer: family and friends in person mostly live in the same area. Concerning I3, we explain the

Table 2 Regression results for I1 and I2

	Dep. Var: contact on social media		
Variables	Model 1	Model 2	Model 3
Geo distance	0.819*	1.062	1.088
Social acquaintance		0.503***	0.512***
Gender	0.694	0.695	0.77
Education	1.283*	1.225	1.21
Income	0.926	0.891	0.888
Motive reward			1.376
Motive connection			1.198
Motive innovation			0.541
Motive generosity			1.148
Constant	1.57	8.784***	6.915**
Observations	172	172	172
Log likelihood	−112.4	−99.31	−98.06
χ^2	9.691	35.87	38.37

***$p < 0.01$, **$p < 0.05$, *$p < 0.1$

Table 3 Regression results for I3

Variables	Odd ratio (real life vs. social media)
Social contact with the project leader	0.309**
Geographical distance	0.883
Social distance	0.536***
Motive reward	1.521
Motive connection	0.404**
Motive innovation	0.973
Motive generosity	0.712
Controls	YES
Constant	10.08*
Observations	170
Log likelihood	−199.1
DF	30
χ^2	59.51

***$p < 0.01$, **$p < 0.05$, *$p < 0.1$

factors, which affect the probability that the donor acquired information on the project in real life vs. in social media. In this case, the previous dependent variable, social contact with the project leader, is considered as an independent variable. Table 3 presents the results expressed as odd ratios, i.e. values smaller (larger) than 1.0 are associated with lower (higher) odds of the outcome real live vs. social media.

Considering the previous evidence discussed in this contribution, this result was unexpected: although crowdfunders usually live in the same area as the project-owner and have a strong social liaison with him/her, they became aware of the project over social media.

As a control, we analysed whether results change when we take into account either the motives[2] behind the funding projects or the socio-demographic characteristics of the crowdfunder. Regressions suggest that the distribution of motives does not vary along any proximity dimension. Results are also robust to changes along any socio-demographic characteristics.

All in all, crowdfunders are likely to be relatives, friends and acquaintances and, for this reason, we observe the evidence that they are both also connected by social media and located in the same geographical area. With regard to the third hypothesis, we find that contact on social media is the primary source of information about a project.

[2] Respondents could specify three out of the following eight motives: it is useful project; it is an innovative idea; I expect a reward; I expect to have a share of the profits; I appreciated past initiatives of the project-owner; I want to help the project-owner; I trust the project-owner; other.

4 Conclusions

Although our database is limited to one country, we think that this research represents a first step towards an original analysis of crowdfunding dynamics in a small emerging market, with an empirical and systematic examination of "crowdfunders", and on their funding selection process.

Family and friends often live in the same area: it seems that proximity remains crucial, as it is for traditional start-up financing. However, a first result from our analysis is that, within the close network of family and friends, information on crowdfunding projects diffuses primarily through social media. Indeed, we observe that the source of information about a project for most of the crowdfunders is social media, even when the project is funded by acquaintances.

This preliminary evidence show us that—through local platforms—the digital nature of the crowdfunding facilitates the speed and the capillarity of the diffusion process, more than reaching out to new individuals.

Our analysis is still ongoing, but we think that the results can give useful indications of management and policy around crowdfunding in different countries and cultural contexts.

References

Aghion, P., & Bolton, P. (1992). An incomplete contracts approach to financial contracting. *Review of Economic Studies, 77*, 338–401.

Agrawal, A. K., Catalini, C., & Goldfarb, A. (2011). *The geography of crowdfunding* (Working Paper No. 16820). Retrieved from National Bureau of Economic Research website: http://www.nber.org/papers/w16820

Agrawal, A. K., Catalini, C., & Goldfarb, A. (2013). *Some simple economics of crowdfunding* (Working Paper No. 19133). Retrieved from National Bureau of Economic Research website: http://www.nber.org/papers/w19133

Berger, A., & Udell, G. (2002). Small business credit availability and relationship lending: The importance of bank organisational structure. *Economic Journal, 112*, 32–53.

Coleman, J. (1990). *Foundations of social theory*. Cambridge: Harvard University Press.

Florida, R. (2002). The economic geography of talent. *Annals of the Association of American Geographers, 92*(4), 743–755.

Florida, R. (2004). *Cities and the creative class*. New York: Routledge.

Goldfarb, A., & Tucker, C. (2011). Advertising bans and the substitutability of online and offline advertising. *Journal of Marketing Research, 48*, 207–227.

Knudsen, B., Florida, R., Stolarick, K., & Gates, G. (2008). Density and creativity in US regions. *Annals of the Association of American Geographers, 98*(2), 461–478.

Lerner, J. (1995). Venture capitalists and the oversight of private firms. *Journal of Finance, 50*, 301–318.

Lin, M., Prabhala, N. R., & Viswanathan, S. (2009). *Judging borrowers by the company they keep: Social networks and adverse selection in online Peer-to-Peer lending* (SSRN Working Paper). Retrieved from http://papers.ssrn.com/sol3/papers.cfm?abstract_id=1355679

Masum, H., & Tovey, M. (2011). *The reputation society: How online opinions are reshaping the offline world*. Cambridge, MA: MIT Press.

Mollick, E. (2014). The dynamics of crowdfunding: An exploratory study. *Journal of Business Venturing, 29*, 1–16.
Rainie, H., Rainie, L., & Wellman, B. (2012). *Networked: The new social operating system.* Cambridge, MA: MIT Press.
Saxenian, A. (1996). *Regional advantage: Culture and competition in Silicon Valley and route 128.* Cambridge: Harvard University Press.

Crowdfunding and Employment: An Analysis of the Employment Effects of Crowdfunding in Spain

Javier Ramos and Bruno González

Abstract This is the first attempt to measure the jobs created by projects funded through crowdfunding (crowd-jobs). This new economic way of financing is already a tangible economic reality made up of 452 active crowdfunding platforms worldwide, which have raised almost $5.1 billion and funded more than 1 million campaigns in 2013.

In Spain, a prototype of an economy in recession, crowdfunding platforms attracted 400 million euros and 2,825 crowdfunding projects in 2012. The funds raised by the successful projects (5,137,648 €) have created around 3,000 direct jobs (crowd-jobs), which represent just 1.61 % of the total target budget (success rate). One year later, the total target budget has decreased (332,145,063 €), however the funds raised by the successful projects have increased (8,526,094 €), especially in the Social and Cultural Sector, creating more crowd-jobs (5,635) and improving the success rate (2.57 %) in 2013.

Since the analysed period only spans 2 years (2012–2013), any conclusion is tentative. All in all, the results seem to suggest that the Spanish crowdfunding market is becoming more efficient, specialised and increasing solidarity, although, again, it is still too soon to consider these tendencies as consolidated patterns and any extrapolation of trends is premature. The economic crisis and the structure of the Spanish economy seem to be responsible for these tendencies, although the expansion of the crowdfunding market should also be considered as a tentative explanatory variable of the observed tendencies in Spain.

Keywords Crowdfunding • Crowd-investment • Crowd-jobs • Economic growth and employment

---

J. Ramos (✉) • B. González (✉)
Instituto Complutense de Estudios Internacionales (ICEI), Madrid, Spain
e-mail: javira02@ucm.es; brungonz@ucm.es

D. Brüntje, O. Gajda (eds.), *Crowdfunding in Europe*, FGF Studies in Small Business and Entrepreneurship, DOI 10.1007/978-3-319-18017-5_7

1 Introduction

For Manuel Castells, one of the most prominent analysts of the "Internet Galaxy", global economy nowadays is only possible because of microelectronic-based technologies and a worldwide infrastructure in telecommunications. These technologies, particularly Information and Communication Technologies (ICTs), enable organisations to: (i) work in real time, (ii) at a global scale, (iii) with a high level of internal decentralisation, as opposed to power-centred and hierarchical Fordist-Weberian models and (iv) create organisational structures in the form of networks that are activated according to specific business projects (Castells, 2001).

ICTs are playing a central role in enabling globalisation by increasing the breadth and speed of communication and helping to reduce costs, which have eased the flow of goods, capital, people and information across borders (OECD, 2013). ICTs are also transforming the productive model by facilitating enterprises' access to global markets, by increasing productivity and the efficiency of business operations. This is done by permitting access to scale markets, reducing transaction costs and lowering initial investment requirements, which improve productivity and growth, especially in SMEs (Raja, Imaizumi, Kelly, Narimatsu, & Paradi-Guilford, 2013).

One of the most innovative and recent products of the expansion of ICTs is crowdfunding. This new form of finance, fully dependent on Web 2.0 to mobilise resources from social networks, opens new windows of opportunity for investment and employment, especially in economies suffering the effects of the crisis. Crowdfunding reduces financial costs and the risk of investment, enables bypassing the traditional banking system and involves people in the creative process without additional costs. Moreover, investors in crowdfunding do not look much at collaterals or business plans, but at values and opinions associated with the project or the firm, which allows entrepreneurs to alleviate the imperative of fast profits, thus increasing the viability of medium-long term economic projects.

However, important limitations are also observable in the expansion of crowdfunding, mostly related to skills and professional preparation to manage e-networks, the lack of legislation to protect ideas and investment, the risk of plagiarism and copycats that significantly increase after crowdfunding projects are exposed to a public audience and the preference for "small" (small numbers of investors and donors, small projects and target budgets), that might condemn crowdfunding to a kind of economic marginality. Moreover, the scope of crowdfunding services (which remains limited), such as the "all-or-nothing model" adopted by most platforms where projects only receive money if they reach their requested target, is somehow inefficient and limits the access to investment (Ramos, 2014).

The intensity of the financial crisis in the EU brings crowdfunding to the forefront of policy controversies on the feasibility, potential and limitations of this new form of finance for economic recovery. The strategy of austerity and budgetary discipline implemented by most EU economies is limiting access to credit and slowing down growth and the creation of employment.

Studies and comparable data on the effects of crowdfunding on employment are still rather limited. It is still missing robust, empirical and differentiated data to properly evaluate the real economic impact of crowdfunding. In order to partially overcome these limitations we have created a database that provides a first picture, although limited in its scope and accuracy, of the crowdfunding-employment nexus in Spain.

In what follows we will analyse first the ICT-Employment nexus (Sect. 2). Section 3 shows the methodology used (Grounded Theory) to approach this nexus and Sect. 4 analyses how the crisis is affecting employment in Europe and especially in Spain. Subsequently, Sect. 5 focuses on the expansion of crowdfunding and its effect on investment and employment in Spain, with the conclusion in Sect. 6.

2 The ICTs-Employment Nexus

Although evidence of the effect of ICTs on employment is still scarce, some estimates attribute the mass adoption of ICTs (Digitisation) to the creation of six million jobs globally, a 1.02 % drop in unemployment rates and a provision of US $193 billion to world economic output in 2011 (Sabbagh, Friedrich, El-Darwiche, Singh, & Koster, 2013). In the EU the contribution of the ICT sector in total GDP has remained relatively constant at 4–5 % of GDP from 1999 to 2008, significantly higher than the GDP annual growth rate (2.2 %). Labour productivity in ICT sectors was 27 % higher than the average productivity in the EU in 2008 and the ICT sectors produced an additional 574 billion euros, which represented 4.7 % of GDP (Turlea, de Prato, Nepelski, & Szewczyk, 2011).

Case study analyses show how companies using ICT (in Germany) employ both fewer unskilled workers and the percentage of skilled workers is relatively higher than in other companies. But it also produces increases in demand for less skilled workers in jobs such as security, restaurants, cleaning and so on (Maurin & Thesmar, 2003). This may explain why the demand for less qualified activities grows as the most innovative sectors grow as well. Only the medium skilled stratum is being reduced (Goos & Manning, 2003).

Recent figures tend to confirm these tendencies. The introduction of ICTs is changing the productive structure of the economy by generating more jobs in both high-skilled and low-skilled sectors, reinforcing tendencies of labour market polarisation (Fernandez-Macias, 2012; Goos, Manning, & Salomons, 2009; Ramos & Ballel, 2009). Similarly, in half of the OECD countries, the loss of jobs associated with a medium level of education was greater than the loss of low skilled jobs. In the remaining countries strong growth in the highest levels of information-processing skills coexist with stable average levels in occupations with the lowest levels of information (OECD, 2013).

ICTs require changes in organisation and efficient life-long learning programmes to maintain improvements in productivity (Ceccobelli, Gitto, & Mancuso, 2012). The short life cycle and fast rhythm of inherent change in these technologies impose the need for continuous retraining of skills and abilities. ICTs help to empower workers' skills and abilities while producing knowledge in a cheaper, faster and massive way. This has made change possible in the economic and productive models in an increasing number of economies.

2.1 Crowdfunding

In its simple form, crowdfunding is an alternative way of finance and exchange where those seeking funding and those looking to invest or donate can be matched. It is alternative because crowdfunding enables the bypassing of the intermediaries of a traditional supply chain, while making funding processes more transparent and democratic (Ramos, 2014).

It is also an alternative because investors in crowdfunding do not look in detail at collateral or business plans, but at the ideas and core values of the firm. Crowdfunding offers tailored financing methods by using not only technical financial instruments, but also people's values and opinions, that fit well the financing needs of start-ups (Lehner, 2013). Investors in crowdfunding frequently participate in the process of product creation, improvement and diffusion, especially when they perceive that the business model is fair for them (Franke & Klausberger, 2008).

Rubinton (2011) suggests that crowdfunding answers three fundamental questions about how our economy operates: (i) who decides which projects deserve financing? (ii) how can we guarantee they represent the projects' target markets? (iii) what can we do to systematically reduce entrepreneurs' exposure to the risk that they will fail to cover their start-up costs? The reasons why crowdfunding seems to be so economically relevant have to do with the way in which crowdfunding works and how crowdfunding users operate.

Crowdfunding allows significant reduction of the financial costs and the risks of investment, which encourage more people with different investment levels to participate in the crowdfunding market (Kleemann, Voß, & Rieder, 2008). Moreover, crowdfunding fosters the emergence of new sectors of activity where funding is difficult to obtain (Baeck, Collins, & Westlake, 2012; Wojciechowski, 2009), with the subsequent positive effects on labour inclusion, especially among the most vulnerable labour groups.

Crowdfunding is not just about connecting projects and capital, but also about involving people in the creative process, what Surowiecki (2005) calls, "the wisdom of the crowd". No other investment form can provide the benefits of pre-sales, market research, word-of-mouth and crowd-wisdom without additional costs (De Buysere, Gadja, Kleverlaan, & Marom, 2012). However, instead of raising the money from a very small group of sophisticated investors, the idea of crowdfunding is to obtain funds from a large audience ("the crowd"), where each individual provides small amounts of money (Lambert & Schwienbacher, 2010).

There are at least four types of crowdfunding. ***Equity-based crowdfunding***: this is the platform for projects offering a share in future profits. The main motivation for investors is to get the return on their investment, along with other rewards or tangible benefits. ***Lending-based crowdfunding***: investors can choose to lend money in exchange for interest when the goal pays-off. ***Reward-based crowdfunding***: participants receive non-financial rewards in exchange for their contribution. It aspires to attract intrinsic or social motivations to support a project. ***Donation-based crowdfunding***: the model seeks to attract donations for specific projects, mainly social projects, usually managed by NGOs. Donors do not receive tangible benefits in exchange for their donation.

In this sense crowdfunding is providing not only the advantages of ICT's direct and indirect source of employment, but is also serving as a new instrument of co-financing. This is one of the most remarkable benefits of crowdfunding, its capacity to bring together ideas, investment and solidarity to foster economic growth and employment.

According to Massolution (2013), there were 452 crowdfunding platforms active worldwide in 2011, which increased to 536 by the end of 2012, and was forecasted to increase to 630 by the end of 2013. Crowdfunding platforms raised $1 billion in 2010, $1.5 billion in 2011, $2.7 in 2012 and $5.1 billion in 2013.

The USA is the largest crowdfunding market, raising 59 % of the total estimated volume of funds raised worldwide ($1.59 billion in 2012), followed by Europe (35 %, $945 million) and the rest of the world (6 %, $159 million).

Crowdfunding first gained popularity as a way to fund creative, philanthropic, and social projects. Although this popularity prevails, entrepreneurial ventures have significantly increased. The most active crowdfunding category in 2012 was social projects made up 30 % of crowdfunded projects. Yet crowdfunding of equity platforms has grown 80 % rising over $25K+ and is expected to grow at a rate of 63 %. Philanthropic projects raised $676 million, but were the slowest growing of the categories at 43 %. Lending-based platforms raised $552 million and are growing at a rate of 78 %.

However, despite this promising early start, crowdfunding may not be so fruitful in the future. For Bradley (2014) the state of crowdfunding is very immature and highly fragmented. Crowdfunding's hype comes primarily from media and is based on imagining crowdfunding's potential to disrupt current models for raising money.

Yet, in spite of the thousands of crowdfunding platforms operating all over the world, most with very little activity, they have globally raised less than $100 billion, very few as compared to $200+ trillion raised by global capital markets (stocks and bonds) (Bradley, 2014).

According to Fundable (2014), the profile of the American crowdfunder is a man aged between 24 and 35 years old. Those campaigns demanding around $7,000 and lasting around 9 weeks are most likely to success. Similarly campaigns that can gain 30 % of their goal within the first week are more likely to succeed.

Social media is critical in crowdfunding success since for every order of magnitude increase in Facebook friends (10, 100, 1,000), the probability of success increases drastically (9 %, 20 %, 40 %). Moreover, there seems to be a direct correlation between the number of outside links to a crowdfund and the success of the fundraise.

Although the number of platforms in Europe is rapidly changing, Massoudi (n.d.) calculates around 395 active crowdfunding platforms, with France being the European country with the highest numbers of platforms (190) followed by UK (58), Germany (31), the Netherlands (27), Spain (18), Italy (16), Belgium (15) and Switzerland (13). In this paper we analysed these figures in Spain, showing a more realistic account, which indicates a higher number of platforms (38 in 2013) in this country.

3 Methodology

This research draws on ***Grounded Theory (GT)*** methods to approach the employment effects of crowdfunding in light of data, without a preformed theory. GT seeks to challenge the dominant deductive way of creating knowledge based upon "validation" of previous theories. Rather than developing a theory and finding evidence to verify or disprove it, the GT set outs to gather data and then systematically create knowledge derived from it (Corbin & Strauss, 2008; Glaser & Strauss, 1967; Nicholas, 2013; Strauss & Corbin, 1998; Walker & Myrick, 2006).

GT is a method where the analyst first provides basic descriptions of the topic at stake in order to produce a conceptual ordering of core and related categories. Subsequently, the analyst engages in inspecting the coded data for identifying properties, tendencies etc. through an analytical procedure of constant comparison, to produce a proposition.

This is not to say that approaches based upon GT are without existing knowledge or other theoretical issues that may be pertinent to developing an accurate analytical framework. This emphasis on data collection rather than on initial hypothesis seeks to overcome certain obsessions with "verification" predominant in mainstream methodological circles.

Moreover, given the novelty and unconventionality of crowdfunding, literature found on this topic is very scarce and often rather predictive. Methodical, reliable and comparable data on crowd-jobs do not exist, beyond certain estimations. This encourages the use of GT methods to approach the blurred connection between finance and employment predominant in crowdfunding practices. This methodology is particularly suitable for fields where novelty and lack of reliable data are the norm rather than the exception.

Although the expansion of crowdfunding is attracting increasing interest on the part of practitioners, entrepreneurs and scholars, there is no systematic analysis on the economic effects of crowdfunding and how this financial instrument helps to create economic activity and employment. In order to overcome these limitations we have followed GT (Strauss & Corbin, 1998).[1] First of all, we have done

[1] (1) Collect data; (2) Analysis of evidence from the data; (3) Fact-finding and replica; (4) Generation of Theory.

extensive data collection and tracking related to projects financed by Spanish crowdfunding platforms over the last 2 years.

The main corpus of data on which this article is based is comprised of analyses of the crowdfunding websites and interviews with most of the crowdfunding managers running the platforms in 2012 and 2013. Managers have showed a very cooperative and supportive attitude by providing us with data on the selected items that have been contrasted with our own data drawn from their websites. Table 1 shows the crowdfunding platforms in Spain that we included in our analysis.

Table 1 Crowdfunding platforms in Spain

Sociosinversores	www.sociosinversores.es	Equity-based
Inverem	www.inverem.es	
Bihoop	www.bihoop.com	
Nuuuki	www.nuuuki.com	
Seedquick	www.seedquick.com	
The Crowd Angel	www.thecrowdangel.com	
Verkami	www.verkami.com	Reward-based
Lanzanos	www.lanzanos.com	
Comproyecto	www.comproyecto.com	
Kreandu	www.kreandu.com	
Libros.com	www.libros.com	
Nvivo	www.nvivo.es	
Projeggt	www.projeggt.com	
Goteo	www.goteo.org	
Kifund	www.projeggt.com/kifund	
MolaFM	www.mola.fm	
TahonaCultural	www.latahonacultural.com	
UnitedFoodRepublic	www.unitedfoodrepublic.com	
Vorticex	www.vorticex.org	
Emprendalia	www.emprendelandia.es	
Montatuconcierto	www.montatuconcierto.com	
MyMajorCompany	www.mymajorcompany.es	
Ith	www.ithcrowdfunding.org	
Bandeed	www.bandeed.com	
Fundlike	www.fundlike.com	
Volanda	www.volanda.com	
Juntalia	www.juntalia.com	
Kuabol	www.kuabol.com	
Migranodearena	www.migranodearena.org	Donation-based
BbvaSuma	www.bbvasuma.com	
DeportistasSolidariosenRed	www.deportistassolidarios.org	
MicrodonacionesHazloPosible	microdonaciones.hazloposible.org	
MiAportación	www.miaportacion.org	
Totsuma	www.totsuma.cat	
Arboribus	www.arboribus.com	Lending-based

Our calculations of the number of wage-jobs created through crowdfunding projects are based upon information provided by the projects' creators, especially those found on the SociosInversores website.[2] Most projects on this site explain not only the financing required, but also the number of jobs they plan to create.[3]

These references have been applied to other projects of a similar nature launched on other crowdfunding websites. In sum the average number of jobs per project in each sector is the following:

- Three jobs average per project in Social Sectors
- Five jobs average per project in Start-up and Entrepreneurship
- Four jobs average per project in Innovation, Technologies and Internet
- Four jobs average per project in Education
- Three jobs average per project in the Cultural Sector

Once data has been collected we move to the conceptual ordering of this data through categories related to crowdfunding and employment. We have encoded the selected data in order to analyse the specific context in which crowdfunding and employment operate in Spain. When analysing evidence from data we notice that although many crowdfunding projects and campaigns, mainly in the field of culture and entertainment, are often related to self-employment (writing a book, painting etc.), there are also projects that necessitate wage-workers to carry out their activities.

1. Number and Types of crowdfunding platforms
2. Types of projects launched on crowdfunding platforms
3. Volume of finance at different scales
    - Total Target Budget submitted
    - Deal flow (an amount of funds raised for funded and non-funded projects)
    - Total target budget funded
    - Success Rate
4. Crowd-jobs
    - Total crowd-jobs created
    - Direct crowd-jobs created
    - Indirect crowd-jobs created

[2] https://www.sociosinversores.es/ (Accessed 26 February 2015).

[3] 3–5 people to start up a tapas bar (chef, waiter and cleaning staff), 3–5 workers in e-business [webpages on different issues (1 general manager, 1 webmaster, 1 salesman and 1 secretary)], 4 workers in sales website (1 commercial manager, 1 in purchase management and 1 for marketing), 5 workers in leisure and sport centre (management, monitors and administration staff), 2–3 workers in development and commercialisation of patents, 3–4 workers in rent and sale store of equipment for disabled people, 2 workers in martial arts schools, 10 workers in a Kindergarten (1 director/general manager, 1 coordinator, 1 commercial staff, 1 accountant, 1 receptionist, 5 teachers) and 10–15 workers in hotel industries and accommodation.

This template will help us to approach the crowdfunding-employment nexus. Unfortunately, neither the crowdfunding sectors nor public institutions carry out follow-up initiatives to check out what goes on once a project has been funded. We know nothing about the sustainability of the funded projects and the jobs created. This is a serious handicap to exploring not only the volume of crowd-jobs created, but also the quality of these crowd-jobs. This is a real challenge for future analysis on the economic effects of crowdfunding.

4 Financial Crisis: Spain as a Case Study

Over the last 5 years the Monetary Union has stood on the brink of collapse. Since 2008, practically all European economies have opted for the same strategy of austerity and budgetary discipline to put their finances back on track. Cutting deficits is a precondition for access to EU rescue packages and to reduce pressure from international financial markets. Yet deficit cutting is reducing economic activity, which leads to reduced revenues and encourages additional pressure to cut deficits and so on.

This coordinated austerity during depression is self-defeating, as debt-to-GDP ratios have not been reduced; on the contrary they will be higher in 2014. Eurozone seasonally adjusted unemployment is hitting a new record of 16.5 million (12 %) and 10.7 % in EU-28 in December 2013. The youth unemployment rate was 23.8 % in the Eurozone and 23.2 % in EU-28, becoming more structural, and therefore more difficult to eradicate. Long-term unemployment continues to rise, reaching 4.6 % of the labour force in 2012, higher than the previous year (4.1 %) (Eurostat, 2013; ILO, 2012).

With all EU economies consolidating deficits simultaneously, this spill-over effect is likely to continue for years to come, especially in Southern Europe. Spain is a paradigmatic case study. The Spanish economic growth model was seen over the last two decades as an "economic miracle" that combined budgetary and fiscal discipline with growth rates above the EU average. This combination translated into employment creation at an unprecedented pace and greater convergence with its European partners in per capita GDP. Yet the miracle was based upon a booming economy, created by cheap credit, construction and low skilled sectors, which benefited from the EU's Structural Funds and the expansionary policies pursued by the European Central Bank to stimulate the Eurozone.

The exposure of the Spanish economy, and particularly the banking sector, to the fate of the housing boom, pushed the Spanish economy into the greatest recession in recent economic history, similar to the one experienced during the 1940s of the twentieth century. The Spanish economy has been downgraded several times to restore market confidence and avoid bank-runs. Since then the following have become policy priorities: strengthening bank balance sheets, increasing guarantee of private deposits, buying toxic assets and restricting short-selling (Ramos & Valera, 2012).

Austerity programs in times of recession have failed to reduce budget deficits because they lead to a downward economic spiral and punishing interest rates. The results in the labour markets are already appreciable. For the fifth year, Spain remained the country with the highest overall unemployment rate, which more than doubled between 2008 and the last semester of 2013 (25.8 % of the labour force, 5,995,000 unemployed workers, 53.2 % of unemployment among the younger stratum of the labour force), bringing Spain back to even higher levels of unemployment than in early 1992. Those worst hit are, unsurprisingly, temporary workers, particularly young people, and those employed in the service and construction sectors (Eurostat, 2013).

In this context, ICTs are widely thought to help economic recovery. The *2013 Employment Package* identifies ICTS as one of the top priorities for growth and employment creation. Similarly, the *Europe-2020 Strategy* promotes a digital market as an opportunity for the EU to promote employment. This strategy seeks to promote smart, sustainable and inclusive growth through five goals in the areas of employment, innovation, education, poverty reduction and climate/energy. Among the "flagship initiatives" used as a reference to meet these goals, the *Digital agenda for Europe*[4] aspires to create a single digital market based on fast/ultrafast Internet and interoperable applications[5] to favour a dynamic economic sector for Europe to benefit from globalisation.

The *Digital Agenda Scoreboard 2013*[6] also stresses the centrality of ICTs as a potential source of growth and employment in the current context of economic crisis. Evidence shows significant improvements in Internet usage—especially among disadvantaged groups—shopping on-line, e-government services, falling roaming prices and broadband coverage.

In what follows, we will try to analyse the volume of finance activity, projects, ideas and employment links to the expansion of crowdfunding practices in Spain. Crowdfunding is becoming increasingly important in providing new ways of financing in an era of financial crisis in a country severely suffering from the effects of the crisis.

---

[4] http://ec.europa.eu/information_society/digital-agenda/index_en.htm (Accessed 26 February 2015).

[5] By 2013: broadband access for all, by 2020: access for all to much higher internet speeds (30 Mbps or above), by 2020: 50 % or more of European households with Internet connections above 100 Mbps.

[6] http://ec.europa.eu/digital-agenda/en/digital-agenda-scoreboard (Accessed 26 February 2015).

5 Crowdfunding and Employment in Spain: Key Figures January 2012–January 2013

There were **19** crowdfunding sites in Spain, which have launched **2,825 projects** during the examined period (January–December 2012), amounting to **430,963,927** € (total target budget submitted) of which **121,367,740** € have been already used to fund projects (deal flow). The success rate (number of projects obtaining the target budget divided by the total number of projects submitted) reaches **1.61 %**, totalling **5,137,647** € (see Table 2).

By sector of economic activity (see Fig. 1), the majority of successful projects belong to the field of culture and entertainment and social projects. Although the employment created in this sector is not huge (**3,143 jobs** and a total of **7,564 indirect jobs**) this is certainly good news for a country that has been losing 100,000 jobs per month over the last 3 years. Moreover, the potential to create more employment is very high since Spanish crowdfunding platforms have raised only 1.61 % of the total target budget in 2012 (see again Table 2).

Among the reasons behind the poor rate of coverage observed, the following seem to be the most significant causes. Most crowdfunding platforms were established in 2012, meaning that crowdfunding is at a very early stage. Moreover, only 9 out of 19 crowdfunding sites provide users with assistance services to improve the quality of the campaign and its chances of success (Goteo, Socios-Inversores, Verkami, Thecrowdangel, Kifund, Injoinet, Comproyecto, LaTahona-cultural, Projecggt).

If the number of languages available in crowdfunding sites is a sign of internationalisation, Spanish crowdfunding sites are still highly nationally oriented. Although the international strength of the Spanish language as a tool of communication and business permits Latin American projects to be presented on Spanish crowdfunding sites, 71.5 %—15 out of 19 sites—are available only in Castilian and other domestic languages (Catalan, Basque, Galician). Three sites are also available in English (La Tahona Cultural, Verkami), some are also available in French and Portuguese. Only SocioInversionistas is also available in the former languages plus Italian, German, Chinese (simplified and traditional), Arabic and Russian. This lack

Table 2 Crowd-investment and crowd-jobs in Spain in 2012

(1) Number of crowdfunding platforms	19
(2) Number of submitted projects	2,825
(3) Total target budget submitted	430,963,927 €
(4) Deal flow (amount of funds raised for funded and non-funded projects)	121,367,740 €
(5) Total target budget funded (amount of funds raised for funded projects)	5,137,647 €
(6) Success rates (point 3 divided by point 5)	1.61 %
(7) Crowd-jobs created	3,143
(8) Crowd-jobs created + indirect jobs	7,564

Source: Own elaboration

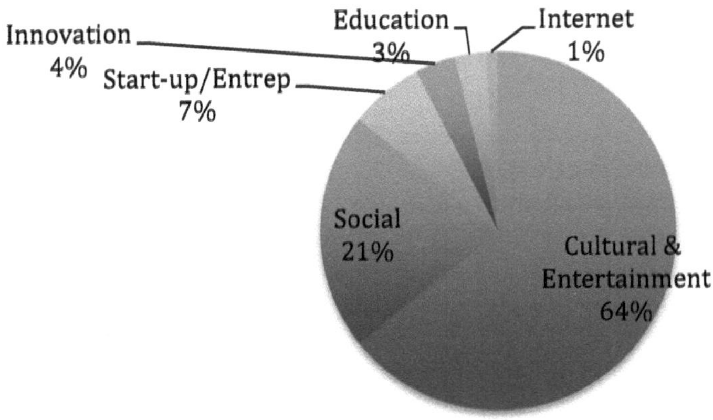

Fig. 1 Success projects by sector of activity 2012. *Source*: Own elaboration

of internationalisation constitutes a serious handicap to crowdfunding expansion in Spain.

There is a certain degree of specialisation with some sites taking the lead in launching and financing social projects (Teaming, Hazloposible, BBVASuma), others in start-ups and entrepreneurship (SociosInversionistas, Projeggt, Thecrowdangel), culture and entertainment (Verkami, Lanzanos, Goteo, Injoinet, Fundyu, Kifund, Comproyecto, Montatuconcierto, LaTahonacultural) innovation, technologies and internet (Migranodearena) and education, which is presented on some sites, though not a majority. Most of the 19 crowdfunding sites in Spain started in 2012, showing promising growth in a year. Yet, the level of activity on six crowdfunding platforms is low, launching less than five projects, and two platforms disappeared during 2012 (Volanda, Nvivo).

For pure entrepreneurial projects only SociosInversores and to a lesser extent Verkami, and Lanzanos seem suitable. This is a typical equity for profits platforms specialising in start-ups, where investors and funders exclusively seek the interest of the pay-back after the lending period. At the other extreme of the spectrum are Teaming, Miaportacion or Hazloposible ranked as the best crowdfunding platforms for social projects (aid & cooperation). These are the prototypical non-commercial platforms highly embedded in non-profit NGOs, whose donors do not seek economic pay-backs, but immaterial rewards in exchange for their donations.

Three platforms (Teaming, Verkami and SociosInversores) represent 71.3 % of all projects launched in 2012 (2,115 out of 2,825 submitted projects) and 99.48 % of the total target budget (332,618,300 €). However, the rates of success vary significantly between these leading platforms. SociosInversores shows a success rate of 6.81 %, among the lowest, far below Verkami (81.39 %), Miaportacion (80.00 %) or Lanzanos (61.08 %). Something similar applies to the total target budget covered. With 10,034,500 € raised, SociosInversores is placed at the top of the ranking, although this amount represents only 3.02 % of its total target budget, again, far below the rest of leading crowdfunding platforms.

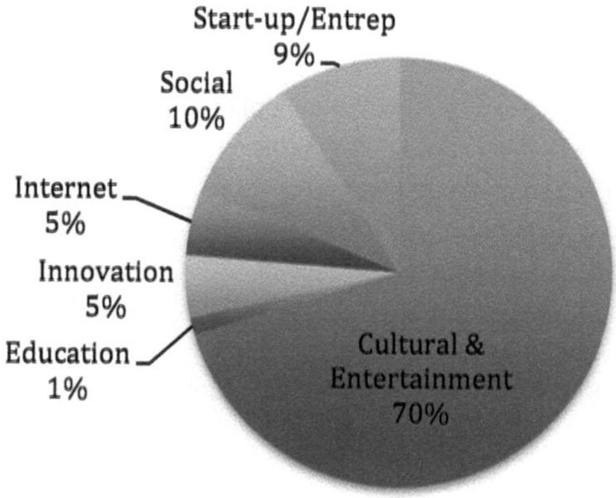

Fig. 2 Crowd-jobs by sector of activity 2012. *Source*: Own elaboration

Most of these jobs belong to the cultural and entertainment sectors (70 %) and social (10 %), but also start-ups and entrepreneurship (9 %), innovation and internet (5 %), and education (0.6 %) (see Fig. 2).

Crowdfunding projects aimed at supporting political anti-corruption campaigns have substantially increased, which is consistent with the movement of political struggle and mobilisation that Spain has been experiencing in the last 5 years. Activists seeking to raise money to pay for bail for other protesters arrested in demonstrations against the crisis or for denouncing corruption have launched the most popular initiatives over the last 2 years.

Furthermore, there are also campaigns to finance films, books and documentaries in favour of certain political issues including: anti-neoliberal globalisation, the environment, gender equality, and the independence of Catalonia and the Basque Country. Although they are not yet significant in number, it is highly likely that these political campaigns will become a solid category in the near future. We therefore consider crowdfunding not only as an alternative mode of fundraising, but also as a new instrument of political mobilisation that deserves additional academic attention. This expansion is also encouraging the emergence of specialised e-firms that help users to connect with specific crowdfunding networks that increase the chances of success, as the site Injoined does.

5.1 Key Figures January 2013–January 2014

Just 1 year later the crowdfunding sector in Spain has suffered some significant transformations. The crisis has limited the flux of investment and has worsened economic activity in general. This has translated into a significant reduction in available funds. Total target budget and deal flow have decreased by 98,818,864 € and 56,180,224 €. Yet, the number of platforms and projects and the success rate have increased in 2013 (see Table 3).

Table 3 Investment and jobs created in 2012 and 2013 in Spain

	2012	2013	Variation
(1) Number of crowdfunding platforms	19	38	+19
(2) Number of submitted projects	2,825	3,207	+328
(3) Total target budget submitted	430,963,927 €	332,145,063 €	−98,818,864 €
(4) Deal flow	121,367,740 €	65,187,516 €	−56,180,224 €
(5) Total target budget funded	5,137,647 €	8,526,094 €	+3,388,447 €
(6) Success rates	1.61 %	2.57 %	+0.96
(7) Crowd-jobs created	3,143	5,635	+2,492
(8) Crowd-jobs created + indirect jobs	7,564	10,117	+2,553

Source: Own elaboration

This may suggest that crowdfunding creators, investors and donors are improving the attractiveness and the quality of projects and are adjusting the expected profits and rewards, making the Spanish crowdfunding sector more efficient and sustainable.

Another consequence of the financial crisis is the increasing importance of the social sector. The number of funded social projects has increased from 101 to 258 in the 2-year time period analysed. The social sector represents 25 % of funded projects at present, significantly higher than 10 % in 2012 (see again Figs. 2 and 3).

Similarly, the employment created in this sector has also increased from 303 to 774, which represents 17 % of total employment created in the Spanish crowdfunding market in 2013 (see Fig. 4).

This tendency is worthy of attention because solidarity is becoming more economically important as a factor of labour and social inclusion, which is attracting increasing investment and donations. New platforms specialising in solidarity and cooperation have been launched in 2013, namely Microdonaciones, BBVASum, Totsuma.

New platforms specialising in business and entrepreneurship have also emerged in 2013, as a logical reaction to the consequences of inactivity, lack of finance and unemployment created by the crisis. These platforms are Inverem, Bihoop, Emprendalia, Seedquick and Arboribus. New platforms have also emerged in sectors of innovation and education (Vorticex, CrowdAngel and Nuuuki) although they still represent a comparatively smaller percentage of the whole crowdfunding market.

The process of platform specialisation is also being reinforced judging by the consolidation of the leading platforms in their fields of specialisation (Lanzanos, Verkami, SociosInversionistas, Goteo), but also by new specialised platforms that have been launched in sectors of activity where crowdfunding was not so widespread. This is the case of Deportistas-SolidariosRED (Sport), and UnitedFoodRepublic

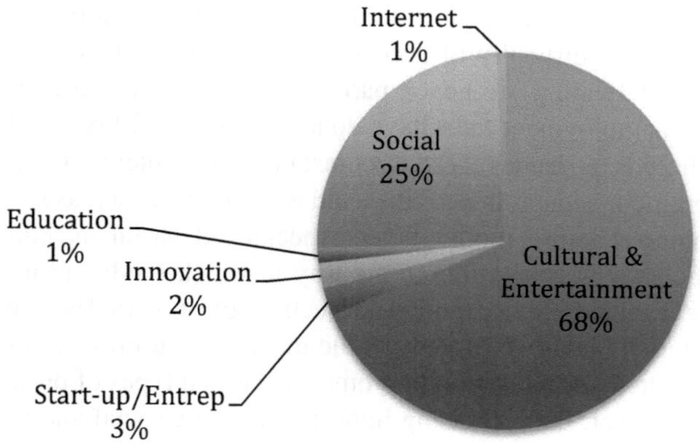

Fig. 3 Successful projects by sector of activity 2013. *Source*: Own elaboration

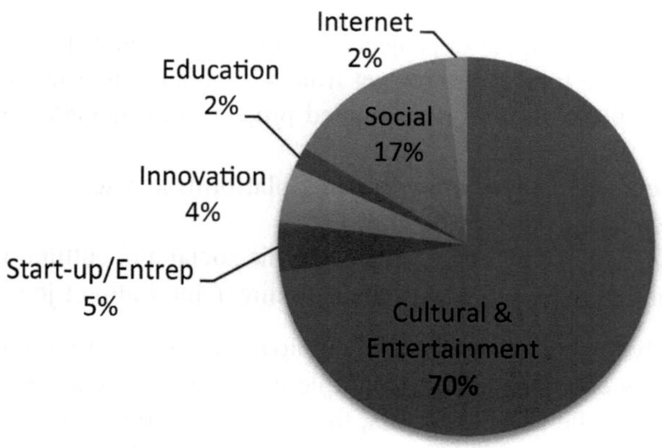

Fig. 4 Crowd-jobs by sector of activity 2013. *Source*: Own elaboration

(Food and cooking). Specialisation is also observable in Kifund and MolaFM (cultural), Microdonaciones (Social), Vorticex (technology) and Inverem (Entrepreneurship).

6 Conclusions

The main purpose of this research is to contribute to a better understanding of how crowdfunding practices are helping creators and entrepreneurs to fund their projects and create employment in Spain. The absence of empirical evidence and specific literature on this subject justified this attempt to provide a first detailed framework to interpret the crowdfunding-employment nexus.

The current economic crisis has brought with it a recessionary spiral that has resulted in a serious difficulty of access to traditional financing channels. Alternative sources of funding are hence particularly interesting in countries such as Spain, where unemployment rates have doubled between 2008 and the last half of 2013 to reach 25.8 %. Under these circumstances, the interest in crowdfunding's capacity to promote economic activities and employment increases.

Crowdfunding is getting more efficient, specialised, social and cultural in Spain. A greater efficiency is perceptible in the way in which funded projects and target budgets have evolved (more funded projects coexist with less investment and smaller total target budgets). Moreover, the most popular crowdfunding platforms are reinforcing their specialisation in promoting certain types of projects, ideas and investment. However, the increasing importance of the social and cultural sectors does not exclude the potential of other type of initiatives more related to start-ups and other more entrepreneurship oriented projects.

The following are the most important tendencies observed:

- An increase in the number of crowdfunding platforms. From 17 in 2012 to 38 in 2013.
- An increase in the number of projects submitted between 2012 and 2013 by 328.
- A decrease in the total target budget from 430,963,927 to 332,145,063 €.
- An increase in the success rate (funded projects/total launched projects) from 1.61 to 2.57 %.
- An increase in specialized crowdfunding platforms and services.
- A 25 % increase in funded social projects.
- A predominance of successful projects in the social and cultural sector.
- A significant increase of crowd-jobs both direct and indirect jobs.

It is too early to generate a theory of employment in crowdfunding markets. We still do not know enough about the multiple interplays between crowdfunding and economic outputs, the success factors, the conditions explaining the expansion of some sectors of activity in crowdfunding, the uncertainty over risks to investors, the potential impact of regulatory change and the role that public institutions can play in promoting the use of crowdfunding services.

Given the rapidly changing nature of crowdfunding and the lack of baseline comparable data, it would be useful to also identify indicators of impact within different areas of use (enterprise, creative industry etc.) to estimate aggregate potential impact on economic growth and employment.

We need to carry out similar studies in other countries that allow comparisons and conclusions to be drawn on how individuals, enterprises and institutional frameworks operate to render the crowdfunding-employment relationship more efficient and consolidated. It would be interesting to compare these tendencies in other economies with different economic and productive models to unravel whether crowdfunding reproduces these models or alternatively creates its own specialisation.

References

Baeck, P., Collins, L., & Westlake, S. (2012). *How the UK's businesses, charities, government and financial system can make the most of crowdfunding* (Nesta Report 2012). Retrieved from http://www.nesta.org.uk/library/documents/CrowdingInwebv3.pdf

Bradley, A. (2014, August 12). *The state of crowdfunding is very immature and highly fragmented* [Blog log post]. Retrieved from http://blogs.gartner.com/anthony_bradley/2014/08/12/the-state-of-crowdfunding-is-very-immature-and-highly-fragmented/

Castells, M. (2001). *The Internet Galaxy*. Oxford: Oxford University Press.

Ceccobelli, M., Gitto, S., & Mancuso, P. (2012). ICT capital and labour productivity: A non-parametric analysis of 14 OECD countries. *Telecommunication Policy, 36*(4), 282–292.

Corbin, J., & Strauss, A. (2008). *Basics of qualitative research: Techniques and procedures for developing grounded theory* (3rd ed.). Thousand Oaks, CA: Sage.

De Buysere, K., Gadja, O., Kleverlaan, R., & Marom, D. (2012). *A framework for European crowdfunding*. Retrieved from http://www.eurocrowd.org/files/2013/06/FRAMEWORK_EU_CROWDFUNDING.pdf

Eurostat. (2013). Database. Statistic explained. Retrieved from http://ec.europa.eu/eurostat/data/database

Fernandez-Macias, E. (2012). Job polarisation in Europe? Changes in the employment structure and job quality, 1995–2007. *Work and Occupations, 39*(2), 157–182.

Franke, N., & Klausberger, K. (2008). *Design communities: Business model of the future?* Retrieved from http://noori.abismo.org/crowdsourcing.pdf

Fundable. (2014). *Crowdfunding statistics*. Retrieved from http://www.fundable.com/crowdfunding101/crowdfunding-statistics

Glaser, B., & Strauss, A. (1967). *The discovery of grounded theory*. Chicago: Aldine.

Goos, M., & Manning, A. (2003). *Lousy and lovely jobs: The rising polarisation of work in Britain*. CEP Discussion Paper. Center for Economic Performance, LSE, London.

Goos, M., Manning, A., & Salomons, A. (2009). The polarization of the European labor market. *American Economic Review Papers and Proceedings, 99*, 58–63.

ILO. (2012). *Global employment trends*. Geneva: International Labour Office.

Kleemann, F., Voß, G., & Rieder, K. (2008). Un(der)paid innovators: The commercial utilisation of consumer work through crowdsourcing. *Science, Technology & Innovation Studies, 4*(1), 5–26.

Lambert, T., & Schwienbacher, A. (2010). *An empirical analysis of crowdfunding* (SSRN Working Paper). Retrieved from http://ssrn.com/abstract=1578175

Lehner, O. M. (2013). Crowdfunding social ventures: A model and research agenda. *Routledge Venture Capital Journal, 15*(4), 289–311.

Massolution. (2013). *The crowdfunding industry report* (Abridged version). Retrieved from http://www.crowdsourcing.org/editorial/2013cf-the-crowdfunding-industry-report/25107

Massoudi, A. (n.d.). *Crowd funding websites & websites to find & connect with angel investors and venture capital-private equity firms*. Retrieved from http://www.strategy-of-innovation.com/pages/Crowd_Funding_Websites_Websites_to_Find_Connect_with_Angel_Investors_and_Venture_CapitalPrivate_Equity_firms-4605700.html

Maurin, E., & Thesmar, D. (2003). *Changes in the functional structure of firms and the demand for skill* (CEPR Discussion Papers No. 3831). Center for Economic Policy Research, London.

Nicholas, J. (2013). *Sharing, collaborative consumption and Web 2.0* (Media@LSE Electronic Working Paper No. 26). Retrieved from http://www.lse.ac.uk/media@lse/research/mediaWorkingPapers/pdf/EWP26-FINAL.pdf

OECD. (2013). *OECD skills outlook 2013: First results from the survey of adult skills*. Paris: OECD. doi:10.1787/9789264204256-en

Raja, S., Imaizumi, S., Kelly, T., Narimatsu, J., & Paradi-Guilford, C. (2013). *Connecting to work: How information and communication technologies could help expand employment opportunities*. ICT Sector Unit, World Bank. Retrieved from http://www-wds.worldbank.org/external/

default/WDSContentServer/WDSP/IB/2013/09/09/000456286_20130909094536/Rendered/PDF/809770WP0Conne00Box379814B00PUBLIC0.pdf
Ramos, J. (2014). *Crowdfunding and the role of managers in ensuring the sustainability of crowdfunding companies*. Institute for Prospective Technological Studies (IPTS), European Commission. Retrieved from http://ftp.jrc.es/EURdoc/JRC85752.pdf
Ramos, J., & Ballel, P. (2009). Globalisation, new technologies (ICTs) and dual labour markets: The case of Europe. *Emerald Journal of Information, Communication & Ethics in Society, 7*(4), 258–279.
Ramos, J., & Valera, A. (2012). From opportunity to austerity: Crisis and social policy in Spain. In M. Kilkey & G. Ramia (Eds.), *Social policy review 24: Analysis and debate in social policy, 2012*. Bristol: Policy Press.
Rubinton, B. (2011). *Crowdfunding: Disintermediated investment banking*. FINE 547 Advanced Finance Seminar.
Sabbagh, K., Friedrich, R., El-Darwiche, B., Singh, M., & Koster, A. (2013). Digitisation for economic growth and job creation. In B. Bilbao-Osorio, S. Dutta, & B. Lanvin (Eds.), *The global information technology report* (pp. 35–43). INSEAD & World Economic Forum. http://issuu.com/politicaspublicas/docs/wef_globalinformationtechnology_rep
Strauss, A., & Corbin, J. (1998). *Basics of qualitative research* (2nd ed.). Thousand Oaks, CA: Sage.
Surowiecki, J. (2005). *The wisdom of the crowd*. New York: Anchor Books.
Turlea, G., de Prato, G., Nepelski, D., & Szewczyk, W. (2011). *The 2011 report on R&D in ICT in the European Union*. JRC-IPTS, European Commission.
Walker, D., & Myrick, F. (2006). Grounded theory: An exploration of process and procedure. *Qualitative Health Research, 16*(4), 547–559.
Wojciechowski, A. (2009). Models of charity donations and project funding in social networks. *Computer Science, 5872*, 454–463.

Non-equity Crowdfunding as a National Phenomenon in a Global Industry: The Case of Russia

Evgeny Torkanovskiy

Abstract Venture capitalists and entrepreneurs all over the world have tried to imitate the success of Kickstarter, Indiegogo and other crowdfunding platforms. Russia has followed suit with the emergence of local platforms for raising capital online in 2010–2013. The moving forces behind this were an eagerness to copy a successful business model, existing language and legislative barriers and the potential capability to raise capital from strangers from afar that might be very important in such a vast country as Russia. However, given the performance of Russian platforms for non-equity-based crowdfunding it is evident that the success of local platforms largely depends on the characteristics of the national market and competition from international platforms. We provide a preliminary exploration of the underlying economics of Russian crowdfunding and its relationship with the international crowdfunding community. We offer a framework for speculating on how crowdfunding may unfold at national level and what the required conditions for its local development might be.

Keywords Crowdfunding • Non-equity • Fundraising • Russia • National platform • Planeta • Boomstarter

1 Introduction

2012 was a very fruitful year for the development of crowdfunding in Russia. April saw the launch of planeta.ru and in August boomstarter.ru saw the light. These two leaders of Russian crowdfunding and several smaller competitors such as kroogi.ru, together.ru, smipon.ru, blagobox.ru, tried to imitate the successful business model developed by Kickstarter and Indiegogo. The level of imitation differed significantly. For example, Planeta positioned itself as a community of creative people who help each other and support noble causes and crowdfunding was just one of the means of interaction within the community, whereas Boomstarter copied diligently

E. Torkanovskiy (✉)
Institute of Economics, Russian Academy of Sciences, Nakhimovsky Prospekt 32, Moscow, 117218 Russia
e-mail: torkanovsky@gmail.com

D. Brüntje, O. Gajda (eds.), *Crowdfunding in Europe*, FGF Studies in Small Business and Entrepreneurship, DOI 10.1007/978-3-319-18017-5_8

Kickstarter's model in a bid not to reinvent the wheel. The teams and costs were quite considerable. Planeta declared in Peganov (2012) that about 20 programmers worked for a year before the launch and $500,000–700,000[1] was invested. Now in an interview with Krauzova (2013) Planeta states that it employs more than 50 people. Boomstarter permanently employs about 40 people and by the end of 2013 had spent $800,000 as its founder declared in an interview with Nikolaeva (2013).

Clearly, the Russian founders were inspired by the success of international crowdfunding platforms. Two years later, major Russian platforms are still loss making but alive, without new money raised from outside financial or strategic investors. What are the reasons for Russian national platforms' emergence, how do they operate and what might the future hold for these national platforms vis-à-vis international heavyweights? We do preliminary research regarding these issues and try to define the market niche occupied by national crowdfunding platforms to speculate about their future. As there is still only limited academic research on crowdfunding in Russia, we use exploratory and descriptive research designs as our research method. We try to form hypotheses on the basis of descriptive research and use exploratory research to get new insights, assess phenomena and develop theory from data analysis, as well as using a deductive approach.

2 Russian Crowdfunding Development and Comparison with International Platforms

Despite emerging at approximately the same time, the fate of the 30 odd crowdfunding platforms in Russia is quite different. Some, such as Time-to-start or RuStarter, have not really taken off the ground due to fierce competition or insufficient funding. Others have found their public and a sustainable business model and are still in business, though with differing levels of success. The first entrant—kroogi.ru created in 2007—is not among the leaders as often is the case in nascent industries.

Russian crowdfunding platforms may be divided into two broad categories based on the motivation for their emergence. In the first group, crowdfunding platforms were created following the needs of the existing Internet community as an additional instrument of social interaction or by a group of active supporters of a particular, often regional, project. Consideration for legal issues is very low in this group as projects are initiated by friends or friends of friends and the platform is just a convenient way to collect funds from these friends, as discussed in SpaceW (2012). The platform is not a money-generating vehicle but a social responsibility or hobby. Thus, the level of technical complexity is rather low, as noted in SpaceW

[1] In this document $ denotes United States dollars. We have made the conversion from roubles, where applicable, for the reader's convenience.

(2012). This is the way kroogi.ru, smipon.ru and some other niche and regional platforms emerged.

Another option is "business" creation where the founders identified a business opportunity and started building a company for collecting funds from complete strangers. The venture's aim is to earn money and/or increase its capitalisation. The technical teams are quite advanced and there are special support teams advising the project creators seeking financing. Projects are admitted to the database after preliminary approval from the platform's team and the content is curated. Much time, effort and money are allocated to overcoming legal and payment difficulties and uncertainties. Lack of legal regulation is a deadly threat for such projects. Boomstarter and Planeta—two Russian crowdfunding leaders—have emerged this way and remain vocal proponents of better legal regulation of the national crowdfunding industry, as evidenced in Likeandplay (2013).

Both leading platforms, Planeta and Boomstarter, strive to become the dominating platform in Russia. Such dominance can produce a catalyst effect for the platform's development as the value of a platform to creators increases with the number of funders, and vice versa, for funders the value of a platform increases with the number of creators and other funders. When one platform is dominating the landscape then more and more funders and creators flock to a single platform creating a practical monopoly that can be used to increase the platform's revenues. At the same time a dominant platform is more attractive as a business for potential investors and acquirers.

Smaller competitors of Planeta and Boomstarter tried to develop niche markets. Blagobox specialises in charities for children with serious diseases. Smipon is basically a Siberian platform collecting funds for projects in the region. Together. ru is collecting funds for charity, principally for orphanages and shelters for children, the homeless, the elderly and other socially disadvantaged people.

As in the rest of the world, crowdfunding in Russia developed primarily for creativity-based industries (the top three categories according to Nikolaeva (2013) on Boomstarter are music, movies and books).

However, despite all the hype surrounding crowdfunding in the Russian media it is not a universal funding solution. The available empirical data shows that the typical successful creator is not a freshly found genius but a well-known, if not famous professional. The emphasis of both leading Russian platforms is on a star-creator who seeks to raise financing for a new project. Typical examples include the production of a TV show by well-known Russian producers Messrs Shenderovich and Mirzoev on Planeta (approx. $170,000) or the financing of the third season of Russian Stand-Up Show on Boomstarter ($15,000). Planeta specifically makes its case as a community of creative people helping each other and consequently the majority of projects are initiated by well-known musicians and artists. The reputation of creators is being used as a powerful antidote to information asymmetry and moral hazard problems. Russian crowdfunding platforms also try to attract projects that can generate a disproportionate share of media attention, because this both expands the existing community of funders (further increasing network effects) and allows the platform to expand into new categories.

At the same time many successful projects emphasise a national component, actively exploiting past glory, folk history and conservation of historic memorabilia (for example, the record breaking project to make a movie about 28 Panfilov soldiers who gave their lives to stop a column of Nazi tanks near Moscow raised $100,000 on Boomstarter). In our view Russian national platforms have more immediate political reactivity than their global competitors and pursue less stringent policies regarding political correctness, as shown by recently started projects following events in Ukraine.

Despite the fact that both leading platforms and some of the smaller competitors accept all types of projects the technology-associated projects do not find a good audience on Russian platforms, raising significantly less than they do abroad ($10,000–15,000 maximum), and according to our calculations the percentage of successful projects in this category is much lower (3–6 % vs. 8–16 % average for the whole platform). This is not logical given the flourishing of the IT industry and the quantity of IT specialists in Russia.

This may be evidence of a trend for national crowdfunding platforms, which needs to be explored further. Russian preliminary data confirms that the local platform is seen as a possible substitute for an international platform for certain types of projects only, whereas other projects and creators (in the case of Russia—IT) migrate to international platforms thus supporting and enhancing their dominance. For example, Kickstarter's record project from Russia is not a movie or show but a computer game—a flight simulator which raised $158,000. Other examples of successful Russian projects on Kickstarter include card games or documentaries on issues such as the Gulags or life behind the Iron Curtain. These latter projects may have had less success on Russian national platforms where national pride and glory or the Russian language are promoted as the major attraction point for funders in many projects.

Overall, on international platforms the chances of raising funding are significantly higher for technological geniuses or unorthodox artists or designers because of these platforms' ability to easily connect a huge crowd of discriminating customers or niche funders whose numbers cannot reach critical mass on national platforms. Thus, projects get funded that would never be able to obtain funding on national platforms.

Interestingly, no Russian platform has indicated an interest in expansion abroad. On the contrary, the regional, local or national component is very often emphasised. This may be an indirect indication that Russian platforms either consider the Russian market big enough to earn sufficient money in this national segment or lack the competitive advantages and resources to promote themselves internationally. Both positions mean that Russian platforms may be targets but not acquirers in potential international mergers.

3 Global Trends on Russian National Platforms

International platforms are also used as alternatives to traditional methods of sale in line with Hardy (2013) or for confirmation of the viability of a business model or product concept. The producer may set up regular production at the expense of future consumers without incurring costs itself. Or, he/she may test a product concept before investing money in the venture—if the response is not positive enough, then he/she may abandon the project as it is going to fail. The crowd serves also as the panel of potential consumers and advisors for the product's future design and features. Crowdfunding also implies independence from a single large investor who may impose his own constraints on the producer. Another important thing is that crowdfunding confirmation currently serves as a substitute for traction for many technology projects and is required by institutional investors (such as venture funds) or angel investors before they start considering the project or committing money. Our research shows that Russian platforms offer this pre-sale test only for creative projects like shows, books, albums, films etc. while technology projects get financing at an earlier stage and such funding is more equivalent to grants.

The funder-consumers in the crowdfunding relationship have a direct influence on the project's outcome and the product they intend to acquire. As a part of a community they may influence the product design and features by interacting directly with the producer. Their level of participation depends on their interest in the project and may vary thus serving the amelioration of a product's utility rather than the acquisition of a ready product. For creative projects obtaining financing on Russian platforms this feedback is less pronounced as crowdfunding is more considered as a means of popularity voting or as an advertising channel, and creators are not looking for feedback for product amelioration.

Simultaneously, doubts persist about the ability of national platforms to fight fraud, effectively ensure quality control, and operate transparently. For example, Boomstarter stresses that with more stringent control of submitted projects on Kickstarter there is a migration of American projects from this international platform to Boomstarter, as proudly revealed by its own Boomstarter Blog (2014). This raises the issue of the quality and level of control of incoming projects. Another confirmation of the acuteness of this issue is the record-breaking fundraising ($50,000) for the so-called Tesla Tower designed to transmit energy without loss from any point on the Earth to another using the Earth's surface. All these examples show that the national platforms largely ignore and do not protect the interests of funders considering them as dumb cash cows. This may require significant government regulation with the start of equity-based crowdfunding in order to protect funders. These concerns may already dissuade many from utilising and contributing through crowdfunding platforms.

The majority of projects on Russian platforms (70–100 % depending on the platform) have non-profit status. In line with Schwienbacher and Larralde (2010) who suggest that the non-profit status of individual projects provides a much higher success rate and higher overall funding amounts than the for-profit status of counterparts on similar crowdfunding platforms; the projects which are seen as for-profit ventures raise significantly less. Charity and philanthropy play an extremely important part in funding on Russian platforms. Individual projects prefer to convey that they do not have for-profit motives thereby establishing both trustworthiness and confidence in a project's relative quality with funders. Gerber, Hui and Kuo (2012) discuss the importance of non-profits in the emerging crowdfunding industry and conclude that the emphasis on being in a donative community is one of the major motivators for crowdfunding participation. Metzler (2011) notes that crowdfunding supporters of non-profits are encouraged by sympathy and empathy towards the cause, feeling guilty for not giving, and strengthening identity and social status. This also explains that for many star-creators a crowdfunding platform is seen as an additional advertising channel paying for itself. It is also worth noting that crowdfunding capital may hardly substitute for traditional sources of financing for the majority of projects displayed on Russian platforms.

One dimension on which crowdfunding usually differs from traditional funding is the spatial allocation of capital. Because transactions occur online rather than in person, factors that influence the geography of traditional forms of early-stage investments may be less important in the crowdfunding setting. Agrawal, Catalini, and Goldfarb (2011) proved that funding is not geographically constrained. Due to the scarcity of available data it is difficult to confirm this in Russia. However, the majority of successful projects tend to be in Moscow or St. Petersburg whereas most funders also reside in major Russian city agglomerations. This may be due to the low level of crowdfunding activity and early followers' relative concentration in city agglomerations. The total number of funders on Boomstarter is a little over 36,000 (as of April 2014).

All Russian non-equity crowdfunding platforms have applied a "provision point mechanism" as described by Bagnoli and Lipman (1989). Specifically, the creator only receives the funds if a funding threshold level is reached (or surpassed) within a certain period of time. Planeta allows the creator to take any amount if more than 50 % of the requested amount is raised. Boomstarter's policy is "all or nothing". By implementing a provision point mechanism, crowdfunding platforms eliminate the risk to funders of providing funds for a project that is unable to raise enough capital to be viable. It should be noted that funds pledged to unsuccessful projects on Boomstarter and Planeta are not returned to the contributor but are placed with the platform in the name of the contributor who can only use these funds for contribution to another project. Thus, the platforms obtain interest-free credit from contributors for unsuccessful projects.

4 Future of Russian Non-equity Crowdfunding

The leading Russian crowdfunding platforms are predominantly for-profit businesses. The two leaders employ a revenue model based on a transaction fee for successful projects equal to 5 % of the total funding amount with another 5 % paid to a payment processing company. Consequently, the platform's objective is to maximise the number and size of successful projects. In 2 years Planeta raised 70,000,000 roubles ($2,000,000) and Boomstarter 50,000,000 ($1,500,000). Thus, the combined revenues of both leaders of Russian crowdfunding did not exceed $200,000 in 2 years, or $50,000 a year each. That is why both platforms try to develop additional sources of revenue like ticket sales or e-commerce of art-related items (CDs, DVDs etc.). Both leaders continue to burn cash in the expectation of growth in the popularity of crowdfunding and the related increase in earnings and capitalisation.

The amounts already invested in leading Russian platforms are quite significant even by international standards. As ter Kuile (2011) noted donating platforms raise on average just 900,000 €.

What are the expectations of Russian platforms for the future? As we noted earlier, economically the platform may turn profitable only thanks to significant growth of the market. Revenues, given our estimates of costs, must grow to $300,000–400,000 per year just to break even. That means $6–8 million of successful projects per year. With the average amount raised remaining at the same level as now ($5,000) that means 1,200–1,600 projects per year. With the most optimistic forecasts of growth of the Russian market for crowdfunding given as 2–3 times per year in 2014–2015, as in Tarasenko (2014), this means that Russian platforms will not break even before 2016. Evidently, financial support is necessary but the return may be not very attractive from an investment standpoint. That is why, as Tarasenko (2014) indicates, platforms search for new financing from different sources, including the State. We may speculate that if only one platform is able to secure financing and survive then it may become the national crowdfunding platform and a successful business. If, however, the present oligopolistic structure is maintained, non-equity crowdfunding in Russia will be a loss-making industry waiting for a consolidator, possibly from abroad.

Another economic reason for the business of crowdfunding platforms is capitalisation growth and merger expectations. The majority, if not all, founders of crowdfunding sites in Russia perfectly understood, as evidenced in their interviews in Bogdanov (2012) and Plenin (2014), that the main function of the crowdfunding platform is money processing which means that, due to legislative requirements, entering a new national market for an international crowdfunding platform is equivalent to starting a new business. This would mean that any crowdfunding platform expanding internationally would be more inclined to acquire a local competitor than start the platform in a new environment from scratch. However, these expectations have not yet materialised and the problems encountered by the crowdfunding platforms in Russia may impact on the realisation of these hopes making international giants follow the example of PayPal and eBay by developing local franchises independently instead of acquiring a local competitor which may be loaded with past problems and reputation issues. Given that the major asset of the crowdfunding platform is its reputation among funders and creators it may prove difficult to align Russian and international platforms without loss of value in such mergers.

5 Conclusion

The demand for emergence of national crowdfunding platforms in Russia is impacted by several factors, including language and the development of payment systems.

The viability of national non-equity crowdfunding platforms depends on local and global factors. Among local we can indicate the receptivity of the local market to a new financing method, its size and rate of growth, the existing barriers to entry for international crowdfunding platforms, language barriers, local legislation and regulation. Among global factors we include barriers for creators to bring their projects to international platforms. As data shows, geography or spatial distance is not a problem.

We expect that local non-equity crowdfunding platforms have two options for development. Either, due to their reputation, the quality of their projects, creators and funders they will remain a second-tier alternative to global players. Or, with an increase in the number of national funders and adequate regulation supporting ease and efficiency of funding, and interest from foreign creators, they will develop into global or, at least, regional players themselves. We assume that international M&A activity in this sector in Russia will be very low in the coming 2 or 3 years given the important role of a platform's reputation and the weak alignment of reputation among local and global players.

References

Agrawal, A. K., Catalini, C., & Goldfarb, A. (2011). *The geography of crowdfunding* (NBER Working Paper No. 16820). Retrieved from http://www.nber.org/papers/w16820

Bagnoli, M., & Lipman, B. L. (1989). Provision of public goods: Fully implementing the core through private contributions. *Review of Economic Studies, 56*(4), 583–601.

Bogdanov, A. (2012). *RuStarter Startup is like Kickstarter, only in Russia* (in Russian). Retrieved from http://siliconrus.com/2012/06/startap-rustarter-kak-kikstarter-tolko-v-rossii/

Boomstarter Blog. (2014, February 10). *Blog on Boomstarter* (in Russian). Retrieved from http://boomstarterru/blog/111

Gerber, E. M., Hui, J. S., & Kuo, P.-Y. (2012). Crowdfunding: Why people are motivated to post and fund projects on crowdfunding platforms. *Proceedings of the International Workshop on Design, Influence, and Social Technologies: Techniques, Impacts and Ethics*. Retrieved from http://www.juliehui.org/wp-content/uploads/2013/04/CSCW_Crowdfunding_Final.pdf

Hardy, W. (2013). *How to perfectly discriminate in a crowd? A theoretical model of crowdfunding* (University of Warsaw, Faculty of Economic Sciences, Working Papers No. 16/2013 (101)). Retrieved from http://www.wne.uw.edu.pl/inf/wyd/WP/WNE_WP101.pdf

Krauzova, E. (2013, March 21). Maks Lakmus: Russian crowdfunding will grow into something very interesting (in Russian). *Computerra*. Retrieved from http://www.computerra.ru/60617/maks-lakmus-rossiyskiy-kraudfanding-vyirastet-vo-chto-to-ochen-interesnoe/

Likeandplay. (2013). *Year of crowdfunding in Russia: Between past and future* (in Russian). Retrieved from http://www.likeandpay.ru/god-kraudfandinga-v-rossii-mezhdu-proshly-m-i-budushhim

Metzler, T. (2011). *Venture financing by crowdfunding*. Bonn: GRIN Verlag.

Nikolaeva, Z. (2013). Ruslan Tugushev, Boomstarter. Far from all projects that seemed interesting raised money (in Russian). *Slon.ru.* Retrieved from http://slon.ru/biz/startup-rating-2013/boomstarter/

Peganov, S. (2012, July 5). Planeta.ru is Russian Kickstarter for Creative Personalities (in Russian). *Zuckerberg Calls.* Retrieved from http://www.siliconrus.com/2012/07/planeta-ru-russkiy-kikstarter-dlya-tvorcheskih-lichnostey/

Plenin, D. (2014, January 17). Ruslan Tugushev: Boomstarter has not been a clone of Kickstarter for a long time already (in Russian). *Firrma.* Retrieved from http://firrma.ru/data/interview/2408/

Schwienbacher, A., & Larralde, B. (2010). Crowdfunding of small entrepreneurial ventures. *SSRN Electronic Journal.* Retrieved from http://ssrn.com/abstract=1699183

SpaceW. (2012, June 13). Interview with S Miru Po Nitke Project Manager (in Russian). *GeekTimes.* Retrieved from http://habrahabr.ru/post/145763/

Tarasenko, S. (2014, January 15). In Russia the crowdfunding market is expected to grow 2–3 times a year (in Russian). *Metro.* Retrieved from http://www.metronews.ru/novosti/v-rossii-zhdut-rosta-rynka-kraudfandinga-za-god-v-2-3-raza/Tponao---vgAwz1tAY1JXk/

ter Kuile, F. A. (2011). *The state of crowdfunding: A review of business models and platforms.* Retrieved from http://futureideas.eu/wp-content/uploads/2013/01/Frank-ter-Kuile_The-state-of-crowdfunding.pdf

Institutions Influencing the Evolution of Crowdfunding in China: A Review of the World Bank Report on Crowdfunding's Potential for the Developing World

Andrea S. Funk

Abstract In the recently published World Bank Report on Crowdfunding [infoDev (Crowdfunding's Potential for the Developing World (Report). World Bank, 2013)], China has been predicted to have great potential: By 2025, Chinese households might invest up to US$50 billion per year in crowdfunding projects. However, as the authors of this report have admitted, they based their approximation primarily on economic data, and thus China's prospective amount of crowdfunding capital may actually be much lower. Not least for international crowdfunding platforms, the development of crowdfunding in the Chinese market is of considerable importance. This paper assesses the World Bank Report's procedural methods and their applicability to China. Moreover, it addresses some mistakes and contradictions that underlie this report. Whilst the report's findings provide a solid insight into crowdfunding's potential for the entire developing world, some key variables used are not applicable to China and therefore adulterate the findings. The author of this paper suggests an extended study, which considers country-specific variables and circumstances.

Keywords Crowdfunding • China • World Bank • Social media engagement

Crowdfunding today is still a phenomenon predominantly occurring in the developed world. Yet, shortly after the establishment of the first crowdfunding platform (CFP) in the USA, in 2008 this new art of finance has been initiated also in less developed regions. In 2011, the first Chinese crowdfunding platform, Demohour, went online. Within its first 2 years of operation, it acquired about US$1 million of funds enabling more than 400 projects to be realised. The recently published World Bank Report on Crowdfunding (WBRC) recognises huge potential for crowdfunding in developing countries, ascribing China the most promising future, with potential annual funds of

A.S. Funk (✉)
Julius-Maximilians-University of Wuerzburg, Wuerzburg, Germany
e-mail: andrea.funk@uni-wuerzburg.de

D. Brüntje, O. Gajda (eds.), *Crowdfunding in Europe*, FGF Studies in Small Business and Entrepreneurship, DOI 10.1007/978-3-319-18017-5_9

up to US$50 billion invested by Chinese crowdfunders.[1] This estimation is based on economic data and the analysis of selected key variables, which determine the number of CFPs resembling the dependent variable of the entire report. Whilst crowdfunding's potential for the emerging Chinese market is beyond question, this paper addresses the World Bank's assumptions, which used parameters which do not hold for China. Moreover, the author suggests some alternative key variables more suitable for research on crowdfunding in China.

1 WBRC's Key Variables for Crowdfunding Engagement

In order to analyse the crowdfunding potential for the developing world, the World Bank created a model including one dependent and several independent variables, which might be disputable.

First, the number of CFPs might not be an accurate measurement for crowdfunding engagement in any country. In order to get an idea of a population's engagement level in its respective crowdfunding market, the authors of the WBRC chose the CFP count as a proxy of the dependent variable. Even though a higher number of platforms in one country might suggest a higher number of active users amongst its citizens, there are countries which are dominated by a few crowdfunding platforms. Then there are other countries having a relatively high number of moderately successful crowdfunding platforms. For example, in the USA, *Kickstarter* and *Indiegogo* obtain most crowdfunding projects, whereas in Germany, there are several competing platforms of a similar size. Nevertheless, in absolute terms, there are many more active crowdfunders in the USA compared to Germany. With regard to China, CFPs are labelled either as *chanpin* (product) or *guquan* (equity shares) platforms, whereas the former term rather refers to reward-based platforms. Yet, the author has identified three different categories of CFPs in China: First, big players like *JD Crowdfunding, Hi.Taobao,* and *Zhongchou Wang,* which are affiliates of large companies having their core business in e-commerce or financial services respectively. These platforms offer a broad spectrum of product- and service-based projects. Second, start-up platforms with a vertical orientation like *Dreamore* (with focus on youths), *Musikid* (music), and *Modian* (games). Third, quasi equity-based crowdfunding platforms like *Angelcrunch, Meng3, Tianshi Jie, Zhongchou Wang* and *JD Equity Crowdfunding.* Moreover, many Chinese prefer to run their own crowdfunding campaign without the help of a crowdfunding platform, but instead leverage their project by tools like *Weixin.* Ultimately, the CFP count might not tell the whole truth of a country's level of crowdfunding engagement.

Moreover, the authors of the WBRC have identified some key variables influencing the CFP count; however, some of these parameters are not applicable to China. As social media is an essential prerequisite for the development of crowdfunding,

[1] In this paper the term "crowdfunder" defines a person who invests financially in a crowdfunding project.

social media engagement has been acknowledged as "the single most predictive factor for the rate of crowdfund emergence" (infoDev, 2013, p. 40). In order to quantify the level of a country's social media engagement, the authors of the WBRC have taken the number of Facebook users as a proxy count. Whilst this assumption might hold for most countries in the world, Facebook is hardly used in China, which is also due to the fact that this social network is officially banned by the Chinese government. Unless one has access to a virtual private network (VPN), Chinese citizens cannot access Facebook via a Chinese server. Nevertheless, the Chinese are highly engaged in social media (Chiu, Lin, & Silverman, 2012), relying on local networks like *Weibo*, *Weixin* (=*WeChat*) or *QQ*. Therefore, Facebook penetration cannot be taken as a proxy for social media engagement in China.

Thirdly, according to the WBRC there is a positive correlation "between the proportion of the population with secondary or tertiary education and the rise of crowdfunding" (infoDev, 2013, p. 37), forming the cognitive key variable for CFP count. However, one should rather consider the quality of education and less the absolute number of a country's graduates, which might be a misleading parameter. In terms of China, the government recently sought an increase in the number of university places in order to address the lack of skilled people. Yet there are millions of Chinese graduates who suffer from unemployment (Branigan, 2008). Moreover, the Chinese education system enjoys a bad reputation, which is reflected by the number of students seeking to study abroad (Siddiq, 2013). Consequently, the proportion of a country's graduates is not a significant variable for the CFP count.

Besides cognitive factors, the WBRC has also identified several normative variables, which as a whole appear to indicate a country's risk aversion tendency; even though each single variable might determine the CFP count to a certain extent, those variables cannot be subsumed to risk aversion. Amongst the category of normative variables, the authors of the WBRC recognised face-saving, uncertainty avoidance, in-group collectivism, and performance orientation, claiming that "the more people are concerned with saving face, the more important they will consider other people's perceptions of them to be and the less likely they are to take risks" (infoDev, 2013, p. 37). Whilst this thesis sounds plausible, one should know that the Chinese mentality is indeed face-saving and quite collectivist; yet, according to Hofstede's cultural dimensions, China shows a rather low level of uncertainty avoidance (The Hofstede Centre, n.d.). Finally, normative variables can be antipodal, and therefore need to be contemplated individually in order to identify a country's risk aversion tendency.

2 Mistakes and Contradictions Within the WBRC

The WBRC has listed one Chinese crowdfund investment platform. According to a more recent report by zero2ipo (2014) there are at least three crowdinvesting platforms operating in China. During her field studies in 2015, the author has identified nine Chinese quasi equity-based CFPs; yet some of these have only been launched recently. In order to run a legal crowdinvesting platform, one needs to apply for a licence from Chinese authorities (He Siyuan, 2015).

The emission of shares by private people and unregistered companies in China is considered illegal (Xinhua Wang, 2012) and could entail draconian punishment (Zui gao renmin fayuan, 2012). He stated that there are increasingly more platforms applying for such a licence (He Siyuan, 2015). Still, platforms differ a lot in terms of conception and operation from our Western understanding. Therefore, one needs to first define the criteria of a crowdinvesting platform, and thereupon determine which platforms actually meet these criteria (zero2ipo, 2014).

Secondly, the graphical presentation and the interpretation of those factors enabling or deterring a crowdfunding ecosystem are dissonant; therefore the reader of the WBRC has to decide him/herself which findings are correct. By drawing a two-dimensional grid demonstrating the positive vs. negative influence of the variables on crowdfunding, and its certainty of correlation, all identified factors have been placed according to their capabilities; yet, in the subsequent discussion, some factors have been interpreted differently. For example, "performance orientation is strongly correlated (if not nearly as strongly as social media penetration) with the number of platforms in a country" (infoDev, 2013, p. 40). However, contemplating the graphical analysis of the WBRC's data (infoDev, 2013, p. 38; Fig. 2.1), performance orientation is one of the least important factors determining CFP count. As a second example, the authors state that "[r]emittance inflows and informal investor rate are both negatively correlated" (infoDev, 2013, p. 40) with CFP count. Whilst the former does not appear in Fig. 2.1, the informal investor rate is recorded as a rather positive factor enabling crowdfunding. In conclusion, the WBRC should be revised, as the discussion of the data deviates from the graphical presentation of the latter.

According to the WBRC, 38 % of all Chinese citizens hold a Facebook account (infoDev, 2013, p. 43; Fig. 2.3), which is somewhat questionable as the use of Facebook in China is an illegal action. In order to quantify a country's crowdfunding potential, the authors of the WBRC have analysed each country's social media penetration; as a proxy of social media engagement, they have contemplated the number of Facebook accounts registered in each country. Even though Chinese excessively use social media (Chiu et al., 2012), they mainly rely on Chinese social media like *Weibo* or *Weixin*; if a Chinese person intends to use Facebook in China, he/she needs to access a VPN. Indeed, such a VPN might be easy to use; however the use of local social media might be rather obvious, not least for reasons of linguistic convenience. Ultimately, the number of Chinese Facebook users, and therefore China's social media penetration, seems to be adulterated. In fact, the actual percentage of Chinese social media engagement based on Chinese social media might be even higher.

3 Institutions Influencing the Evolution of Crowdfunding in China

The WBRC has identified a range of influencing variables determining the future growth of crowdfunding in developing countries; still, for a reliable appraisal of the Chinese crowdfunding market the author suggests some further factors should be stressed, which have country-specific significance.

In line with the WBRC, the author highlights the importance of "a regulatory framework that leverages the transparency, speed, and scale" (infoDev, 2013, p. 8). In December 2014, the Chinese government quietly published draft regulations for equity crowdfunding and requested for comments. Whereas these regulations are quite strict, they are still rather guidelines than binding law and lack some clarity; therefore, crowdinvesting in China is still at a "trial and error" stage. Foremost, equity CFPs are obliged to register at the Securities Association of China (SAC) and apply for membership. Moreover, they need to hold net assets of at least RMB 5 million. The board of such a platform needs to comprise of several senior experts in equity crowdfunding and the fields of finance or IT. Like in the US, crowdinvesting is only open for accredited investors, who either hold net assets of RMB 10 million or have financial assets of at least RMB 3 million and a minimum annual income of RMB 500,000 for the past three years. An investor could also simply become accredited by investing a minimum sum of RMB 1 million in a single project. Apart from the above, there are further rules and restrictions. Yet, the fact that there is some regulation in fact demonstrates the government's awareness of crowdfunding's potential in China (Roche, 2015). The future will show how these regulations will further be implemented.

Furthermore, the importance of social media engagement for the establishment of a crowdfunding ecosystem is indisputable; though its level should be estimated by suitable proxies. In China, the microblog *Weibo* is the most popular social network amongst Internet users, followed by *Weixin* and *QQ* (Chiu et al., 2012). In order to assess Chinese social media penetration, one would have to analyse the usage of the latter. Ultimately, even though Facebook is less prevalent in China, there are Chinese equivalents, which might be essential for the future of crowdfunding in China.

Finally, whilst estimating the size of a crowdfunding market one should not exclusively rely on economic and financial data, but also consider whether wealthy people are willing to invest into crowdfunding projects. According to the WBRC, its projections regarding the size of crowdfunding markets are based on "the number of households capable of making crowdfunding investments; the amount in U.S. dollar equivalents (using purchasing power parity) available to invest in securities-based crowdfunding; and the amount of money investors will reallocate from both savings and their equity holdings" (infoDev, 2013, p. 40). First, as mentioned above, today equity crowdfunding in China still differs from the western understanding of crowdinvesting and is rather intransparent, which might impair the World Bank's estimation of China's potential crowdfunding capital. Secondly, there is no guarantee nor estimate of the likelihood that people who hold enough funds are also willing to invest these into crowdfunding projects, instead of depositing or spending them otherwise. Conversely, current Chinese crowdfunders are mainly comprised of rather penniless students, who are willing to spend their remaining monthly budget on interesting projects (Du Mengjie, 2013); and a limited number of accredited investors (Roche, 2015). Overall, in order to make a solid estimate of China's future crowdfunding market, one needs to have a clear understanding of the composition and motivations of Chinese crowdfunders.

4 Conclusion

The World Bank Report on Crowdfunding's Potential for the Developing World (WBRC) ascribed to China a promising crowdfunding future, with up to US$50 billion annual funds of investment for crowdfunding projects. However, as the authors of the report have also mentioned, this number should not be taken for granted as the Chinese market holds some huge challenges for crowdfunding. The authors of the WBRC identified a range of key variables, in their estimation determining the evolution of a crowdfunding ecosystem. However, some variables do not hold for China, some are not distinctive enough for the Chinese market, and some are even adulterated; above all, Facebook as a proxy for social media engagement cannot be applied to China as the Chinese government has banned its citizens from using the most popular social network. In envisioning the size of the Chinese crowdfunding market one should analyse some further variables which are characteristic for China; e.g. the (potential) regulatory framework; the extent of alternative social media; and the composition of Chinese crowdfunders. Inarguably, China has a huge potential for crowdfunding; however, its actual crowdfunding capability is yet to be determined.

References

Branigan, T. (2008, December 4). *Millions of Chinese graduates out of work after five-fold rise in university places*. Retrieved from http://www.theguardian.com/world/2008/dec/04/china-higher-education-graduate-jobs

Chiu, C., Lin, D., & Silverman, A. (2012). *China's social-media boom* (Report). Retrieved from https://s3-ap-northeast-1.amazonaws.com/mckinseychinavideos/PDF/McKinsey-Chinas-Social-Media-Boom1.pdf

Du Mengjie杜梦杰. (2013, August 19). *Interview with Du Mengjie杜梦杰, founder and CEO of the crowdfunding platform Dreamore/Interviewer: Andrea S. Funk*. University of Wuerzburg, Germany.

He Siyuan 何思远. (2015, February 20). *Telephone interview with He Siyuan 何思远 Co-founder of the crowdfunding platform ifundu/interviewer: Andrea S. Funk*. University of Wuerzburg, Germany.

infoDev. Finance and Private Sector Development Department. (2013). *Crowdfunding's potential for the developing world* (Report). Washington, DC: World Bank.

Roche, C. (2015, May 6). *Interview with Conor Roche, Associate Director at BOP Consulting in China/Interviewer: Andrea S. Funk*. University of Wuerzburg, Germany.

Siddiq, H. (2013, November 18). *More Chinese students want a US education, but fewer stay for a job*. Retrieved from http://www.scmp.com/comment/insight-opinion/article/1356828/more-chinese-students-want-us-education-fewer-stay-job

The Hofstede Centre. (n.d.). *What about China?* Retrieved from http://geert-hofstede.com/china.html

Xinhua Wang 新华网. (2012, May 21). 吴英集资诈骗案重审改判死缓 [*Re-investigation of Wu Ying's case of fraudulent fundraising; she has been sentenced to death with extension*]. Retrieved from http://news.xinhuanet.com

Zero2ipo. (2014). 中国众筹模式运行统计分析报告 [*Report on data analysis on the operation of different kinds of crowdfunding in China*] (unpublished report).

Zui gao renmin fayuan 最高人民法院. (2012). 最高人民法院关于审理非法集资刑事案件具体应用法律若干问题的解释 [*Declaration of the National Supreme Court regarding the correct implementation of regulations on the prosecution of illegal fundraising*]. Retrieved from http://www.court.gov.cn/

Part III
Analysis of Specific Application Areas in Crowdfunding

The Perfect Regulation of Crowdfunding: What Should the European Regulator Do?

Sebastiaan N. Hooghiemstra and Kristof de Buysere

Abstract More and more SMEs use crowdfunding to raise funds from a large audience by means of a cost-effective effort. Crowdfunding helps SMEs to overcome the demand for capital for early-stage (equity) financing. The traditional availability of financing, such as bank lending, venture capital and angel investments, are not available to most start-ups and other SMEs. Offerings are, thus, more and more promoted through crowdfunding portals. Funds through this channel of financing are typically raised from a larger number of contributors in the form of relatively small contributions. It is therefore very obvious that more and more firms have started to use this medium for this goal. Regulations on the national and European level, however, heavily limit mechanisms to promote offers and campaigns to a wide range of potential investors. In addition, company laws and banking and securities regulations hinder the emergence of an ecosystem with platforms that can offer the infrastructure for internet-based campaigns. This paper particularly explores these (mainly European) obstacles, and proposes remedies.

Keywords SMEs • Public offerings • Crowdfunding • Private company law • MiFID

1 Introduction to Crowdfunding

SMEs represent 99 % of the businesses in Europe and they create a large number of jobs and innovations (De Buysere, Gajda, Kleverlaan, & Marom, 2012; Milhaupt, 1998). SMEs, however, face an enormous capital funding gap (Bradford, 2012). Available sources of capital fall short in meeting the demand for early-stage

---

The legislation and bibliographic references used in this contribution are current as of 17 February 2015.

S.N. Hooghiemstra (✉)
University of Liechtenstein, Vaduz, Liechtenstein
e-mail: b_hooghiemstra@hotmail.com

K. de Buysere
Tilburg Law School, Tilburg, The Netherlands

D. Brüntje, O. Gajda (eds.), *Crowdfunding in Europe*, FGF Studies in Small Business and Entrepreneurship, DOI 10.1007/978-3-319-18017-5_10

(equity) financing (Sjostrom, 2004). The traditional availability of financing, such as bank lending, venture capital and angel investments[1] are not available to most start-ups and other SMEs. Banks tend not to lend to SMEs that do not have collateral, cash flow, or an operating history (Fisch, 1998), whereas venture capital funds tend to focus on companies that have passed the initial start-up phase (Cable, 2010). Angel investors look in general for high-growth, high-return investment opportunities, leaving no traditional sources of capital willing to fund the SME funding gap.

More and more SMEs use crowdfunding to raise funds from a large audience by means of a cost-effective effort. Offerings are published and promoted through online crowdfunding portals. Such offerings are only open for a specific period of time. Funds through this channel of financing are typically raised from a larger number of contributors in the form of relatively small contributions. It is therefore obvious that firms have started to use this medium for this goal. Regulation on the national and European level, however, heavily limits the mechanisms that promote offers and campaigns to a wide range of potential investors. In addition, company laws and banking and securities regulations hinder the emergence of an ecosystem that can offer the infrastructure for internet-based campaigns. This paper particularly explores these (mainly European) obstacles and proposes remedies.

In the following, what crowdfunding is (Sect. 2) will be explored first, and to what extent (European) securities laws (Sect. 3) and national company laws are restricting crowdfunding offerings for SMEs (Sect. 4). Furthermore, the pitfalls for crowdfunding platforms under (European) securities laws are identified (Sect. 5), before a proposal for a harmonised European regulatory framework will be made (Sect. 6). Finally, the paper concludes (Sect. 7).

2 What Is Crowdfunding?

Crowdfunding can be defined as a collective effort from a large number of individuals, who support individual projects and businesses with small contributions initiated by entrepreneurs (SMEs) or organisations (De Buysere et al., 2012).[2] Usually, the raising of capital is done through social networks, facilitated by specialised platforms on the Internet. Depending on the taxonomy that is used, there are generally at least four forms of crowdfunding (Pope, 2011; Röthler & Wenzlaff, 2011) that correspond to the different motivations funders have:

[1] Angel investments are investments conducted by wealthy individuals with substantial business and entrepreneurial experience. See, for example, Art. 6 Regulation (EU) No 345/2013 of the European Parliament and of the Council of 17 April 2013 on European venture capital funds.

[2] European Commission (2014) Communication from the Commission to the European Parliament, the Council, the European Economic and Social Committee and the Committee of the Regions—Unleashing the potential of Crowdfunding in the European Union, Com (2014) 172 final, p. 3.

donation-based, reward- and early sales-based, lending-based, and revenue sharing and equity-based. One important aspect that can however be observed with all types of crowdfunding, is that the expectation of risk-adjusted returns is, in most cases, not the primary driver for funders to support a project or business (National Council on National Council on Economic Education, 2005). Donation-based crowdfunding, for example, is usually a (donor) contract without existential reward at all. The funders are satisfied when a certain project can be realised (De Buysere et al., 2012). Reward- or pre-sales-based crowdfunding focuses on funders that want to get a product or service as a reward for their investment, whereas investors investing in lending-based, revenue sharing and equity-based crowdfunding aim to obtain a financial return (De Buysere et al., 2012). This paper only concentrates on equity-based crowdfunding.

3 Crowdfunding Offerings Under (European) Securities Laws

Crowdfunding offerings are publicly promoted and therefore might need to publish a prospectus under the Prospectus Directive.[3] A prospectus must be published when an offer of securities is made to the public within the European Economic Area (EEA) (Leuering & Rubner, 2012).[4] The definition of an "offer of securities to the public" refers to a communication in any form or by any means presenting sufficient information on the terms of the offer and the securities to be offered so as to enable an investor to decide to purchase or subscribe for securities.[5] Crowdfunding offerings made via a crowdfunding platform would typically fall within the scope of this definition.[6] However, if it is established that there is an offer to the public, a number of exemptions from the prospectus requirement are listed in the Prospectus Directive. The most important "exemption" is actually a limitation

[3] A prospectus contains key financial and non-financial information that a company makes available to potential investors when it is issuing securities to raise capital. See for the information that a prospectus needs to contain: Directive 2003/71/EC of the European Parliament and of the Council of 4 November 2003 on the prospectus to be published when securities are offered to the public or admitted to trading and amending Directive 2001/34/EC (OB L 345/64) as amended by Directive 2010/73/EU of the European Parliament and of the Council of 24 November 2010, OJ L 327, 31 December 2003, 1 (hereafter: "Prospectus Directive"); Commission Regulation (EC) No 809/2004 of 29 April 2004 implementing Directive 2003/71/EC of the European Parliament and of the Council as regards information contained in prospectuses as well as the format, incorporation by reference and publication of such prospectuses and dissemination of advertisements, OJ L 149, 30 April 2004, 1 (hereafter: "Prospectus Regulation").

[4] European Economic Area, European Union, including Liechtenstein, Iceland and Norway.

[5] Art. 2(1)(d) Prospectus Directive.

[6] European Securities and Markets Authority, Opinion of 18 December 2014 (ESMA/2014/1378), Investment-based crowdfunding, pp. 12–13; European Securities and Markets Authority, Advice of 18 December 2014 (ESMA/2014/1560), Investment-based crowdfunding, p. 13.

of the scope of the Prospectus Directive rather than an exemption, as the Directive does not regulate public offerings which do not exceed a value of 5,000,000 €.[7] Those may however be regulated on the national level. Art. 3(2) of the Prospectus Directive also contains a number of exemptions which apply to securities offerings irrespective of the 5,000,000 € threshold. These apply to the following types of offerings[8]:

(a) *an offer of securities addressed solely to qualified investors; and/or*
(b) *an offer of securities addressed to fewer than 150 natural or legal persons per Member State, other than qualified investors; and/or*
(c) *an offer of securities addressed to investors who acquire securities for a total consideration of at least €100,000 per investor, for each separate offer; and/or*
(d) *an offer of securities whose denomination per unit amounts to at least €100,000; and/or*
(e) *an offer of securities with a total consideration in the Union of less than €100,000, which shall be calculated over a period of 12 months.*

Under these exemptions, no EEA-Member State may in any case require a prospectus to be prepared for offerings of less than 100,000 €. However, many crowdfunding campaigns may exceed the 100,000 € threshold. The problem is that for offerings between 100,000 € and 5,000,000 € the choice is left to the individual Member States whether they grant an exemption on offerings up to 5,000,000 € or not.[9] This has resulted in many different national regimes ranging from full prospectus regimes to complete exemptions.[10] It is important in this regard to note that the company offering its shares must comply not only with the regulations of its home Member State, where it is established, but also with the prospectus requirements of the host Member State where the shares are being offered to the public.

Thus, companies face considerable problems in structuring an offer of securities so as to fall within one of the exemptions from the requirement to produce a prospectus. The variety of national implementations of the Prospectus Directive thus deprives start-ups from raising funds on a cross-border basis.

---

[7] Art. 1(2)(h) Prospectus Directive.

[8] Art. 3(2) Prospectus Directive.

[9] Some countries, like the UK, even have a country-specific regime for financial promotions to which the Prospectus Directive does not apply. See: Section 21 Financial Services and Markets Act 2000.

[10] In Estonia, Germany, Latvia and Lithuania a prospectus under the national prospectus rules needs to be prepared when offered amount is 100,000 € or more (Estonia; § 12(5) Securities Market Act; Germany: § 3(2) sub-paragraph 1 Nr. 5 Securities Prospectus Act; Latvia: Art. 16 (2) sub-paragraph 5 Law on the Financial Instruments Market; Lithuania: Art. 5(5) Law on Securities); In Norway the amount is 1,000,000 € (Section 7-2 Securities Trading Act); In Finland 1,500,000 € or more (Section 3(4), chapter 4 Securities Markets Act); In the Netherlands and Sweden 2,500,000 million euros (Netherlands: Art. 53 Exemption Regulation FSMA; Sweden: § 4 Financial Instruments Trading Act); In Denmark, Spain and the UK 5,000,000 € or more (Denmark: Art. 43(1) Securities Trading Act; Spain: Art. 30 Securities Market Act; UK: Section 85, 86 FSMA 2000).

4 Pitfalls for Crowdfunding Offerings: National Company Laws

An additional layer of limitations in Europe that may apply to public offerings derives from national company laws (Pietrancosta, 2006). Start-ups usually opt for "cheap" company regimes, which effectively are closely held company types. Closely held company types in various Member States in Europe impose cumbersome limitations on offering equity to potentially large numbers of investors in a crowdfunding campaign. These limitations may either be derived from (i) public offering limitations by national company laws or (ii) substantial formalities imposed by national company laws upon equity raising and share issues. This second layer substantially erodes the attractiveness of Prospectus Directive public offering exemptions, and of national prospectus exemptions.

4.1 Public Offering Limitations by National Company Laws

Many Member States that have implemented the Prospectus Directive do not distinguish between private and public companies in the obligation to publish a prospectus.[11] Crowdfunding businesses established as a private limited company may in these Member States want to offer stakes to the public, and are thus either subject to or exempt from the requirements imposed by the Prospectus Directive. However many Member States, such as the UK, have left their national company laws untouched.[12] These laws prohibit private limited companies in their national company laws from making public offers. Businesses established as a private limited company might for that reason not be able to benefit from the public offering exemptions under the Prospectus Directive. They will need to establish themselves as an "expensive" public limited liability company to be saved from this restriction. The effect of the exemptions offered by the Prospectus Directive is thus eroded by the limitations of national private company laws to publicly offer securities.

---

[11] See in the UK: Section 85 Financial Services and Markets Act 2000.

[12] In France, companies by default are prohibited from offering shares to the public: as a sanction for violating this rule, every subscription contract will be void. Public limited companies are saved from that rule, but closely held companies (limited liability companies) are not. See French Civil Code Art. 1841, as amended by Order No 2009-80 from 15 January 2009, Art. 15; See for the UK: Section 755 (1) Companies Act 2006: a private company limited by shares or limited by guarantee and having a share capital must not: "(a) offer to the public any securities of the company, or (b) allot or agree to allot any securities of the company with a view to their being offered to the public".

4.2 Formalities Imposed by National Company Laws

A similar problem arises when national company laws impose substantial formalities on private limited companies in the case of equity raises and share issues. These limitations may be formalities, such as notarised shareholder resolutions[13]/ subscriptions,[14] or votes requiring qualified majorities[15] (and for instance also during voting on the acceptance of new shareholders). The latter prevents them from actually offering units to third parties that do not yet belong to a closed circle of persons close to the firm. For that reason, the units are also not considered as negotiable (tradable) securities, which often exclude them from the Prospectus Directive, but not necessarily from the Member State-specific promotion regimes. In many cases, closely held companies are thus unsuitable for crowdfunding as these are legal structures aimed at resolving intrashareholding conflicts, whereas in crowdfunding managerial agency problems between the entrepreneur and shareholder have typically taken over from intrashareholder conflicts. Formalities in national company laws thus also erode the benefits of the exemptions offered under the Prospectus Directive and the national prospectus rules.

5 Crowdfunding Platforms Under (European) Securities Laws

Not only entrepreneurs but also platforms face important legal restrictions in promoting crowdfunding campaigns. As a result, two business models are used for crowdfunding platforms. Crowdfunding platforms for company funding either try to "engineer" a transaction model around the legal barriers, or they organise themselves as an "eBay" business model (De Buysere et al., 2012).

[13] A capital raise in Belgium and Italy requires in many cases a resolution or notification evidencing the execution of the capital raise. This does generally not require any intervention of new investors. See for Italy: Art. 2481bis Italian Civil Code; See for Belgium: Art. 308 Belgian Companies Code.

[14] Notarised subscription statements for capital raises are, for instance, required by Germany. See § 55 German Private Limited Liability Companies Act.

[15] Spain requires for private limited companies (Sociedad de Responsabilidad Limitada; SRL's) the agreement of half of the shareholders during a general meeting of shareholders. See for example Art. 199 Spanish Corporate Enterprises Act; or take, for instance, French SARL's (Société à Responsabilité Limitée), where resolutions of an ordinary general meeting require a majority of more than 50 % of the share capital. Decisions regarding capital increases will be made by the extraordinary general meeting since modification of statutes requires a majority of more than 75 % of the share capital. See Art. L223-30 Commercial Code.

Platforms using the transaction-engineered model usually offer their investors investment-type contracts,[16] or securities in an intermediate vehicle. Intermediate holding vehicles may either be set up for each crowdfunding campaign/business individually,[17] or for all portfolio firms on a platform.[18] After a crowdfunding campaign has been successfully conducted, the intermediary entity may either continue to act as the owner of the equity stakes in the crowdfunding campaigns/ businesses, or they may distribute the stakes among the investors. The latter may take place in various ways. The platform may either directly transfer the shares from the intermediary vehicle to the investor, underwrite the equity raise on behalf of the investors on the basis of a power of attorney, or sell options from the intermediary entity to investors that investors may exercise if a crowdfunding campaign has been successfully conducted (De Buysere, 2012). Either way the platform is an intermediate vehicle that acts as counterparty to investors, putting them in a similar position to if the shares of the portfolio firm(s) had been underwritten in the traditional way.

The eBay model, on the contrary, only provides the technical means whereby potential investors and investees can get in contact with each other. Therefore, the platform operator itself does not constitute a party in the equity raise that may ultimately result. The eBay model is more suitable to some investor preferences that dislike the constructions under transaction-engineered crowdfunding platforms.

Each model has its own limitations or regulatory uncertainties. However, as platforms want to overcome the problems related to crowdfunding offerings, as discussed above, the transaction-engineered model is in practice almost exclusively used. Innovestment in Germany,[19] for example, uses the notion of silent partnerships instead of direct equity, such as stocks or similar company and partnership law instruments. Silent partnerships are not considered as securities in some countries, and can therefore escape the scope of some regulations (Klöhn & Hornuf, 2012), such as the Prospectus Directive and Markets in Financial Instruments

---

[16] Might be perceived by some financial market authorities as a derivative, and thus, a security under the Prospectus Directive or a financial instrument under the Markets in Financial Instruments Directive (MiFID).

[17] Symbid in the Netherlands, for instance, solves the difficulty of selling equity in private companies by using project-specific cooperatives. Cooperatives have the property that membership capital can easily be increased or decreased without many formalities.

[18] MyMicroInvest in Belgium, for instance, uses equity-like contracts, in that intermediate vehicles are offered instead of shares, as it would be impossible to allocate cash flows of portfolio companies to the specific shareholders of the vehicle.

[19] Crowdfunding platforms in Germany run counter to so many legal obstacles in raising equity that most of them are, instead of equity-based, lending-based. After the introduction of the planned crowdfunding legislation, lending-types of crowdfunding using subordinate loans ("Nachrangdarlehen") and profit participating loans ("partiarische Darlehen") will also be subjected to specific regulation. See Gesetzentwurf der Bundesregierung, Entwurf eines Kleinanlegerschutzgesetzes (Status: 10 November 2014). http://www.bundesfinanzministerium.de/Content/DE/Downloads/Gesetze/2014-11-12-kleinanlegerschutzgesetz.pdf?__blob=publicationFile&v=2 (Accessed 24 February 2015; hereafter: German Crowdfunding Draft Law).

Directive (MiFID).[20] However, this interpretation is not followed in every country. In many countries, there is no interpretation available and this creates legal uncertainty.

Depending upon whether crowdfunding platforms are legally structured as transaction-engineered, or on the eBay business model, platforms might face different legal problems. Transaction-engineered platforms might particularly be required to obtain an authorisation for accepting reclaimable funds under the Capital Requirements Directive IV (CRD IV), they may qualify as an alternative investment fund (AIF) under the Alternative Investment Fund Managers Directive (AIFMD), or may be deemed subject to an authorisation as an investment service/ activity under MiFID. The eBay business model, apart from the company law problems discussed above, only seems to run counter to the latter. These problems will be subsequently discussed.

5.1 Accepting Reclaimable Funds (CRD IV, E-Money Directive)

Crowdfunding platforms usually "control" the process of the monetary commitment of investors in the timeframe between an investor's commitment and the actual completion of the campaign. The purpose of this is to avoid cumbersome formalities when collecting money from investors before the equity raise (De Buysere et al., 2012).[21] Problems, however, might pop up especially when investors reclaim funds if a campaign fails, or if investors allocate it to another project. In such a situation the reclaimable funds may be considered by financial market authorities as bank deposits for which crowdfunding platforms need an authorisation[22] as a credit institution.[23] The upfront "uploads" of funds, or the availability of re-allocatable funds after failed campaigns, may also be problematic

[20] Directive 2014/65/EU of the European Parliament and of the Council on markets in financial instruments and amending Directive 2002/92/EC and Directive 2011/61/EU, OJ 173/349, 15 May 2014 (hereafter: MiFID II); Regulation (EU) No 600/2014 of the European Parliament and of the Council of 15 May 2014 on markets in financial instruments and amending Regulation (EU) No 648/2012, OJ L 173/84, 15 May 2014 (hereafter: MiFIR).

[21] European Securities and Markets Authority, Opinion of 18 December 2014 (ESMA/2014/1378), Investment-based crowdfunding, pp. 34–37.

[22] Directive 2013/36/EU of the European Parliament and of the Council of 26 June 2013 on access to the activity of credit institutions and the prudential supervision of credit institutions and investment firms, amending Directive 2002/87/EC and repealing Directives 2006/48/EC and 2006/49/EC, OJ L 176/338, 27 June 2013 (hereafter: "CRD IV"); Regulation (EU) No 575/2013 of the European Parliament and of the Council of 26 June 2013 on prudential requirements for credit institutions and investment firms and amending Regulation (EU) No 648/2013, OJ L176/1, 27 June 2013 (hereafter: "CRR").

[23] Art. 4(1) Nr 1 CRR defines a credit institution as "an undertaking whose business is to receive deposits or other repayable funds from the public and to grant credits for its own account".

when a system of virtual credit is used.[24] This could be classified as electronically storing a monetary value to be used for payment transactions, and requires a license as a credit institution or electronic money institution.[25] Both licenses are too expensive for an equity crowdfunding platform to obtain. Platforms that are unable to meet these requirements may enter into an agreement with a licensed payment service provider that will act as the acceptor of the reclaimable funds (De Buysere et al., 2012).

5.2 Continued Ownership (UCITSD, AIFMD, VC-Regulation, EU-SEF-Regulation)

Transaction-engineered platforms, that act as a central counterparty between investors and investees, may come under the scope of either European or national regulations on collective investment undertakings.[26]

On the European level, collective investment undertakings are either UCITS[27] or AIFs.[28] The latter also includes venture capital and social entrepreneurship funds under the European Venture Capital Funds (EuVECA) and European Social

Following Art. 9 CRD IV, taking deposits or repayable funds from the public may exclusively be undertaken by credit institutions.

[24] Directive 2013/36/EU of the European Parliament and of the Council of 26 June 2013 on access to the activity of credit institutions and the prudential supervision of credit institutions and investment firms, amending Directive 2002/87/EC and repealing Directives 2006/48/EC and 2006/49/EC, OJ L 176/338 (hereafter: "E-money Directive").

[25] See Art. 1 E-Money Directive.

[26] Directive 2009/65/EC of the European Parliament and of the Council of 13 July 2009 on the coordination of laws, regulations and administrative provisions relating to undertakings for collective investment in transferable securities (UCITS) (recast), OJ L 302, 17 November 2009, 32 (hereafter: "UCITSD"); Directive 2011/61/EU of the European Parliament and of the Council 8 June 2011 on Alternative Investment Fund Managers and amending Directives 2003/41/EC and 2009/65/EC and Regulations (EC) No 1060/2009 and (EU) No 1095/2010, OJ L 174, 1 July 2011, 1 (hereafter: "AIFMD"); Regulation (EU) No 345/2013 of the European Parliament and of the Council of 17 April 2013 on European venture capital funds, OJ L 115/1, 25 April 2013 (hereafter: "EuVECA-Regulation"); Regulation (EU) No 346/2013 of the European Parliament and of the Council of 17 April 2013 on European social entrepreneurship funds, OJ L 115/18, 25 April 2013 (hereafter: "EuSEF-Regulation"); Proposal for a Regulation of the European Parliament and of the Council on European Long-term Investment Funds, COM(2013) 462 final, 26 June 2013 (hereafter: "ELTIF-Regulation"); Proposal for a Regulation of the European Parliament and of the Council on Money Market Funds, COM(2013) 615 final, 4 September 2013 (hereafter: "MMF-Regulation").

[27] UCITS: undertakings of collective investment in transferable securities. See Art. 1 (2) UCITSD.

[28] Art. 4(1)(a) AIFMD; European Securities and Markets Authority, Opinion of 18 December 2014 (ESMA/2014/1378), Investment-based crowdfunding, pp. 20–24; European Securities and Markets Authority, Advice of 18 December 2014 (ESMA/2014/1560), Investment-based crowdfunding, pp. 21–24.

Entrepreneurship Funds (EuSEF) Regulation,[29] which can be voluntarily opted in to by investment managers.[30]

Intermediary vehicles that are set up by crowdfunding platforms will in any case not qualify as a UCITS as they do not offer redemption possibilities, nor do they comply with the investment restrictions as laid down in the UCITSD.[31] These vehicles, on the contrary, could fall within the broad definition of being an AIF within the scope of the AIFMD. The AIFMD however only applies to investment fund managers that have at least 100 million euros assets under management.[32] Besides, the AIFMD only regulates the management and marketing of AIFs to professional investors. The AIFMD leaves the regulation of AIFs marketed to retail investors to the Member States.[33] Although the legal pooling of assets resembles a collective investment undertaking (Zetzsche, 2012a), intermediary vehicles cannot be regarded as (retail) AIF,[34] as the platform will not discretionarily manage the investments made by the investors, which is a pre-requisite for all types of collective investment undertakings (Zetzsche, 2012a). The platform only makes a pre-selection, whereas the investors ultimately decide by themselves whether they invest in a project/business or not.[35] Intermediary vehicles as set up by crowdfunding platforms thus in general do not qualify as collective investment undertakings.

5.3 *MiFID Regulated Activities*

Another set of rules that shapes the organisation of crowdfunding platforms is the Market in Financial Instruments Directive (MiFID).[36] Platforms might need to

[29] European Securities and Markets Authority, Opinion of 18 December 2014 (ESMA/2014/1378), Investment-based crowdfunding, p. 25; European Securities and Markets Authority, Advice of 18 December 2014 (ESMA/2014/1560), Investment-based crowdfunding, pp. 25, 26.

[30] Collective investment undertakings regulated by the proposed MMF- and ELTIF-Regulation also (might) qualify as AIFs. See Art. 1 ELTIF-Regulation and Art. 1 MMF-Regulation. Both regulations, however, apply to collective investment undertakings with a pre-defined investment policy that does not correspond to crowdfunding portfolio companies.

[31] See Art. 50 et seq. UCITSD.

[32] See for these high thresholds: Art. 3(2)(a) AIFMD.

[33] Art. 43 AIFMD.

[34] It is important to note in this regard that the AIFMD does not allow another interpretation of the definition of AIF by individual Member States when these are marketed to retail investors. See European and Securities Market Authority, Guidelines of 13 August 2013 (ESMA/2013/611), Guidelines on key concepts of the AIFMD, p. 4.

[35] See European and Securities Market Authority, Guidelines of 13 August 2013 (ESMA/2013/611), Guidelines on key concepts of the AIFMD, p. 29.

[36] European Securities and Markets Authority, Opinion of 18 December 2014 (ESMA/2014/1378), Investment-based crowdfunding, p. 14; European Securities and Markets Authority, Advice of 18 December 2014 (ESMA/2014/1560), Investment-based crowdfunding, p. 15.

obtain a prior authorisation for investment activities/services which relate to financial instruments.[37] A platform may qualify as one of the following investment services/activities under MiFID (De Buysere et al., 2012)[38]:

- Investment advice;
- The placing of financial instruments;
- The execution of orders on behalf of clients;
- The reception and transmission of order in relation to one or more financial instruments[39];
- Services related to underwriting.

Whether an equity crowdfunding platform will fall under any of these MiFID investment activities/services depends in particular upon the national interpretation of financial market authorities (Weitnauer & Parzinger, 2013). These differ on a country-per-country basis. Regardless of the kind of interpretation used, platforms fall in any case outside the scope of MiFID if the instruments issued by private companies and/or the equity platform are not considered to be "transferable securities".[40] The latter explains the predominance of the transaction-engineered model compared to the eBay model. The transaction-engineered model, when properly structured, ensures that the activities of the platform fall outside the scope of MiFID without having to take into account the business forms and the type of instruments that are issued by the individual crowdfunding companies. Whether an instrument is considered to be a transferable security or not again depends on several different national interpretations. Both the differing interpretations regarding investment activities/services, and the definition of financial instruments, create uncertainty for crowdfunding platforms operating on a cross-border basis.[41] For this reason, some large platforms[42] have been authorised as MiFID firms to operate cross border

[37] See for definition of financial instruments: Annex I Section C of the MiFID II.

[38] These are listed in Annex I Section A MiFID II; European Securities and Markets Authority, Advice of 18 December 2014 (ESMA/2014/1560), Investment-based crowdfunding, pp. 16–19.

[39] In the Netherlands, equity crowdfunding platforms are usually only considered to fall within the scope of this MiFID II investment activity/service. See AFM (Autoriteit Financiële Markten), DNB (De Nederlandsche Bank) en AFM geven interpretatie over crowdfunding. http://www.afm.nl/~/media/Files/crowdfunding/interpretatie-dnb-afm.ashx (Accessed 24 February 2015).

[40] Art. 4(1) No 15 MiFID II. See for instance the Dutch guidance on what constitutes a transferable security: AFM, Beleidsregel verhandelbaarheid. European Securities and Markets Authority, Opinion of 18 December 2014 (ESMA/2014/1378), Investment-based crowdfunding, p. 15.

[41] European Securities and Markets Authority, Advice of 18 December 2014 (ESMA/2014/1560), Investment-based crowdfunding, p. 28.

[42] See for a list of platforms in the Netherlands: http://www.afm.nl/~/media/Files/registers/register-crowdfunders-170714.ashx

under the European passport for one (or more) of the relevant activities (De Buysere et al., 2012).[43] Due to legal problems, crowdfunding platforms throughout Europe nevertheless use a wide variety of transaction designs. These transaction models are often heavily reliant on national exemptions or national interpretations of harmonised rules. Therefore, crowdfunding campaigns that are offered on a cross-border basis are usually problematic and rarely sustainable.

6 Towards a European Regulatory Proposal

What should the European regulator do? In order to answer this question, first the costs and benefits of crowdfunding need to be assessed in order to determine whether regulation is socially desirable, before a European approach will be proposed.

6.1 The Lack of Investor Information, Exit, Voice and Loyalty

Crowdfunding regulation needs to be based upon the balancing of two conflicting goals: fostering capital formation and investor protection (Bradford, 2012; Meredith, 2011; Pope, 2011). SMEs face an enormous capital funding gap in meeting the demand of capital for early-stage (equity) financing (Sjostrom, 2004). This has two main causes. Firstly, informational inefficiency leads to a mismatch between source of capital and potential investment opportunities (Agrawal, Catalini, & Goldfarb, 2010). Secondly, the traditional availability of financing, such as bank lending, venture capital and angel investments are not available to most start-ups and other SMEs. Crowdfunding platforms improve capital formation as they reduce the search costs, but investor protection remains an issue not only in the relationship between investors and entrepreneurs, but also in the relationship between investors and platforms (Campbell, 2006).

A first set of potential problems relates to the relationship between the investor and the entrepreneur. Information asymmetries exist in crowdfunding projects as the entrepreneur holds all the cards and investors have little information about the SME and little control over what the entrepreneur does. Investing in SMEs is

[43] In these cases the MiFID II specific requirements, such as client classification and the requirements with regards to inducements, might create problems.

very risky. Crowdfunding platforms make it possible for relatively unsophisticated investors to invest in ventures facing high liquidity and business failure risk.[44] In addition, SMEs are more likely to be prone to fraud and self-dealing (Dent, 1992).[45]

Crowdfunding platforms are typically not able to resolve these problems. SMEs themselves usually provide very limited information. Apart from this, crowdfunding portals conduct very limited due diligence in picking the investment project, and do not monitor the entrepreneurs. The low level of sophistication of the investors (Klöhn & Hornuf, 2012), and the impersonal nature of crowdfunding also do not provide the incentives (Olson, 2004) and the possibility to individually negotiate control rights and negative covenants for investors to protect themselves against self-dealing. Fraud may be partly condemned as the emergence of more platforms and the increased competition among platforms led to more pre and post-investment communication, fraud detection and vetting services (De Buysere et al., 2012). Collective wisdom is, however, limited in providing "smart money" (Surowiecki, 2004) to SMEs. Liquidity, business failure and self-dealing problems remain.

A second set of problems applies to the relationship between the investors and the platforms.

The remuneration model in most crowdfunding platforms' business models that has evolved over time increases the risk of conflicts of interests. Most platforms are remunerated based upon successful crowdfunding campaigns. These "success fees" are independent of the eventual success of the business venture. In the short-term, platforms thus have the incentive to offer a high number of unprofitable ventures to the market (Klöhn & Hornuf, 2012). Especially "money chasing deals", i.e. too much money chasing too few deals, might be a problem due to the large amount of platforms on the market (Gompers & Lerner, 2000).

In some cases an intermediary may even play a dual role. Some platforms operate a co-investment model, whereby a VC fund completes investment rounds or provides funding in the form of seed capital (Collins & Perrakis, 2012). Platforms might use their superior information to generate better investment opportunities than the investors participating through its platform. Some platforms, being aware of this conflict of interests issue, have implemented a rule to prevent this, in

---

[44] European Securities and Markets Authority, Opinion of 18 December 2014 (ESMA/2014/1378), Investment-based crowdfunding, pp. 10–12.

[45] Dent mentions self-dealing, such as excessive compensation, misuse of corporate opportunities, dilution of investors' interest and other issues similar to those faced by investors in closely held companies.

which per single campaign 50 % of the investments are made by the platform, and the other 50 % by the public.[46] Equity crowdfunding platforms generally, however, do not prevent additional deals being carried out outside of the platforms (De Buysere et al., 2012).

Any crowdfunding regulation proposed in the future therefore has to keep the transaction cost to investors, entrepreneurs and platforms, on the one hand, low; whereas on the other hand it should mitigate risks and preserve investor protection.

6.2 A European Legislative Proposal

Recently various legal initiatives have been initiated in Europe[47] to foster crowdfunding and close the liquidity gap for SMEs. Following the development of various differing legal initiatives in Europe the result is a regulatory landscape that is fragmented. This fragmentation along national lines poses challenges for platforms, entrepreneurs and investors. Only harmonisation on the European level may overcome these problems. In this Section will be discussed what considerations by the European legislator should be taken into account when proposing legislation for crowdfunding in the future.[48] The recently enacted/proposed legislation for equity-based crowdfunding in Finland,[49]

[46] This is in practice known as the 50/50 rule.

[47] Various legislative initiatives have also been initiated outside the EEA. As this research is limited to the EEA, these have not been taken into account. See for the US: Jumpstart Our Startups Act, Pub. L. 112-06, 126 Stat. 306 (2012). http://www.gpo.gov/fdsys/pkg/BILLS112hr3606enr/pdf/BILLS-112hr3606enr.pdf (Accessed 25 July 2014); See for New Zealand: Financial Markets Conduct (Phase 1) Regulations 2014 (2014/50); See for Canada: the "Start-up Exemption" in Saskatchewan (SK), as adopted last December 2013, (The Securities Act, 1988 (General Order 45-925)) and the "Crowdfunding Exemption" consultation, initiated by a collaborative effort between Ontario, Manitoba, Quebec, New Brunswick and Nova Scotia (The Ontario Securities Commission, Introduction of Proposed Prospectus Exemptions and Proposed Reports of Exempt Distribution in Ontario—Supplement to the OSC Bulletin, March 20, 2014 Volume 37, Issue 12 (Supp-3) (2014), 37 OSCB).

[48] European Securities and Markets Authority, Opinion of 18 December 2014 (ESMA/2014/1378), Investment-based crowdfunding, pp. 12–13.

[49] Finland did not enact special regulation. Instead, the Finnish Financial Market Supervisory Authority published guidelines in which they mandatorily require equity crowdfunding platforms to obtain an authorisation under MiFID. See Finnish Financial Market Supervisory Authority, Guidelines on Equity Crowdfunding, 26 June 2014, Section "Obligation to publish a prospectus under the Securities Markets Act". www.finanssivalvonta.fi/en/Authorisations/crowdfunding/Pages/Default.aspx (Accessed 24 February 2015).

France,[50] Germany,[51] Italy,[52] Spain,[53] and the UK[54] will be taken into account.[55]

[50] Ordonnance no 2014-559 du 30 mai 2014 relative au financement participatif, JORF 31 mai 2014. This ordinance, that entered into force on 1 October 2014, introduced a full-fledged crowdfunding regime in the French Monetary and Financial code (hereafter: "CMF") that has been elaborated in more detail in the AMF regulation. See Ministère des Finances et de Comptes Publics, Décret no 2014-1053 du 16 septembre 2014 relatif au financement participatif, JORF 17 septembre 2014 (hereafter: AMF Regulation).

[51] Technically speaking the new proposed legislation aims at platforms which are issuing subordinate loans ("Nachrangdarlehen") and profit participating loans ("partiarische Darlehen"). Platforms issuing silent participations to investors ("Stille Beteiligungen") are not exempt from publishing a prospectus under the special proposed German crowdfunding regime. See the German Crowdfunding Draft Law. The German Crowdfunding Draft Law applies to mezzanine financial products, which expose investors economically to equity-like instruments, and merely are used by platforms to circumvent regulations. Therefore, this draft proposal is for the purpose of this paper being considered as targeting equity-based crowdfunding.

[52] See Consob, resolution No. 18592, July 12, 2013, providing for a set of rules on fund raising for innovative start-ups via crowdfunding online portals (hereafter: "Consob Regulation"). The Regulation implements Art. 50-quinquies and 100-ter of the Legislative Decree No. 58 of 24 February 1998 introduced by Art. 30 of the Italian Law Decree No. 179 of 18 October 2012 (hereafter: "Italian Crowdfunding Decree", modified by the Parliament and subsequently converted into Law No. 221 of 17 December 2012 (commonly known as, "Decreto Crescita bis").

[53] The text of Spanish Crowdfunding law has been officially passed by the Spanish Congress, but has on the time of writing this book chapter not yet entered into force. For the purpose of this book chapter, the law is assumed to have entered into force. See Projecto de Ley 121/000119, de fomento de la financiación empresarial, 27.01.2015, Título V Régimen jurídico de las Plataformas de Financiación Participativa (hereafter: "Spanish Crowdfunding Law"); See for the two initial Draft Bills: Anteproyecto de Ley XX/2014, de fomento de la financiación empresarial, 05.03.2014 and 17.10.2014, Título V Régimen jurídico de las Plataformas de Financiación Participativa.

[54] FCA 2014/13, Crowdfunding and the Promotion of Non-Readily Realisable Securities Instrument 2014: This legislative act came into force on the 1 April 2014. It amends the Financial Services and Markets Act 2000 and several FCA sourcebooks, such as, amongst others, the Senior Management Arrangements, Systems and Controls sourcebook (SYSC), the Interim Prudential sourcebook for Investment Businesses (IPRU(INV)) and the Conduct of Business sourcebook (COBS). In addition, the Code of Principles of the UK Crowdfunding Association applies mandatorily to its members. This Code of Principles can be found at: www.ukcfa.org.uk/code-of-practice-2 (Accessed 24 February 2015).

[55] In Portugal, the political party *Partido Socialista* presented a crowdfunding draft bill that has been consultated with the Portugese parliament and other relevant stakeholders. See Projeto de Lei 419/XII, Aprova o Regime Jurídico do Financiamento Colaborativo, 30.04.2013; See also Projeto de Lei 419/XII/2ª, Aprova o Regime Jurídico do Financiamento Colaborativo, 11.12.2013; Romania published a crowdfunding draft law in September 2014. See Proiect LEGE privind dezvoltarea finanţărilor participative (crowdfunding). http://imm.gov.ro/cms/0/publicmedia/getincludedfile?id=520 (Accessed 24 February 2015). The draft laws of Portugal and Romania do not contain a unique approach compared to the Member States addressed in this contribution. They will, therefore, not be further discussed.

6.2.1 Restrictions on the Offering

Finland,[56] France,[57] Germany,[58] Italy,[59] Spain[60] and the UK[61] clearly see equity crowdfunding as being beneficial.[62] Given the problems with limited investor information, voting (voice) and exit rights, they have introduced restrictions on the offerings or on the companies making the offerings. By taking this approach, all these Member States researched aim at minimising investor losses without destroying its utility to entrepreneurs raising capital. There is, however, limited consistency in the legal measures applied to reach this goal. Finland,[63] France[64] and Germany[65] primarily rely on investor disclosure, Spain on a combination of the self-certification of investors and a maximum cap per project/participation[66] (Pope, 2011), whereas Italy[67] and the UK[68] solely rely upon the self-certification of investors. The question arises of what legal measures should be taken in possible Europe-wide regulation. In answering this question, all three options will be discussed.

[56] See Finnish Financial Market Supervisory Authority, Guidelines on Equity Crowdfunding, 26 June 2014, www.finanssivalvonta.fi/en/Authorisations/crowdfunding/Pages/Default.aspx (Accessed 24 February 2014).

[57] See Autorité de contrôle prudentiel et de résolution (ACPR) and Autorité des marchés financiers (AMF), Un Nouveau Cadre pour Faciliter le Développement du Financement Participatif, 30.09.2013. p. 2.

[58] German Crowdfunding Draft Law, pp. 47, 48.

[59] See the recitals of the Consob Regulation.

[60] See Spanish crowdfunding law, p. 5.

[61] FCA, The FCA's regulatory approach to crowdfunding over the internet, and the promotion of non-readily realisable securities by other media—Feedback to CP13/13 and final rules, PS 14/4, March 2014, pp. 5, 6; FCA, The FCA's regulatory approach to crowdfunding (and similar activities), CP 13/13. pp. 36–38.

[62] See for an overview of the considerations of other legislators in Europe, North America and Israel: European Crowdfunding Network, 2014.

[63] See Finnish Financial Market Supervisory Authority, Guidelines on Equity Crowdfunding, 26 June 2014, Section "Obligation to publish a prospectus under the Securities Markets Act". www.finanssivalvonta.fi/en/Authorisations/crowdfunding/Pages/Default.aspx (Accessed 24 February 2015).

[64] Art. L. 411-2 (1bis) CMF; Art. 217-1 and Art. 314-106 AMF Regulation.

[65] Apart from investor disclosure, Germany requires also an investment cap per project offered and an investment cap per investor per project. The latter is, however, only required to obtain an exemption from the prospectus requirement as laid down in the Investment Products Act. See German Crowdfunding Draft Law, pp. 47, 48.

[66] Art. 69 Spanish Crowdfunding Law.

[67] Art. 17 (3) and (4) Consob Regulation, part II Consolidated law on Finance and the related implementing regulations.

[68] See for the UK: COBS 4.7.7 R (2).

6.2.1.1 Disclosure

Most investors involved in crowdfunding are unsophisticated. Finland, France, Germany and Spain have therefore introduced minimum disclosure requirements for SMEs wishing to fund themselves by means of crowdfunding.

Finland does not provide any detailed harmonised disclosure requirements for equity crowdfunding. Instead, equity crowdfunding platforms are considered as investment firms and the standard information duties contained in MiFID apply.[69] Apart from this, investors in public offerings without an obligation to publish a prospectus[70] have to be provided with "sufficient information on factors that may have a material effect on the value of the shares". According to the Finnish guidelines, the level of the disclosure obligation should be considered in proportion to the target group's investment experience, investors' knowledge of the securities or issuers in question and any other specific features of the offer.[71] The information to be provided will be almost the same as required for a Finnish national prospectus if a more limited level of information cannot be justified by the target group's investment experience or knowledge.[72]

In France a light-prospectus[73] of a few pages, instead of a full-prospectus, is required for transactions up to 1,000,000 €.[74] The light-prospectus[75] is a statement prepared by the issuer that is published on his/her website and contains information on[76]:

- the crowdfunding project/business;
- the degree that the issuers themselves are financially participating in the project/business;
- shareholder rights and how to exercise them;
- the liquidity of the securities issued;
- the subscription conditions; and
- the specific risks involved with investment in the project/business.

[69] See Finnish Financial Market Supervisory Authority, Guidelines on Equity Crowdfunding, 26 June 2014, Section "Investment-based crowdfunding and authorisation". www.finanssivalvonta.fi/en/Authorisations/crowdfunding/Pages/Default.aspx (Accessed 24 February 2015).

[70] These are offerings less than 1,500,000 €. See chapters 3–5 Finnish Securities Markets Act.

[71] See Finnish Financial Market Supervisory Authority, Guidelines on Equity Crowdfunding, 26 June 2014, Section "Obligation to publish a prospectus under the Securities Markets Act". www.finanssivalvonta.fi/en/Authorisations/crowdfunding/Pages/Default.aspx (Accessed 24 February 2015).

[72] See FIN-FSA, Regulations and Guidelines, 6/2013; See also: Finnish Financial Market Supervisory Authority, Guidelines on Equity Crowdfunding, 26 June 2014, Section "Obligation to publish a prospectus under the Securities Markets Act". www.finanssivalvonta.fi/en/Authorisations/crowdfunding/Pages/Default.aspx (Accessed 24 February 2015).

[73] Art. 325-38, 314-106 AMF Regulation.

[74] See Arts L.411.2 (I bis) CMF, D.411-2 CMF.

[75] Art. L. 411-2 (I bis) CMF. Art. 217-1, 314-106 AMF Regulation.

[76] Art. 217-1 AMF Regulation.

Germany exempts all equity crowdfunding offerings from publishing a prospectus[77] for offerings in which:

- the maximum investor contribution per project is 10,000 €[78];
- the total amount offered per project does not surpass 1,000,000 €; and
- the platform on which the offer is promoted is authorised/registered in accordance with the Trade Regulations Act,[79] or the Banking Act.

Instead, Germany requires a small information leaflet (Vermögensinformationsblatt; VIB) to be published which is signed and distributed to investors investing more than 250 € in a project.[80] This leaflet contains key information on the offerer and offering in not more than just a few pages.

On the contrary, Spanish crowdfunding platforms are obliged to publish on their website information on the project,[81] the issuer[82] and the particular offering of securities.[83]

Compared to the German solution, Spain requires much more detailed information to be disclosed that clearly increases the cost of crowdfunding (Bradford, 2012). Especially, the information on issuers and offerings required under the Spanish Crowdfunding Law seems to miss the most important facet of the argument for exempting offerings under the Prospectus Directive: for offerings below a certain size, the cost of any minimum disclosure exceeds the benefits (Bradford, 2012).

6.2.1.2 Maximum Cap per Project and Participation

Germany and Spain limit the total amount of the offering and the total amount that each individual investor may invest.[84] Spain for this purpose, however, differentiates between accredited and non-accredited investors. The cap per investor/participation in Spain only applies to non-accredited investors.[85]

---

77 The national prospectus regime under the Investment Products Act. See for the proposed § 2a (3) Investment Products Act: German Crowdfunding Draft Law, pp. 8, 9.

78 This is the proposed maximum cap per participation per investor. The proposed investment cap per individual in Germany is wealth-based and can be lower. See for details: *infra* par. 6.2.1.2.

79 § 34f Trade Regulations Act ("Gewerbeordnung").

80 Proposed to be implemented in § 2a(3) and § 13 Investment Products Act. See German Crowdfunding Draft Law, pp. 47, 48.

81 Art. 70 Spanish Crowdfunding Law.

82 Art. 78 Spanish Crowdfunding Law.

83 Art. 79 Spanish Crowdfunding Law.

84 Proposed to be implemented in § 2a(3) Investment Products Act. See German Crowdfunding Draft Law, pp. 47, 48; Spain: Art. 68 Spanish Crowdfunding Law.

85 See for the difference between accredited and non-accredited investors: *infra* par. 6.2.1.3.

SMEs under the German proposed regime that wish to fund themselves by means of crowdfunding may not make an offering of more than 1,000,000 €.[86] The Spanish limit per offering is set at 2,000,000 € for campaigns or rounds that involve non-accredited investors and 5,000,000 € for accredited investors.[87] In addition, Germany proposes a cap of 10,000 € and Spain introduced a cap of 3,000 € that individuals may invest per crowdfunding project.[88] The investment cap of 10,000 € proposed in Germany only applies to investors that have declared to platforms by means of self-certification:

- to have a freely available income consisting of cash deposits and financial instruments that exceeds 100,000 €; or
- to invest not more than two average monthly net incomes in a project.

Investors in Germany who do not comply with the above-mentioned optional self-certification procedure may only, without restrictions, invest up to 1,000 € per project.

In Spain individuals are on an aggregated basis, not be allowed to invest more than 10,000 € in various projects on any single platform over a 12 month period.[89] The latter applies to all of an individual's crowdfunding investment in any given year and not on a per-offering basis. Only crowdfunding investments are considered in applying this annual cap. Moreover, the cap is applied on an annual basis to avoid computational issues.

The maximum cap per project and participation proposed by Germany and Spain are understandable considering the fact that SMEs are risky and losses are likely. A set cap on the amount forces unsophisticated investors to diversify their investments minimizes investor losses and is set low enough that most people could afford to lose that amount.

6.2.1.3 Self-Certification

The cap per investor/participation, as proposed in Germany, is a wealth-based limit which does not differentiate between sophisticated and unsophisticated investors. It also unduly offers retail investor protection to sophisticated investors. Italy, Spain and the UK have found a solution for this. They rely on the self-certification of investors.[90] Under the Italian Crowdfunding Law an investor is required to fill out a

[86] Proposed to be implemented in § 2a(3) Investment Products Act. See German Crowdfunding Draft Law, pp. 47, 48.

[87] Art. 68 Spanish Crowdfunding Law.

[88] *Ibid.*

[89] Art. 82 Spanish Crowdfunding Law.

[90] Germany also relies upon self-certification for determining the cap per participation per project. Germany, however, does not allow in any case, sophisticated investors, such as angel investors, to invest amounts exceeding 10,000 € per project.

questionnaire giving evidence that they understand the risks of equity investments and that their personal estate will not be compromised.[91] In addition, investors are granted a set of rights to exit their investment in the following situations:

- retail investors, bank foundations, and registered incubators have a granted 7 days withdrawal right[92];
- retail investors, bank foundations, and registered incubators are entitled to waive the investment if something new happens or a material mistake is discovered that influences the investment decision after the investment has been made, but before the offer is closed[93];
- retail investors are entitled to either a withdrawal or tag-along right (Feld & Mendelson, 2013),[94] if the founders sell or the control of the company changes[95];
- any investment contract stipulated by a consumer through the Internet is subject to a 14 days withdrawal right.[96]

Spain distinguishes between accredited and non-accredited investors. The Spanish Crowdfunding Law does not contain any limits in the amount that accredited investors may invest in a project through crowdfunding platforms.

Non-accredited investors, however, are restricted to an annual investment limit per project of 3,000 € and 10,000 € for all crowdfunding platforms combined.

[91] This applies to small investments up to 500–1,000 € per year for individuals and 5,000 € per year for companies. See Art. 17(3) and (4) Consob Regulation, See also Part II of the Consolidated Law on Finance and its implementing regulations.

[92] See Art. 13(5) Consob Regulation. See also the withdrawal right under the Consumer Protection Directive. See Directive 2011/83/EU of the European Parliament and of the Council of 25 October 2011 on consumer rights, amending Council Directive 93/13/EEC and Directive 1999/44/EC of the European Parliament and of the Council and repealing Council Directive 85/577/EEC and Directive 97/7/EC of the European Parliament and of the Council, L 304/64, 25 October 2011 (hereafter: "Consumer Protection Directive").

[93] Art. 25(2) Consob Regulation allows such a waiver for a maximum of 7 days after the relevant news came up. Professional investors, as defined by the CONSOB Regulation, are not entitled to this waiver.

[94] A tag-along right is a contractual clause, particularly used in venture capital deals, which allows minority shareholders to sell his or her (minority) stake if a majority shareholder sells his or her stake. In this way, minority shareholders are protected against a change of control.

[95] Following Art. 21(1)(a) Consob Regulation companies must, however, have enacted such rights in their statuses before being admitted to crowdfunding. These rights would be valid throughout their innovative start-up status which is considered to be 3 years. Professional investors do not benefit from this rule.

[96] This protection is laid down by the Art. 64 Italian Consumers Code which implements the Consumer Protection Directive.

Accredited investors are:

- professional clients under MiFID;
- companies with more than 1,000,000 € in assets, a turnover of 2,000,000 €[97] or shareholder's equity of 300,000 €[98];
- private investors with an income of more than 50,000 € per year or assets of over 100,000 € who expressly waive their treatment as non-accredited investor[99]; and
- investors who have obtained investment advice from an authorized investment concerning projects which do not have the obligation to publish a prospectus and are offered on a crowdfunding platform.[100]

In the UK equity-based crowdfunding is subject to a restrictive promotion regime.[101] This promotion regime[102] only allows offerings to particular categories of investors, such as professional and retail clients who are either certified high net worth[103] or are certified[104] or self-certified[105] sophisticated investors.[106] The Financial Conduct Authority (FCA), in addition, has updated this in its recent crowdfunding legislation by:

- setting out the limits on type of investors a platform may deal with[107]; and
- permitting two new categories of potential investors:
  - retail clients who invest on the basis of an investment advisory or management service[108]; and

---

[97] For SMEs only this requirement applies for being acknowledged as an accredited investor. See Art. 81(2)(d) Spanish Crowdfunding Law.

[98] Art. 81(2)(b) Spanish Crowdfunding Law.

[99] Art. 81(2)(c) Spanish Crowdfunding Law.

[100] Art. 81(3) Spanish Crowdfunding Law.

[101] Loan-based crowdfunding is being perceived by the FCA to represent a lower risk to investors than equity-based crowdfunding. Accordingly, lending-based crowdfunding is exclusively protected by disclosure. See FCA, The FCA's regulatory approach to crowdfunding over the internet, and the promotion of non-readily realisable securities by other media—Feedback to CP13/13 and final rules, PS 14/4, March 2014. p. 39; COBS 14.3.6A.G. See also FCA, The FCA's regulatory approach to crowdfunding (and similar activities), CP 13/13. pp. 28–31.

[102] COBS 4.7.7 R. – 4.7.10 R. FCA, The FCA's regulatory approach to crowdfunding (and similar activities), CP 13/13, pp. 37–38. See also FCA, The FCA's regulatory approach to crowdfunding over the internet, and the promotion of non-readily realisable securities by other media—Feedback to CP13/13 and final rules, PS 14/4, March 2014. pp. 35–43.

[103] COBS 4.7.9 R; COBS 4.12.6 R.

[104] COBS 4.7.9 R; COBS 4.12.7 R.

[105] COBS 4.7.9 R; COBS 4.12.8 R.

[106] COBS 4.7.7 (2) R.

[107] COBS 4.7.9 R.

[108] COBS 4.7.8 R.

- retail clients that certify that they have not/will not invest more than 10 % of their investible income, net of their primary residence, pensions and life cover in unlisted share or debt securities over the 12 months periods prior to and following the investment.[109]

The self-certification of investors as introduced by Italy, Spain and the UK differentiates between sophisticated and unsophisticated investors. All three require equity crowdfunding platforms to collect information regarding the wealth and financial knowledge of individual investors. One could argue, however, that self-certified income and financial knowledge is essentially the same as no standard at all (Bradford, 2012). Investors who want to invest more would quickly learn to exaggerate their income or financial knowledge.

6.2.1.4 Proposal?

The best proposal to reduce barriers on the European level concerning crowdfunding offerings would be to introduce a combination of self-certification, a cap for investors/offerings, and investment information on a pan-European basis.

Offering restrictions would rely upon the self-certification of investors[110] to delineate sophisticated from unsophisticated investors. All investors would be required to fill out some questions giving evidence that they understand the risks of equity investments and that their personal estate will not be compromised.[111] Investors passing this test would qualify as "self-certified investors". The "unsophisticated investors" mandatorily would have to watch a brief educational film. The film would function as a substitute for sub-1,000,000 € offerings that are excluded from the scope of the Prospectus Directive. The use of a brief educational film or quiz with feedback for unsophisticated investors would have to take no more than a few minutes to complete. Such information would inform the potential risks and rewards of crowdfunding and also allows regulators to control the information presented. Moreover, research shows that in general (unsophisticated) investors either do not pay attention to investor disclosure or they do not understand it (Lusardi, 2006). Applying this proposal forces investors to engage and take advantage of the information provided As with any investor information, however, there is no guarantee that investors actually pay attention.

---

[109] COBS 4.7.10 R.

[110] This is already widely used under the HNWI criteria under Art. 6 EuVECA/EuSEF Regulation. However, the regime should be tailor made for crowdfunding.

[111] This applies to small investments up to 500–1,000 € per year for individuals, and 5,000 € per year for companies. See Art. 17 (3) and (4) Consob Regulation.

For exempt offerings between 1,000,000 € and 5,000,000 €, the introduction of a key information document modelled after the PRIIP-Regulation could be considered.[112] This document would have to contain standardised information up to a maximum of five pages regarding the issuer, type of business, investment risks, any past performance and practical information.[113] The latter would complete a pan-European harmonised regime introduced for sub-5,000,000 € offerings that would be excluded from the scope of the Prospectus Directive.

Unsophisticated investors would have to be subject to an investment cap of 1,000 € per project per year to foster diversification, limiting investment risks. The latter is set low enough so that most people could afford to lose this amount. No cap for crowdfunding investments on an aggregated basis for unsophisticated investors would be introduced as this would lead to excessive administrative costs for crowdfunding platforms. An additional mandatory funding goal entitling all investors to a withdrawal right until the funding goal is reached, should be deemed sufficient to protect retail investors.

6.2.2 Light Company Law Structures

Introducing a special business form on the European level that applies to crowdfunding could be introduced to fully utilise the potential of cross-border European crowdfunding offerings. SMEs typically choose relatively "cheap" private limited company regimes. However, by choosing such a private limited company they unintentionally run counter to limitations in various Member States when publicly offering crowdfunding campaigns to investors. These problems vary from imposing substantial formalities in the case of raising equity to direct limitations on any public offering. This currently leads to legal uncertainty and high transaction costs that only a pan-European regime could overcome.

Applying some features from public company types to cheaper private limited companies could be the solution to this problem (De Buysere et al., 2012). Recently, France, for example, in its Commercial Code, replaced the typical (voting) procedures related to the General Meeting of Shareholders of

[112] Regulation (EU) No. 1286/2014 of the of the European Parliament and of the Council of 26 November 2014 on key information documents for packaged retail and insurance-based investment products (PRIIPs), OJ L 352, 9 December 2014, 1 (hereafter: "PRIIP-Regulation"). See also Commission Regulation (EU) No 583/2010 of 1 July 2010 implementing Directive 2009/65/EC of the European Parliament and of the Council as regards key investor information and conditions to be met when providing key investor information or the prospectus in a durable medium other than paper or by means of a website, OJ L 176, 10 July, 1 (hereafter: "KIID-Regulation").

[113] This is comparable to the brief information leaflet as proposed by Germany in its draft law. Mäschle (2012) proposes a different proposal for equity offerings.

closely held companies (société par actions simplifiée; SAS), with those of the French Public Limited Company (sociétés anonymes; SA) for crowdfunding offerings.[114] Applying the features of public company types to private limited companies that take away the problems related to the acceptance of new shareholders would certainly accommodate the demands of business life (De Buysere et al., 2012).

6.2.3 Restrictions on Crowdfunding Sites

Depending on how equity crowdfunding platforms are legally structured, platforms might face different legal problems, such as a mandatory obligation to obtain authorisation as a credit institution for accepting reclaimable funds, as a collective investment undertaking or any of the investment activities/services under MiFID. By introducing a special (proposal for a) regulation that regulates equity crowdfunding platforms, Finland, France, Germany, Italy, and Spain have partly resolved the problems discussed above. The introduced legislation in the individual Member States, however, shows limited consistency in licensing and business organisation requirements, leading to a fragmented legal landscape for equity crowdfunding platforms. By pointing out several general common principles, the considerations by the European legislator that should be taken into account when proposing pan-European legislation for equity crowdfunding in the future will be discussed.

6.2.3.1 Licensing/Registration Requirements

Requiring financial intermediaries[115] to be subject to licensing/registration is a common feature in European financial law (Zetzsche, 2012b). European financial law requires licensing to promote fairness, honesty and professionalism by those who provide financial services, on the one hand, while ensuring that intermediaries remain financially solvent on the other.[116] Unsurprisingly, licensing/registration

---

[114] See Art. L. 411-2 (1bis) CMF, Art. L 227-2-1 Commercial Code.

[115] Examples of such financial intermediaries, amongst others, are credit institutions and portfolio managers. See CRD IV and MiFID II.

[116] See the licensing requirements in, for example, CRD IV, UCITSD, AIFMD and MiFID II.

requirements on a cross-sectoral basis all embody more or less the same requirements. Some of these common requirements required by Finland,[117] France,[118] Germany,[119] Italy[120] and Spain[121] when licensing/registering as a crowdfunding platform,[122] include:

- fit and proper requirements for the key management[123];
- minimum capital requirements (details do vary)[124];
- an adequate business organisation[125]; and
- penalties if the platforms no longer meet the requirements of the applicable legislation.[126]

Despite these common requirements, there still exist considerable differences between the licensing/registration regimes throughout the EEA.

[117] See Section 10 Finnish Investment Services Act.

[118] Art. L. 532-1, Art. L- 547-1, Art. L. 547-3 CMF.

[119] See, in particular, § 32(1) Banking Act and § 34f Trade Regulations Act.

[120] Art. 7-12 Consob Regulation. The registration duty in Italy only applies to "innovative start-ups". The definition of "innovative start-ups" contains strict requirements regarding its core business and seems to limit equity crowdfunding to high-tech start-ups. See Art. 25 Italian Crowdfunding Decree. Its scope, compared to the other countries researched, is very limited.

[121] Art. 53–59 Spanish Crowdfunding Law.

[122] In Spain platforms have to obtain an authorisation of the Spanish Financial Market Authority (*Comisión Nacional del Mercado de Valores*). The Spanish Central Bank (*Banco de España*) needs to confirm the authorization for platforms that also offer crowdlending. See Art. 53 Spanish Crowdfunding Law.

[123] Finland: Section 10 Finnish Investment Services Act; France: Art. L. 547-3 CMF; Germany: § 32 Banking Act, § 33 Securities Trading Act; Italy: Art. 9 Consob Regulation; Spain: Art. 55 (e) Spanish Crowdfunding Law.

[124] Finland: Section 10 Finnish Investment Services Act; Germany: § 10 et seq. Banking Act, § 33 Securities Trading Act; Spain: a minimum share capital of 60,000 € or a professional liability insurance is required with a minimum coverage of 400,000 € per year. Depending upon the total amount of offerings, the own minimum capital required may be higher. See Art. 56 Spanish Crowdfunding Law.

[125] Finland: Section 10 Finnish Investment Services Act; France: Art. 325-41–325-49 AMF Regulation; Germany: § 32 Banking Act, § 33 Securities Trading Act; Italy: Art. 7, Annex I Consob Regulation; Spain: Art. 55 (h) Spanish Crowdfunding Law.

[126] Finland: chapter 8 Finnish Investment Services Act; Germany: § 54 et seq. Banking Act, § 38 et seq. Securities Trading Act, Italy: Art. 12, 22, 23 Consob Regulation; Spain: Titel V, Chapter VI, Spanish Crowdfunding Law.

In Finland equity crowdfunding platforms[127] need to apply for a permit for acting as an investment firm.[128] All platforms[129] are considered to be engaged in the "reception and transmission of orders in relation to one or more financial instruments".[130] Consequently, the standard MiFID authorisation procedure applies to equity crowdfunding platforms. Depending upon the scope of their activities, Finnish equity crowdfunding platforms may also provide other investment services, such as investment advice[131] and duties typically undertaken by arranger banks.[132]

In France, equity crowdfunding platforms, which are authorised as a special investment firm, have to be a member of a special organisation that monitors its Members.[133]

Germany requires either equity crowdfunding platforms to be registered as a financial investment broker (*Finanzanlagenvermittler*) in accordance with § 34f Trade Regulations Act,[134] or authorised as an investment firm within the scope of the Banking Act.[135]

Italian equity crowdfunding platforms are required to fulfil an additional number of rules and principles. A minimum stake of 5 % of each crowdfunding campaign, for instance, needs to be subscribed by a professional investor by the end of the offer.[136] Any existing shareholders agreements also have to be notified to (potential) investors.[137] Apart from this, all investments being offered have to be finalised by a broker-dealer. This broker-dealer has to comply with the MiFID and requires that the broker-dealer checks that the subscriber's investment profile matches the investors' risk appetite.[138] The Italian Consob Regulation applies a simplified process for small investors. For these crowdfunding campaigns the MiFID

[127] The Finnish guidelines distinguish between loan-based crowdfunding and securities crowdfunding. The former does not require any specific regulation and it is not subject to supervision by the Finnish Financial Market Supervisory Authority.

[128] See Finnish Financial Market Supervisory Authority, Guidelines on Equity Crowdfunding, 26 June 2014, Section "Investment-based crowdfunding and authorisation". www.finanssivalvonta.fi/en/Authorisations/crowdfunding/Pages/Default.aspx (Accessed 24 February 2015).

[129] All platforms that perform investment services that relate to a financial instrument as an investment object. Depending on the interpretation of the Finnish Financial Market Supervisory Authority on what constitutes a "financial instrument" this might offer an opportunity for platforms to transact around this obligation.

[130] Chapter 1, Section 11, sub-section 1(1) Finnish Investment Services Act.

[131] Chapter 1, Section 11, sub-section 1(5) Finnish Investment Services Act.

[132] See in particular Chapter 1, Section 11, Sub-section 1(2) and Sub-section 1(7) Finnish Investment Services Act.

[133] Art. L. 547-4 CMF, Art. 325-51–325-67 AMF Regulation.

[134] The Trade Regulations Act requires certain criteria to ensure professionalism among the staff handling investment projects.

[135] § 31 et seq. Banking Act, § 31 et seq. Securities Trading Act. See German Crowdfunding Draft Law, pp. 47, 48.

[136] Art. 24(2) Consob Regulation.

[137] Art. 24(1)(b) Consob Regulation.

[138] Art. 17(3) Consob Regulation.

requirements applicable to broker-dealers do not apply.[139] These platforms do not have to comply with the MiFID and its requirements relating to the subscriber's profiling and proclivity to risk assessment.

Spain requires equity crowdfunding platforms, in addition to the requirements mentioned above, to:

- fulfil a number of accounting, auditing and other prerequisites[140];
- inform users about investment risks[141]; and
- restrict the marketing of and the participation in the campaigns offered on their platform.[142]

It can therefore be said that there are major differences between the licensing/registration regimes within the EEA that can be regarded as a major obstacle to the cross-border provision of services by equity crowdfunding platforms.

6.2.3.2 Business Organisation

Along with licensing/registration requirements, Finland, France, Germany, Italy and Spain have established organisational requirements for equity crowdfunding platforms. Similarly, the absence of a common European legal framework has resulted in different types of organisational rules.[143] To some extent, however, similar rules on the organisation of a platforms' business can be observed.[144] These rules include, inter alia:

- commitments to fairness, honesty, and acting in the investor's best interests[145];
- conflict of interests rules[146];
- rules on the platform's remuneration.[147]

---

[139] Art. 17(4) Consob Regulation.

[140] Art. 55, 57 Spanish Crowdfunding Law.

[141] Art. 61 Spanish Crowdfunding Law.

[142] Art. 63 Spanish Crowdfunding Law.

[143] See for Finland: Section 10 et seq. Finnish Investment Services Act; France: Art. L. 547-9 CMF, Art. 325-35–325-40 AMF Regulation; Germany: § 31 et seq. Banking Act, § 31 et seq. Securities Trading Act; Italy: Art. 13 Consob Regulation; Spain: Titel V, Chapter III Spanish Crowdfunding Law.

[144] *Ibid.*

[145] Finland: Section 10 Finnish Investment Services Act; France: Art. L. 547-9 (1) CMF; Germany: § 31 et seq. Banking Act, § 31 Securities Trading Act; Italy: Art. 13(1) Consob Regulation; Spain: Art. 60 Spanish Crowdfunding Law.

[146] Finland: Section 10 Finnish Investment Services Act; France: Art. L. 547-9 (4) CMF, Art. 325-42 AMF Regulation; Germany: § 31 et seq. Banking Act, § 34 Securities Trading Act; Italy: Art. 13(1) Consob Regulation; Spain: Art. 62 Spanish Crowdfunding Law.

[147] Finland: Section 10 Finnish Investment Services Act; France: Art. 325-37 AMF Regulation; Germany: § 31 et seq. Banking Act, § 34 Securities Trading Act; Italy: Art. 7 Consob Regulation, Annex 2, Organisational Structure. point 12.

Comparable rules throughout the researched Member States can also be observed for accepting reclaimable funds by equity crowdfunding platforms. All Member States researched require equity crowdfunding platforms not licensed as credit institutions to separate investor funds from the platforms' own funds.[148] Except for France, the same holds true for platforms holding funds that will be used to electronically store and represent money in accounts.[149] Unlike for lending/ donation-based-platforms in some Member States,[150] no exemption or light license can be granted to platforms in these Member States to accept reclaimable funds. Platforms are only able to comply with these requirements by entering into a contract with third-party licensed service providers (De Buysere et al., 2012).[151]

Finland, France, Germany, Italy and Spain have all established organisational requirements for equity crowdfunding platforms. Despite some similarities, the present diversity that still exists hinders platforms from providing services on a cross-border basis in Europe. It is therefore necessary to undertake a process of convergence related to business organisational rules, both to ensure a level playing field and to establish a single market for equity crowdfunding platforms.[152]

6.2.3.3 Towards a Cross-Border Dimension for (Equity) Crowdfunding Platforms

A recent consultation of the European Commission regarding crowdfunding highlighted that only 38 % of the equity-based crowdfunding platforms operate cross-border while almost half of them would like to extend their business to other EU Member States in the future.[153]

Currently, the huge potential of crowdfunding in the EEA has not been unleashed, as various recent national legal initiatives have led to a fragmented market for crowdfunding offerings.

---

[148] Finland: Section 6, 7, 7a Payment Institutions Act; France: Art. 511-5 CMF; Germany: Section 2 Payment Supervision Services Act; Italy: Art. 17(6), 25(1) Consob Regulation; Spain: Art. 52(1) Spanish Crowdfunding Law; UK: the Payment Services Regulations 2012. See FCA, The FCA's regulatory approach to crowdfunding (and similar activities), CP 13/13, p. 22.

[149] All platforms are exempted that do not electronically store more than 3,000,000 € on a monthly basis. See Arts L. 522-11-1, art. D. 522-4 CMF.

[150] France: Arts L 511-5 and L. 511-6 CMF; Spain: Art. 50 Spanish Crowdfunding Law; UK: CASS 1a, 7,7A.

[151] The European Crowdfunding Network proposes to exempt electronic money institutions with less than 5 million euros outstanding credit.

[152] Examples are other types of regulation of financial intermediaries, such as credit institutions and portfolio managers under CRD IV and MiFID II.

[153] European Commission (2014) Communication from the Commission to the European Parliament, the Council, the European Economic and Social Committee and the Committee of the Regions—Unleashing the potential of Crowdfunding in the European Union, Com (2014) 172 final. p. 8.

Only a fully harmonised European regulatory framework introducing a European passport for (equity) crowdfunding platforms may overcome these problems. Such a European passport would only require crowdfunding platforms to obtain one single authorisation/registration from any competent authority within the EEA to be able to offer their services on a cross-border basis throughout the whole EEA. Connecting all platforms, investors and entrepreneurs by creating a European crowdfunding market would lead to more supply and demand for crowdfunding platform services, that would significantly enhance the liquidity of the market. At the same time, more supply and demand would lead to more competition and an improvement in the quality of the services offered by platforms. Such a true internal market would therefore lead to greater market efficiency and economies of scale in the crowdfunding market.

To fully exploit these benefits, the European passporting rules for (equity) crowdfunding platforms would require:

- an application for the licensing requirements by the platform to the Competent Authority of the home state;
- a review of the European provisions by this Competent Authority;
- a notification from the Competent Authority of the home state to the authorities of the host state;
- and a minimum waiting period before the intermediary may provide services in the host state.

In addition, equity crowdfunding platforms that wish to establish a branch in another Member state would be required to:

- show that it meets the organisational requirements to conduct business according to the rules in the host state; and
- subject itself to supervision within a limited scope in the host state.

Complying with an expensive authorisation/registration procedure would however only be economically feasible for big crowdfunding platforms that are able to spread their costs over many projects offered.[154] To counter this problem, platforms that fall below a threshold of 100 million euros in total crowdfunding offerings should be exempt from obtaining a mandatory authorisation/registration. Platforms not complying with the European common crowdfunding legislation would not benefit from the European passport, and could be subject to national regulation. They should however be offered the possibility to opt in to the European passport regime to be able to exploit all the benefits related to it.

It can therefore be concluded that only a fully harmonised European regulatory framework introducing a European passport for (equity) crowdfunding platforms would allow both SMEs and crowdfunding platforms to fully tap the benefits of the European capital market.

[154] See Cohn (2012) for criticism in the US.

7 Conclusion

More and more SMEs use crowdfunding to raise funds from a large audience by means of a cost-effective effort. The traditional availability of financing, such as bank lending, venture capital and angel investments are not available to most start-ups and other SMEs. Crowdfunding helps SMEs to overcome the demand of capital for early-stage (equity) financing. Regulation on the national and European level, however, heavily limits entrepreneurs and equity crowdfunding platforms in promoting offers and campaigns to potential investors. As a result, legislators in various Member States, such as Italy, Spain, the UK and France have enacted or are about to enact legislation to overcome these problems. The various national initiatives, however, lead to a fragmented market for equity crowdfunding offerings. Only a fully harmonised European regulatory framework may overcome these problems. By introducing such a regime, both SMEs and crowdfunding platforms would be able to fully tap the European capital market.

References

Agrawal, A., Catalini, C., & Goldfarb, A. (2010). *The geography of crowdfunding* (NET Institute Working Paper No. 10-08). Retrieved from http://ssrn.com/abstract=1692661. doi:10.2139/ssrn.1692661

Bradford, C. S. (2012). Crowdfunding and the Federal Securities Laws. *Columbia Business Law Review, 1*, 1–150. Retrieved from http://ssrn.com/abstract=1916184

Cable, A. J. B. (2010). Fending for themselves: Why securities regulations should encourage angel groups. *University of Pennsylvania Journal of Business Law, 13*(1), 107.

Campbell, R. B., Jr. (2006). Regulation A: Small businesses' search for "A Moderate Capital". *Delaware Journal of Corporate Law, 31*(1), 77.

Cohn, S. R. (2012). The new crowdfunding registration exemption: Good idea, bad execution. *Florida Law Review, 64*(5), 1441–1443.

Collins, L., & Perrakis, Y. (2012). *The venture crowd—crowdfunding equity investment into business*. Retrieved from http://www.nesta.org.uk/sites/default/files/the_venture_crowd.pdf

De Buysere, K. (2012). *The 'new' venture capital cycle: Obstacles in using the internet for equity raising campaigns*. Unpublished manuscript.

De Buysere, K., Gajda, O., Kleverlaan, R., & Marom, D. (2012). *A framework for European crowdfunding*. Retrieved from http://www.europecrowdfunding.org/files/2013/06/FRAMEWORK_EU_CROWDFUNDING.pdf

Dent, G. W., Jr. (1992). Venture capital and the future of corporate finance. *Washington University Law Quarterly, 70*(4), 1029–1036.

European Crowdfunding Network. (2014). *Interpretations of existing regulation concerning crowdfunding in Europe, North America and Israel*. Retrieved from http://www.eurocrowd.org/files/2014/12/ECN-Review-of-Crowdfunding-Regulation-2014.pdf

Feld, B., & Mendelson, J. (2013). *Venture deals*. Hoboken, NJ: Wiley.

Fisch, J. E. (1998). Can internet offerings bridge the small business capital barrier? *Journal of Small and Emerging Business Law, 57*(2), 78.

Gompers, P. A., & Lerner, J. (2000). Money chasing deals? The impact of fund inflows on the valuation of private equity investments. *Journal of Financial Economics, 55*. doi:10.2469/dig.v30.n3.710

Klöhn, L., & Hornuf, L. (2012). Crowdinvesting in Deutschland. *Zeitschrift für Bankrecht und Bankwirtschaft, 24*(4), 237–266.

Leuering, D., & Rubner, D. (2012). Prospektpflicht des Crowdfunding. *NJW-Spezial, 25*, 463.

Lusardi, A. (2006). *Financial literacy and financial education: Review and policy implications* (NFI Policy Brief No. 2006-PB-11). Retrieved from http://ssrn.com/abstract=923437

Mäschle, O. (2012). *Which information should entrepreneurs on German crowdinvesting-platforms disclose?* Retrieved from http://www.wiwi.unirostock.de/fileadmin/Institute/VWL/VWLInstitut/RePEc/pdf/wp127thuenen.pdf

Meredith, B. C. (2011). *Testimony on crowdfunding and capital formation*. Retrieved from http://www.sec.gov/news/testimony/2011/ts091511mbc.htm

Milhaupt, C. J. (1998). The small firm financing problem: Private information and public policy. *Journal of Small and Emerging Business Law, 2*, 177–195.

National Council on Economic Education. (2005). *What American teens and adults know about economics*. Retrieved from http://www.councilforeconed.org/cel/WhatAmericansKnowAboutEconomics_042605-3.pdf

Olson, M. (2004). *Die Logik des kollektiven Handelns: Kollektivgüter und die Theorie der Gruppen*. Tübingen: Mohr Siebeck.

Pietrancosta, D. A. (2006). The 'Public Offering of Securities' concept in the new prospectus directive. In G. Ferrarini & E. Wymeersch (Eds.), *Investor protection in Europe* (pp. 339–364). Oxford: University Press.

Pope, N. D. (2011). Crowdfunding microstartups: It's time for the Securities and Exchange Commission to approve a small offering exemption. *University of Pennsylvania Journal of Business Law, 13*(4), 101–129. Retrieved from http://ssrn.com/abstract=1916985

Röthler, D., & Wenzlaff, K. (2011). *Crowdfunding schemes in Europe* (EENC Report). Retrieved from http://www.eenc.info/wp-content/uploads/2012/11/DR%C3%B6thler-KWenzlaff-Crowdfunding-Schemes-in-Europe.pdf

Sjostrom, W. K., Jr. (2004). Relaxing the ban: It's time to allow general solicitation and advertising in exempt offerings. *Florida State University Law Review, 32*(1), 1–2.

Surowiecki, J. (2004). *The wisdom of crowds. Why the many are smarter than the few and how collective wisdom shapes business, economies, societies, and nations*. New York, NY: Doubleday.

Weitnauer, W., & Parzinger, J. (2013). Das Crowdinvesting als neue Form der Unternehmensfinanzierung. *Zeitschrift Gesellschafts- und Wirtschaftsrecht*, 153–159.

Zetzsche, D. A. (2012a). Scope of the AIFMD. In D. A. Zetzsche (Ed.), *The alternative investment fund managers directive* (pp. 39–70). The Hague: Kluwer Law International.

Zetzsche, D. A. (2012b). The AIFMD and the joint principles of European asset management law. In D. A. Zetzsche (Ed.), *The alternative investment fund managers directive* (pp. 747–755). The Hague: Kluwer Law International.

Impact of Debt Crowdfunding for Civic Projects on the Optimal Portfolio of a Socially Responsible Investor

Polina K. Kirilova

Abstract Investors strive for profit, but many are also socially responsible. They want to do their fair share, for example supporting the local community. Traditionally, they can donate money to charities. The rise of crowdfunding offers them another possibility to fulfil their social goals. They can directly back projects or give small low-interest loans to finance civic projects. This paper provides an example of how a socially responsible investor's optimal portfolio changes when the possibility of supporting civic projects by the means of low-interest loans is introduced.

Keywords Crowdfunding • Investment theory • Socially responsible investing

1 Introduction

Investors usually wish to maximise their monetary returns, but they are also often additionally interested in being socially responsible (Derwall, Koedijk, & Horst, 2011; Hamilton, Jo, & Statman, 1993; Schueth, 2003; Utz, Wimmer, Hirschberger, & Steuer, 2014). For instance, they wish to help improve the region they and their children live in. They might do this by giving to charities or finding other ways to support the community.

In recent years crowdfunding has emerged as a possibility of gathering financing for all types of projects. There are four typical forms of crowdfunding (Mollick, 2014; Moritz & Block, 2014). In exchange for their (small) investments, the funders (also called "backers") may not receive any material return. This form of crowdfunding is very close to traditional charity. It is possible that the backer receives a special "reward" which is not (yet) available to non-backers. Equity crowdfunding is rare (and legally challenging), but a share of the future earnings or IPO-return is often offered. This paper will concentrate on debt crowdfunding. In this form the lender expects a fixed rate of return. In civic projects in particular, this interest rate will probably not be too high. As the investment is usually not too big

P.K. Kirilova (✉)
FernUniversität in Hagen, Hagen, Germany
e-mail: polina.kirilova@fernuni-hagen.de

D. Brüntje, O. Gajda (eds.), *Crowdfunding in Europe*, FGF Studies in Small Business and Entrepreneurship, DOI 10.1007/978-3-319-18017-5_11

itself, the return is not the only (or often even main) reason for the funding. The backer wishes to support the local infrastructure by providing the debt capital needed to fulfil the project (Striver, Barroca, Minocha, Richards, & Roberts, 2015).

As the lent money is used to improve the infrastructure in the community, there is a positive effect on the investor's social responsibility target (Pitluck, 2012). This paper will show how the possibility to lend money to back civic projects via crowdfunding affects the optimal investment portfolio of an investor, who wishes to bear his fair share of social responsibility while maximising his profits. The simple example proves that debt crowdfunding positively affects the optimal portfolio of investors, who do not solely pursue higher monetary returns.

2 Methodology

The method applied to determine the optimal investment portfolio is based on the linear optimisation [for an extensive introduction to the usage of linear optimisation for investment portfolio optimisation see Hering (2008)]. What is novel is that the non-pecuniary target components are modelled separately, instead of using monetary equivalents. Therefore, it is no longer possible to immediately link the result to the traditional net present earnings value.

To satisfy his non-monetary target, the investor sets a separate social responsibility target value S, expressed in "social responsibility units" (SRUs), which he sees as his fair share. Then he needs to determine how much each opportunity for action contributes to this target. The trade-off between monetary and social responsibility targets is addressed indirectly, as the contribution of high-profit investments to the social responsibility target may be set negatively, thus increasing the amount of positive SRU contributions needed to satisfy the social responsibility constraint.

The linear optimisation approach calculates the optimal investment and financing programme, which maximises the monetary target function value under the social responsibility constraint. In the following, it is assumed that the investor's monetary target is wealth accumulation (highest possible asset value at the planning horizon). The approach is shown below:

$$\max . \mathrm{M}; \mathrm{M} := M_n$$

$$-\sum_{j=1}^{m} g_{jt} {}^{*} x_j \leq b_t \text{ for } t = (0, 1, \ldots, n-1)$$

$$-\sum_{j=1}^{m} g_{jn} {}^{*} x_j + M_n \leq b_n$$

$$-\sum_{j=1}^{m} s_j{}^*x_j \leq -S$$

$$0 \leq x_j \leq x_j^{max} \text{ for every } j$$

b_t	predetermined payment balance at point in time t
g_{jt}	payment resulting from opportunity for action j at point in time t
j	opportunity for action
M	monetary target value
M_n	monetary target contribution at the planning horizon
m	number of opportunities for action
n	planning horizon
S	social responsibility target value
s_j	social responsibility target value contribution of the opportunity for action j
t	point in time
x_j	times opportunity for action j is executed
x_j^{max}	maximum times opportunity for action j can be executed

3 Optimal Portfolio Without Crowdfunding

Our socially responsible investor has just inherited 3,000 ($b_0 = 3{,}000$) monetary units (MU). He intends to use some of this inheritance to do his fair share to help improve the community he and his family live in (S = 50 SRU), and finance a trip abroad with the rest (max M). As his youngest child is still very young, the trip will take place 3 years from now ($M := M_n$ with $n = 3$). As he is very busy, he does not have much time to investigate investment possibilities and only considers a few opportunities for action. To satisfy his social responsibility target, he intends to donate to a local charity. These donations are possible at any point in time and equal 5 SRU for every 100 MU donated. In $t = 0$ he considers buying shares in the company Moneymaker. Each share costs 100 MU, provides annual dividends of 8 MU, and can be sold at the planning horizon for 102 MU. For each Moneymaker share, the investor feels obliged to increase his social responsibility target by 1 SRU. The investor does not want to borrow further money and is not able to put aside any money at any point in time. Therefore, he only operates with the 3,000 MU available at $t = 0$. Any surplus at any period is transformed into cash holdings, as no reinvesting is possible and the interest rates are negligible. The taxation differences have been already considered in the payment streams. Table 1 summarises the opportunities for action. The linear optimisation approach results in the following optimal portfolio (Table 2).

Table 1 Opportunities for action without crowdfunding

j	Description	g_{j0}	g_{j1}	g_{j2}	g_{j3}	s_j
1	Moneymaker share	−100	8	8	110	−1
2	Donation in t = 0	−100	0	0	0	5
3	Donation in t = 1	0	−100	0	0	5
4	Donation in t = 2	0	0	−100	0	5
5	Donation in t = 3	0	0	0	−100	5
6	Cash holdings t = 0	−100	100	0	0	0
7	Cash holdings t = 1	0	−100	100	0	0
8	Cash holdings t = 2	0	0	−100	100	0

Table 2 Optimal portfolio without crowdfunding

j	x_j	Description	$g_{j0} \times x_j$	$g_{j1} \times x_j$	$g_{j2} \times x_j$	$g_{j3} \times x_j$	$s_j \times x_j$
1	30	Moneymaker share	−3,000	240	240	3,300	−30
2	0	Donation in t = 0	0	0	0	0	0
3	2.4	Donation in t = 1	0	−240	0	0	12
4	2.4	Donation in t = 2	0	0	−240	0	12
5	11.2	Donation in t = 3	0	0	0	−1,120	36
6	0	Cash holdings t = 0	0	0	0	0	0
7	0	Cash holdings t = 1	0	0	0	0	0
8	0	Cash holdings t = 2	0	0	0	0	0
Predisposed payments balance			3,000	0	0	0	/
Monetary target			/	/	/	2,180	/
Social responsibility target			/	/	/	/	50

Without crowdfunding, the investor's best strategy is as follows: Buy 30 Moneymaker shares at t = 0 for 3,000, donate the dividends each year (240 MU each), sell the Moneymaker shares at t = 3 for 3,060 and donate further 880 MU. 2,180 MU are left for the family trip.

4 Optimal Portfolio with Crowdfunding

Our socially responsible investor was just about to buy 30 Moneymaker shares, when his wife asked whether he had considered crowdfunding. Browsing the local platform, he now finds a civic project searching for debt crowdfunding. A local entrepreneur wants to reopen the recently closed open-air swimming pool. As the investment is not very lucrative and the local bank is not interested in the project, crowdfunding is the only chance to fulfil this project. The entrepreneur needs the funds in t = 0 and offers to pay back 104 % at t = 3. As our investor wants his children have a place to swim nearby and believes others do too, he assesses the social responsibility contribution of each 100 MU he lends the swimming location reopening project 4 SRU as represented in Table 3. Solving the resulting linear optimisation approach leads to the following optimal portfolio (Table 4):

Table 3 Opportunities for action with crowdfunding

j	Description	g_{j0}	g_{j1}	g_{j2}	g_{j3}	s_j
1	Moneymaker share	−100	8	8	110	−1
2	Donation in t = 0	−100	0	0	0	5
3	Donation in t = 1	0	−100	0	0	5
4	Donation in t = 2	0	0	−100	0	5
5	Donation in t = 3	0	0	0	−100	5
6	Cash holdings t = 0	−100	100	0	0	0
7	Cash holdings t = 1	0	−100	100	0	0
8	Cash holdings t = 2	0	0	−100	100	0
9	Crowdfunding	−100	0	0	104	4

Table 4 Optimal portfolio with crowdfunding

j	x_j	Description	$g_{j0} \times x_j$	$g_{j1} \times x_j$	$g_{j2} \times x_j$	$g_{j3} \times x_j$	$s_j \times x_j$
1	10	Moneymaker share	−1,000	80	80	1,100	−10
2	0	Donation in t = 0	0	0	0	0	0
3	0	Donation in t = 1	0	0	0	0	0
4	0	Donation in t = 2	0	0	0	0	0
5	0	Donation in t = 3	0	0	0	0	0
6	0	Cash holdings t = 0	0	0	0	0	0
7	0.8	Cash holdings t = 1	0	−80	80	0	0
8	1.6	Cash holdings t = 2	0	0	−160	160	0
9	20	Crowdfunding	−2,000	0	0	2,080	60
Predisposed payments balance			3,000	0	0	0	/
Monetary target			/	/	/	3,340	/
Social responsibility target			/	/	/	/	50

The investor now only buys 10 Moneymaker shares at t = 0 for 1,000 MU and lends the other 2,000 MU via the crowdfunding platform. The dividends from the Moneymaker share (80 MU each year) represent cash holdings. At the planning horizon the Moneymaker shares are sold for 1,020 MU and the entrepreneur pays back 2,080 MU. The family trip may now cost up to 3,340 MU.

5 Discussion of the Results

Because of crowdfunding, the investor can now afford a longer trip without disturbing his social conscience. In the example, the crowdfunding loan even completely substituted all donations. Of course, the example was kept very simple and included only "pure" instruments—company shares, chosen only by their returns, and general donations to a local charity. It is possible to achieve higher SRU-contributions by donating directly to charity projects, without online platforms. Furthermore, the investor may differentiate between the corporate social responsibility engagement of the companies, or even invest directly in local small and middle sized companies [the local bias of crowdfunding has been proven empirically (Lin & Viswanathan, 2014)]. All of these possibilities share one disadvantage—they all require very intensive research. Many possibilities are not apparent and must be hunted down. Much of the necessary information is hidden or not available at all. Even after all data is gathered, there is rarely any comparability given. In conclusion, it is unlikely that the average investor will have the time or zest to inform himself about all of these possibilities. The information about crowdfunding projects is available online, usually in a platform standard. This means that more investors are likely to consider crowdfunding than other special instruments (Burtch, Ghose, & Wattal, 2013).

Furthermore, some platforms only process the funds if the funding goal is met. In such cases, the backer knows that he will only actually invest if the project manages to convince enough other investors, who may or may not be better informed than he is [for the likelihood to support crowdfunding projects based on different criteria see Brem and Wassong (2014)]. Finally, the investors can diversify by splitting their contributions between projects.

6 Conclusion

Crowdfunding as a new possibility to directly back projects deserves special attention because it is more than merely an online based investment or a charity vehicle. It is important to study how this new instrument (or actually instruments, as each type of crowdfunding deserves special attention) differ(s) from the classic ones. In order to be able do this properly, a reliable legal framework is required.

This paper gave an exemplary study as to how debt crowdfunding to civic projects affects the portfolio of a socially responsible investor. As a result, the monetary target achievement increased without violating the social responsibility fairness.

To focus on this effect, the example was kept very simple. Scope for further research includes, but is not limited to: More complex models, which consider more types of investments, explicitly address the tax consequences or no longer assume certainty, as well as empirical studies.

References

Brem, A., & Wassong, N. (2014). Wer investiert warum? Eine Analyse von Investmententscheidungen bei Crowdfunding-Projekten. *Zeitschrift für KMU und Entrepreneurship, 62* (1), 31–56.

Burtch, G., Ghose, A., & Wattal, S. (2013). An empirical examination of the antecedents and consequences of contribution patterns in crowd-funded markets. *Information Systems Research, 24*(3), 499–529.

Derwall, J., Koedijk, K., & Horst, J. T. (2011). A tale of values-driven and profit-seeking social investors. *Journal of Banking and Finance, 35*(8), 2137–2147.

Hamilton, S., Jo, H., & Statman, M. (1993). Doing well while doing good? The investment performance of socially responsible mutual funds. *Financial Analysts Journal, 49*(6), 62–66.

Hering, T. (2008). *Investitionstheorie* (3rd ed.). Munich: Oldenburg.

Lin, M., & Viswanathan, S. (2014). *Home bias in online investments: An empirical study of an online crowdfunding market*. doi:10.2139/ssrn.2219546

Mollick, E. (2014). The dynamics of crowdfunding: An exploratory study. *Journal of Business Venturing, 29*(1), 1–16.

Moritz, A., & Block, J. (2014). Crowdfunding and Crowdinvesting: State of the Art der wissenschaftlichen Literatur. *Zeitschrift für KMU und Entrepreneurship, 62*(1), 57–90.

Pitluck, A. Z. (2012). The silence of finance and its critics: Portfolio investors in the world-system. In S. J. Babones & C. Chase-Dunn (Eds.), *Routledge handbook of world-systems analysis* (pp. 206–214). London: Routledge.

Schueth, S. (2003). Socially responsible investing in the United States. *Journal of Business Ethics, 43*(3), 189–194.

Striver, A., Barroca, L., Minocha, S., Richards, M., & Roberts, D. (2015). Civic crowdfunding research: Challenges, opportunities and future agenda. *New Media and Society, 17*(2), 249–271.

Utz, S., Wimmer, M., Hirschberger, M., & Steuer, R. E. (2014). Tri-criterion inverse portfolio optimization with application to socially responsible mutual funds. *European Journal of Operational Research, 234*(2), 491–498.

What Makes Crowdfunding Projects Successful 'Before' and 'During' the Campaign?

Alessandro Marelli and Andrea Ordanini

Abstract This paper sets out to deepen the understanding of crowdfunding campaigns, and investigates a hand-collected database of 500 projects taken from Kickstarter.com, the biggest crowdfunding website in terms of revenue. Through a logistic regression and mediation model, our study tries to explain which are the predictors that can help reaching the funding goal of a crowdfunding initiative.

The first part of the study aims at predicting the chances of projects being successful based on a pool of *ex-ante* predictors. The results revealed that the presence of a video explaining the product's features and adding special offers for early backers are highly correlated with a higher probability of success. In contrast, displaying a Facebook profile with less than 500 friends, having the time to market too long and setting the funding goal too high will lower the odds of success.

The second part of the study consists of a mediation model carried out in order to understand the relationship between the *ex-ante* predictors, a list of proposed mediators that change during the campaign, and the rate of funding. We were able to discover two important effects: the presence of special offers for early backers and showing commitment in the platform by helping other projects are two good mediators influencing the relationship between the number of purchases of the product and the rate of funding.

Keywords Crowdfunding • Success • Predictors • Mediation

A. Marelli
Bocconi University, Via Rontgen, 1, 20136 Milan, Italy
e-mail: a.marelli89@gmail.com

A. Ordanini (✉)
Department of Marketing, Bocconi University, Via Rontgen, 1, 20136 Milan, Italy
e-mail: andrea.ordanini@unibocconi.it

D. Brüntje, O. Gajda (eds.), *Crowdfunding in Europe*, FGF Studies in Small Business and Entrepreneurship, DOI 10.1007/978-3-319-18017-5_12

1 Introduction

Crowdfunding specifically refers to a joint effort by many individuals, grouped as a "large audience", in order to support a cause, a company or an organisation with small donations (Belleflamme, Lambert, & Schwienbacher, 2014). Crowdfunding is getting more and more popular these days, thanks to a few big successful campaigns and a lot of smaller projects getting successfully funded. Over the last year the industry itself has grown to be a $5 billion market worldwide (Massolution, 2013), with hundreds of new campaigns posted every day.

The concept of exploiting a large number of people, asking for small amounts of money to carry out specific capital-intensive tasks, was born in Germany during the seventeenth century. The model was called "praenumeration" and it was used by editors to finance book prints. The customers were buying a subscription fee that was then used to cover the required capital to start the print itself. A similar method was used in 1884 by the American Committee to raise funds for the Statue of Liberty's pedestal. The famous journalist Joseph Pulitzer started a fundraising campaign in his journal, The New York World, asking for help to get the $100,000 needed. More than 160,000 donors contributed to the cause, with more than three-quarters of the donations amounting to less than a dollar, making a total of $101,091 in just 5 months.

The real game changing feature came with the Internet: crowdfunding campaigns can now be addressed to a "broad geographic dispersion of investors" (Agrawal, Catalini, & Goldfarb, 2011), and this has huge benefits both in terms of visibility and also in terms of feedback. In fact, any crowdfunding website is, first of all, a community: a tool with a large network of passionate people that provide not only financial help but also add creativity to the projects, an online environment that allows the work to take place and the community to interact (Brabham, 2008). Jennings (2000), refers to these entrepreneurs as "new media artists": individuals exploiting communication channels and technology to create a new economic, social and artistic business model. Belleflamme, Lambert, and Schwienbacher (2013) pointed out that crowdfunding, being so popular, is now being used not only as a way to collect money from crowds of individuals, but also as a marketing technique for gaining worldwide visibility for innovative projects, beyond financing purposes.

Over the years this phenomenon then blossomed into four main categories. First, there is equity-based crowdfunding, where the entrepreneur gives out shares of his start-up in exchange for funds. Debt-based models are similar both to peer-lending and to the equity-based typology. In this case the entrepreneur does not sell any share of his firm, but instead asks for a loan. Donation-based crowdfunding is instead mostly used for charity initiatives since it is based on donations that get the crowd nothing in return. Finally, there is reward-based crowdfunding in which the entrepreneur is pledging money and, as a reward, the backers will receive the product (or the service) the firm is offering (Ordanini, Miceli, Pizzetti, & Parasuraman, 2011). This model is the most popular one and is the focus of our analysis. Our empirical analysis will indeed be applied to the largest reward-based platform—Kickstarter—which has collected since its beginning over $1 billion and hosted more than 60,000 projects.

2 Research Question

Since this method of collecting money is getting popular, we would like to understand why certain campaigns get funded while others cannot reach the funding goal. Entrepreneurs have lots of alternative ways to collect start-up capital: banks, bootstrapping, business angels, venture capitals and government funds, however crowdfunding is getting more and more popular due to two features: first of all it allows entrepreneurs to display their products to the whole world, and second of all, it does not employ any standard financial intermediaries with the complication this process usually brings.

The purpose of this article is to study and depict key factors of successful campaigns on a crowdfunding platform, in a similar way to Mollick (2014), but using a different set of predictors and analysis. The success of a crowdfunding campaign can be influenced by a set of different variables and the aim of this article is to carry out a detailed study, looking at the different aspects influencing the success or the failure of a campaign. The present study investigates what potentially affects and attracts backers, leading to a successfully funded project. The aim of the research is to answer to the following question:

What are the determinants of a successful crowdfunding campaign?

3 Database and Sampling

Our sample was created by looking at Kickstarter projects that had just ended their campaign period. The database has been created over a period of 3 months (August–October 2013), hand collecting 30 variables for each of the last 500 projects, in chronological order.

The variables taken into account were of two different macro-categories: one category regards the variables that could be observed "ex-ante" at the very beginning of the campaign, and will not change during the campaign itself (such as the product price, the category, the background of the entrepreneur). The second macro-category regards the variables that do change throughout the campaign such as the number of comments, the number of Facebook shares, the number of backers.

All the information was taken from Kickstarter itself or using other websites like Kicktraq that does a web-scrape of the platform. Social networks such as LinkedIn or Twitter were exploited to gain additional information.

The sample results turned out to be in line with Kickstarter's official statistics: out of the total, 222 projects were successfully funded, which means that the average success rate is 44.4 %, in line with the overall success rate provided by Kickstarter's official stats: 43 %. As this sample was created for the last 500 projects, there could have been problems regarding the distribution of projects among categories. Luckily, both the number of projects per category and amount of money collected through successful campaigns per category are comparable to the official stats.

The average successful project has a funding goal of $9,830 and receives $30,386 given by a mean of 327 backers. On the other hand, the average unsuccessful project asks for $32,000 but manages to obtain just $1,760, by convincing on average 25 people to pledge for a reward.

4 Variables

The previous literature has studied which projects are successfully funded based on the industry, the amount pledged, and the geographic dispersion of the entrepreneurs (Mollick, 2014). The goal of this study is to take a step forward and analyse the peculiar aspects of a project from the point of view of a potential customer. Each project has been deeply analysed through several variables that are supposed to influence the rate of funding, grouped in four different categories. Table 1 summarises all variables included in the two steps of the analysis, and below we detail the meaning of each variable.

4.1 Campaign Descriptive Variables

This set of variables is general descriptor of the campaign. The rate of financing is worth mentioning here since it is our dependent variable and makes a division between successful and unsuccessful projects: if the rate is higher than 1 (100 %), then the goal (also referred to as the "amount asked") is reached and the platform will deliver the payment to the entrepreneur.

4.2 Product Related Variables

The first set of features regards the product itself, as it is the principal reason that drives a potential buyer to purchase or not. In order to analyse the product, it has been decided to consider different variables.

First, we use time to market (in weeks). It is a variable that clearly has an impact on the purchasing decision: in theory, the shorter the delivery time, the better it

Table 1 Variables used to analyze crowdfunding success

Descriptive variables	
Date	Date on which the campaign is closed
Project name	Name of the project
No. backers	Total number of people that invested money in the project
Amount received	Total amount of money pledged
Average funds	Amount received/No. backers
Amount asked	The funds the entrepreneur requires to start the business
Dependent variable	
Rate of financing	Amount received/Amount asked If equal to or greater than 1, the project is successful and the entrepreneur receives the money. If the campaign does not succeed (does not reach the amount asked) the pledge will be given back to the backer
Product related	
Industry	Industry of the firm: Art, Comics, Dance, Design, Fashion, Film and Video, Food, Games, Music, Photography, Publishing, Technology, Theatre
Time to market	Expected delivery date of the product (weeks)
Product price	Minimum pledge to obtain the offered product
Number of purchasers	Number of purchasers of the basic price
Shipment	Whether or not there is a differential shipment price
Complementarity	Whether and if the project is complementary to any other product This can be used specifically for games and technology products. The categories are: "Arduino", "Android", "Apple", "Software", "Ouya"
Offer description	
Video	Whether or not there is a video used to quickly explain the product offered
Length	Length of the description, number of words—proxy of the level of detail
Number of deals	Count of the possible pledges a backer can make
Early backer/limited edition offer	Whether or not there is a limited edition offered for Kickstarter only, or a limited number of lower price pledges to boost the kick-off of the campaign (e.g. "the first 50 backers pay $79 instead of $99")
Over-purchase	Sum of the backers that pledged more than the basic product price
Entrepreneur	
Entrepreneurial background	The background of the entrepreneur, as stated by himself in the offer. Entrepreneurs are classified as "Artistic", "Engineering", or "Freelance"
Previous project	Whether or not the entrepreneur has already submitted other projects to Kickstarter. This variable takes values "No", "Yes—Successful" or "Yes—Unsuccessful"
No. of previous projects	Number of previous projects submitted by the entrepreneur
Networking	
Facebook friends	Number of Facebook friends of the entrepreneur
Facebook shares	Number of shares on Facebook
Page visits	Number of page visits from Twitter—proxy of the viral effect of the page
Backed	Number of Kickstarter projects backed by the entrepreneur

is. The longer the time, the greater the uncertainty and, as in basic finance, for a longer waiting time the expected value for the project should be higher. However, projects with a longer delivery time may be more complex and so worth waiting for: this kind of project may still be very attractive to customers. We do not have any clear expectation from the influence of this variable on the rate of success since a lower time would reduce uncertainty, while a longer time may be needed for more complex and valuable products.

We then consider product price and the number of purchases. Given that the offered products are very heterogeneous, the prices show a great variation, especially intra-industry. For example, Comics usually have a very low price when considering the PDF downloadable copy, while some projects like 3D printers that are very popular projects on Kickstarter can easily pass the $1,000 mark. Since the same project can be presented with multiple prices, according to the level of customisation, the services attached or even the delivery time, it has been decided to take into account the cheapest price that allowed the backer to get the basic product. This rule applies also to Comics and Music, where the digital downloadable copy is always the least expensive, but at the same time is also the one that does not have any additional shipment cost. We expect projects with a lower price to be more successful than project with higher prices.

We also include shipment. At the moment this article is being written, Kickstarter accepts projects only from US, Canada and UK citizens. It is possible for people outside these countries to upload projects, but they need to have a bank account opened by a citizen of the countries previously listed. Canada and UK were added in 2013, so for the first 4 years of life of the platform the site was mainly related to the US market. This has led to a trend in which the shipment costs used to be free of charge within USA and people usually should add at least $10 for international shipment. This of course affects all potential customers outside the US, especially when the starting price of the product is very little and the shipment costs can even double the product price. We expect an inverse relationship between shipment price and successful projects because basically they shrink the plausible audience.

Finally, we looked at the role of complementarity. Stand-alone projects have to find a target market, a pricing strategy and key features to meet the customer's needs. Complementarity meanwhile can ease the job of an entrepreneur since he can build upon an already established market and rely upon a set of customers that just want to add value to their products.

This study wants to go into this in depth and find out whether being complementary can help a project to be successful. We expect a positive correlation between the two variables.

4.3 *Offer Related Variables*

The third group of variables refers to the way in which the product is offered: the presence of a video, the level of detail of the description, the product price and the number of deals. As we already stated, each day up to 100 new projects are submitted on Kickstarter and it is crucial not only to hook potential backers, but also to give them all the information needed to make the purchase decision. The creation of a good offer is a pure marketing effort, so the following features are key to achieving success.

Starting with video, Kickstarter itself, in the instructions regarding how to create a project, states: "A video is strongly encouraged but not required. More than 80 % of projects have videos, and those that don't have a much lower success rate." (Kickstarter, 2015). A video is a critical feature since it can convey all the needed information in a short amount of time: in a couple of minutes the entrepreneur himself can explain the features of the projects and show how it works. We do not expect that having a video leads to success, but in contrast we expect the lack of any video to have a huge impact on the success rate of the projects; it should act like a conditional but not sufficient feature.

In this study we also use the length of description as a proxy variable for the level of detail given to the customers. As we know from contracting theory (Kaplan & Stromberg, 2000), agency costs play a crucial role in a market where there is a great asymmetry of information. The entrepreneur must give any potential backer all the information needed to carry out the purchasing decision. The video itself usually provides just a brief explanation on what the product is and what it does, but the ones that really want to buy a product need more: this is where the description kicks in. It is usually a long descriptive text that explains how the product is manufactured, which steps have already been covered, what still needs to be done to obtain a final product, and all possible information needed. In this study we assume that the longer the description, the higher the level of detail provided to the potential backer. Hence, we suppose that a longer description will be associated with a higher success rate.

As already stated, the offer description is one key element in any submitted project. We also suppose the number of possible deals offered to the customer to be related to the level of refinement of the marketing strategy: there are projects that display just a couple of deals while others reach up to 30. As Iyengar and Lepper (2000) showed, customers given too much choice can be paralysed by it. An increase in the number of deals can thus make it very confusing for potential customers.

Further variables considered here are the presence of early backers related to a limited edition offer, and the over-purchase phenomena. A study from Chitika (2003) shows that 94 % of searches on Google do not go beyond the first page (Gravitate Online, 2011): in this fast information world in order to hook customers you have to gain visibility. In order to do so, some projects started using tricks to get to the "Popular this week" page on Kickstarter. The algorithm that puts projects on that page is unknown, but still it is quite obvious that gaining a lot of purchases in a short amount of time is what is needed to get there. In order to do so, using techniques taken from scarcity marketing some entrepreneurs started asking lower prices for a limited batch of the product that the first backers would buy. Another option is to price discriminate later entrants, as some entrepreneurs do, with more categories of limited batches.

An additional method that uses scarcity marketing is selling limited editions of the product so as to give a higher value, in case the firm actually gets successful in the future. The variable "over-purchase" refers to this second category of deals, since here we counted the number of backers that purchased at higher prices than the basic product. This can be due not only to higher prices but also to a compensation mechanism in which, as a collective, people are more likely to help with money when they really support a project.

4.4 Entrepreneur Related Variables

The fourth set of features that may influence the success of the campaign regards the entrepreneur itself: in particular we want to identify whether the background of the entrepreneur, his skills and the number of previous projects submitted are taken into account by potential customers when performing the purchasing decision process. Kickstarter provides a page where the entrepreneur himself can describe his studies and what are the skills that allowed him to create the product. There is a clear dichotomy in the behaviour of the proposers when considering this section of the site: some clearly spent a lot of time picturing themselves in the most detailed possible way. The other pattern of behaviour is just related to the life of the entrepreneur and the people that inspired him in doing this work, without giving any hint related to scholastic or work background. This second pattern is more frequent in industries related to more artistic skills, such as Music, Publishing or Art.

Starting from the entrepreneurial background, the profile of the entrepreneur may play an important role when people are supposed to lend you money on the basis of just a project. Studies on the "anatomy" of entrepreneurs (Wadhwa, Aggarwal, Holly, & Salkever, 2009) show that the usual profile comes from a middle-class family, has a bachelor degree or is a master student, and tends to have an engineering background. "Engineering" and "Artistic" backgrounds are, by far, the most well represented; the rest of the entrepreneurs fall in the category "unknown/freelance" where they do not provide any hint regarding their education, but just describe themselves as "passionate". Another small category is represented by "companies", in which the profile is not the one of the entrepreneur but is the one of the company itself. Similar to what was done with the "industry" variable, collecting the studies of the entrepreneurs has a value in identifying trends and in comparing these trends with the evidence concerning start-ups financed through traditional methods.

In this category we also consider if there is a previous project from the same person, and if so how many previous projects were proposed by him/her in the past. The "previous project" variable is important because it shows whether or not this is the first product that the entrepreneur has submitted to the platform. Even if at first glance it would be normal to assume entrepreneurs with projects that have already succeeded will be more likely to raise funds, a certain pattern of behaviour can radically change the outcome. While one would expect previous entrepreneurs that did not reach the funding goal will struggle more in successive projects, the results can be less obvious due to a clear trend: projects that fail to succeed are usually reuploaded with a lower funding goal. This leads to a higher rate of success. We actually do not have any clear expectation regarding the effect of this variable due to this phenomenon, although Kappel (2009) comparing the model of crowdfunding as ex-ante financing concluded that, unlike post-facto funding, projects do not require established track records to work.

4.5 Networking Variables

The final category of variables here considered regards networking and social networks. Every day nearly 100 projects are submitted on the platform, and to gain visibility it is crucial to reach the right potential backers. Knowing the importance of gaining visibility, the platform itself has Facebook and Twitter shares already embedded to make it easier for the project to go viral.

First of all, we focus our attention on the number of Facebook friends and Facebook shares. The vast majority of entrepreneurs, when presenting themselves to potential backers, provide their Facebook profile: we suppose that a high number of Facebook friends can be a key element to make the campaign skyrocket. Friends should play a role with a word-of-mouth endorsement to their other Facebook friends: this way they can create a buzz that will help reaching potential backers. The higher the number of friends, the higher the number of social interactions within a potential audience, so the higher the number of potential backers.

5 The Analysis

5.1 First Step: Logistic Regression on Ex-Ante Variables

As a first step of the analysis, we performed a logistic regression taking a dummy variable based on the rate of financing as a dependent variable, with the following values: 1 = project financed; 0 = project non-financed. Out of the pool of predictors we collected we decided to select the variables that can be observed "ex-ante", the ones that are not going to change during the campaign. These variables are

Table 2 Logit regression to predict crowdfunding success on ex-ante campaign variables (significant parameters in bold)

	β Coeff	Std. Err.	Wald	Sig.	Exp β
Amount asked	−0.038	0.009	16.721	0.000	0.963
Number of projects previously backed	0.091	0.024	14.598	0.000	1.095
Entrepreneur's background[a]					
Artistic	0.473	0.275	2.970	0.085	1.606
Company	0.453	0.334	1.843	0.175	1.573
Engineer	−0.152	0.631	0.058	0.810	0.859
Other	−0.095	0.404	0.055	0.814	0.910
Complementarity of the product	0.233	0.502	0.215	0.643	1.262
Number of Deals	0.077	0.024	10.42	0.001	1.080
Special offers for early backers	0.560	0.233	5.75	0.016	1.750
Number of Facebook friends[b]					
0–500	−0.604	0.260	5.401	0.020	0.547
500–1,000	0.052	0.357	0.021	0.885	1.053
>1,000	0.059	0.311	0.036	0.850	1.061
Campaign's description length	0.000	0.000	0.617	0.432	1.000
Product price	0.002	0.001	3.437	0.064	1.002
Presence of previous successful projects	0.475	0.275	2.984	0.084	1.608
Presence of previous unsuccessful project	−0.243	0.288	0.712	0.399	0.784
Free shipment[c]					
Other countries	0.376	0.48	0.613	0.434	1.457
Only US	−0.081	0.224	0.131	0.717	0.922
Time to market	−0.028	0.010	7.958	0.005	0.972
Presence of a video	1.227	0.404	9.241	0.002	3.410
Constant	−1.61	0.521	9.558	0.002	0.200

[a]Reference category: freelance
[b]Reference category: no Facebook profile
[c]Reference category: no free shipment

important because they allow us to predict whether or not a campaign could reach its funding goal at the very moment the campaign is published online. Table 2 shows the results of the logit regression, revealing which are the predictors displaying a significant relationship with crowdfunding success, and their coefficients.

Specifically, the first two columns of Table 2 include beta coefficients with their standard errors of estimations. Coefficients reveal the increase in the chance of achieving success by increasing by one unit the corresponding variable. The columns with the Wald statistics and the significance levels (sig.) reveal the test for significance of the above described coefficients: if Sig. is below 0.05, it means that the corresponding beta coefficient is statistically different from zero, and the variable can be considered as a predictor of the crowdfunding success. The final column contains the exponentiated coefficients, or Odds ratios, which present the beta coefficients in a different form: they reflect the change in the probability to succeed compared to the probability to fail.

Out of the 14 ex-ante variables included, just 7 turned out to be significant, but also the non-significant results reveal interesting insights. First of all, the independent variable taking into account the background of the entrepreneur (*Entrepreneur's Background*) resulted as a non-significant predictor (sig. >0.05), which means that backers do not seem to care about the certificates or accomplishments of the entrepreneurs: the potential backers are probably evaluating the campaign by looking at the product itself and not at the person who is offering it. Another fact that may confirm this pattern is the fact that the variables related to the presence of *previous projects*, both successful and unsuccessful, also are not significant. Another interesting non-significant outcome regards *complementarity*: this result seems to suggest that users of this platform seek innovative products and are not interested in products complementary to already established goods. Novelty is then an important characteristic of the products to be considered when looking at these campaigns.

Moving to the significant variables (sig. <0.05) Video has the highest coefficient ($\beta = 1.227$) and is strongly significant: this shows a powerful positive impact on the probability of success. The exponentiated Beta coefficient (in Table 2 "Exp β. (Coeff)") tells us that projects with a video are 3.41 times more likely to succeed. This also confirms Kickstarter's statement saying that a video increases the possibility of having a successful campaign.

The second strongest positive correlation ($\beta = 0.56$) regards the presence of *special offers for early backers*. When present, the odds ratio of success nearly doubles ($\text{Exp}(\beta) = 1.75$), meaning that this marketing tool is strongly effective. As we said, adding this offer has multiple advantages since it does not limit its effect in helping the first backers to make a purchasing choice based on a scarcity of time but, when it successfully makes the project skyrocket, it helps the campaign by giving it visibility on the first page in the section "Popular this week".

The predictor *Backed*, reflecting how many projects the entrepreneur has backed on the platform, is also positively correlated ($\beta = 0.091$), and the odds ratio for entrepreneurs that helped other projects increases by 1.095. This shows that community commitment is appreciated within Kickstarter. The final positively correlated variable is *Deals* ($\beta = 0.077$), meaning that segmenting the potential backers with a high number of offers will make the likelihood of success higher by an odds ratio of 1.08.

Facebook Friends as a whole category is significant ($p = 0.043$), and is divided into four categories: from 0 to 500, from 500 to 1,000, more than 1,000 and "Facebook not connected" which means that the entrepreneur has not disclosed his digital profile and so it is not possible to obtain this data. The first category, from 0 to 500, is strongly correlated but negatively ($\beta = -0{,}604$), while the other two categories are highly not significant. The only conclusion we can draw is that the odds ratio ($\text{Exp}(\beta) = 0.547$) of success of people that have less than 500 friends is half that of the ones not having a public disclosure of their profile.

Time to market is also negatively correlated ($\beta = -0.028$) and it shows a high level of significance ($p = 0.005$). However the odds ratio effect is quite low, with an exponentiated Beta of 0.972. This unravels the balance between the projects that have a short delivery time and so are more attractive, with the projects that are worth waiting for: being negatively correlated with success this means that longer times are really interesting for backers. Another view could point out that Films are the category with a higher number of projects in the database and is also the one with the highest number of failed projects. Usually, projects in that category have longer delivery times than other products; on the other hand, Music and Comics tend to be very successful and have shorter delivery times, these two categories also have great weight in our database.

The last significant variable is *Amount Asked,* which represents the goal of the campaigns. The correlation is negative ($\beta = -0.038$) and the odds ratio is smaller than 1 (0.963). As we stated in the database section, there is a significant difference in mean goals of successful projects ($9,830) versus the unsuccessful ones (nearly $32,000). This does not mean that "big" projects have a hard time reaching their goals; from our experience doing the screening, this is more due to a general greediness that some entrepreneurs show in thinking that reaching the goal is relatively easy, or trying to recover sunk costs.

5.2 Second Step: Mediation Model on Ex-Ante Variables

The analysis carried out so far included independent variables that could be observed before the start of the campaign. Using a mediation model, we now shift to study how the variables that come into play during the campaign can actually change crowdfunding success.

The mediation model seeks to identify the effect of mediators in the interaction between the independent variables and the dependent one. Rather than looking at the direct causal correlation between the independent variables and the dependent one, the mediator model assumes that there is a third variable (or more) in the relationship called mediator, that influences the relationship. Mediation occurs when this third variable plays an important role in shaping the relationship between the independent and the dependent variables.

The question asked here is a little bit different from the previous one: in the logistic regression we investigated whether or not the project would have been successful considering the "ex-ante" observable predictors. In this model we will try to understand which effect mediators have on the rate of financing, so the research question will not be whether or not the project is successful, but how much it has managed to raise and what the variables that influenced this result are. This is a significantly different approach compared to most of the extant research.

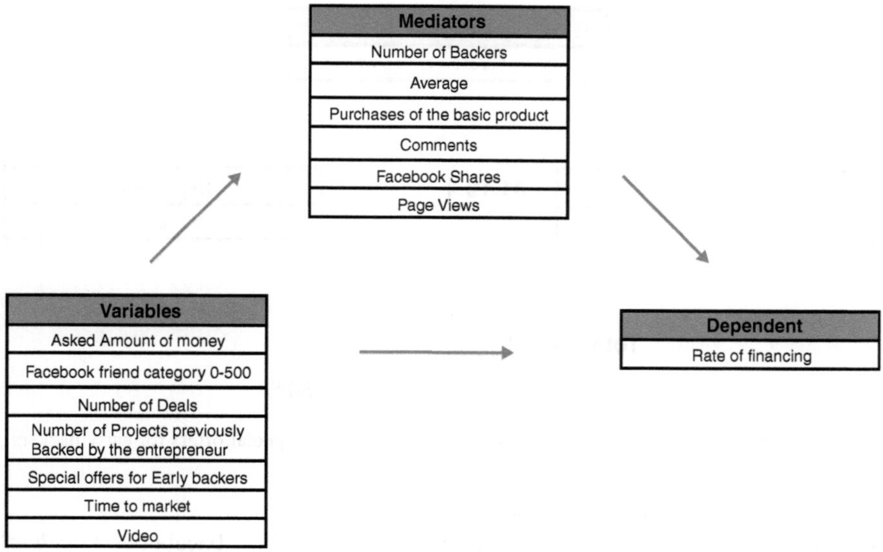

Fig. 1 The mediation model: how the effects of ex-ante variables on crowdfunding success are mediated by campaign variables

There are four effects tested in a mediation model (Baron & Kenny, 1986):

- The first effect is called "direct effect", and taps the relationship between the independent and the dependent variable.
- The second one (A) is the effect that the independent variable has on the mediator.
- The third effect (B) is the effect the Mediator has on the dependent variable.
- The fourth effect is called "indirect effect" and is computed as $A \times B$.

Figure 1 shows the mediation model, in which the total effect is given by the sum of the direct and the indirect effect.

The extent to which the indirect effect contributes to the mediation process makes it possible to distinguish between full mediation (no direct effect) and partial mediation. In this analysis we estimate the standard errors of the model using the Bootstrapping method from Preacher and Hayes (2004), since we are dealing with a relatively small database and we want to avoid potential heteroscedasticity issues.

As independent variables we use all the seven variables that proved to be significant in the previous test, for which there is a potential direct effect to be mediated. This way we can reduce the noise in the analysis and make it simpler to spot interesting effects. As mediators we use the variables that change during the campaign, such as:

- The number of people giving money to the project *(Number of Backers)*
- The average amount pledged *(Average)*
- The number of people that actually decided to buy the smallest pledge that made it possible to obtain the project, without any added value *(Purchasers of the basic product)*

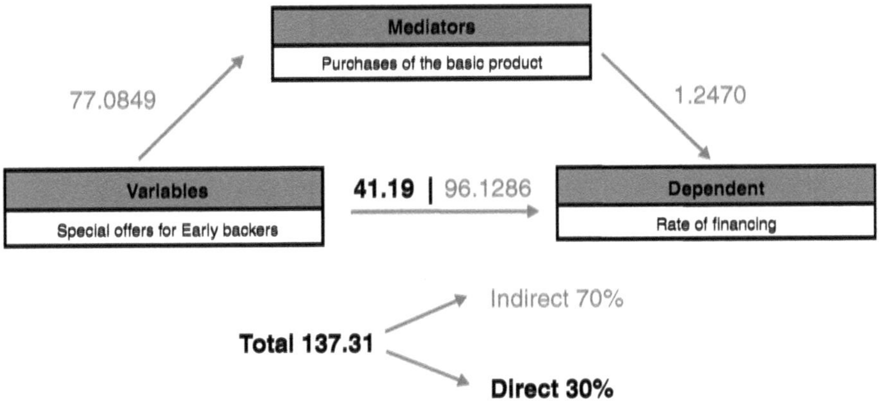

Fig. 2 The mediating role of purchases of the basic product on special offers for early backers

- The number of comments *(Comments)*
- The number of times the campaign has been shared on Facebook *(Facebook shares)*
- The number of Page views obtained via Twitter, that is a proxy of the number of total page views that we could obtain *(Page Views)*.

Moving to the results of our mediation model, out of these six potential mediators, only the variable *purchases of the basic product* turns out to be an eligible mediator, and it mediates two effects on the rate of financing: (i) that of special offers for early backers, and (ii) that of the number of previous projects backed by the entrepreneur. In the first case, Fig. 2 shows the results.

The presence of special offers for early backers strongly mediates the effect of the number of purchases of the basic product. In fact the indirect effect (96.128) is much greater than the direct (41.19).

The relationship is straightforward, since early backers are actually purchasing at a discounted price, so it is a variable that naturally leads to purchases (even if these deals are not counted in the number of purchases of the basic product). When the limited stock of discounted products runs out, the following backers will have to buy at least the basic product. This is a great example of a good marketing technique, since we are not only seeing that the scarcity of a discounted price leads to more purchases, but we can also see that once the stock is exhausted the fact that it was bought by other people works as a positive endorsement to the following potential backers. Since our expectation on the effect of signalling done by references has been proved wrong by the first analysis, we could assume that "internal signalling" made by the community has a stronger effect than an article on a website. This is actually in line with marketing studies suggesting that peer-endorsement is considered more trustworthy by 92 % of the population than brand information. Some of these effects were also found in a study that pointed out that herd behaviour, typical of microfinance, can be found in crowdfunding (Burtch, Ghose, & Wattal, 2011). Ward and Ramachandran (2011) also analysed

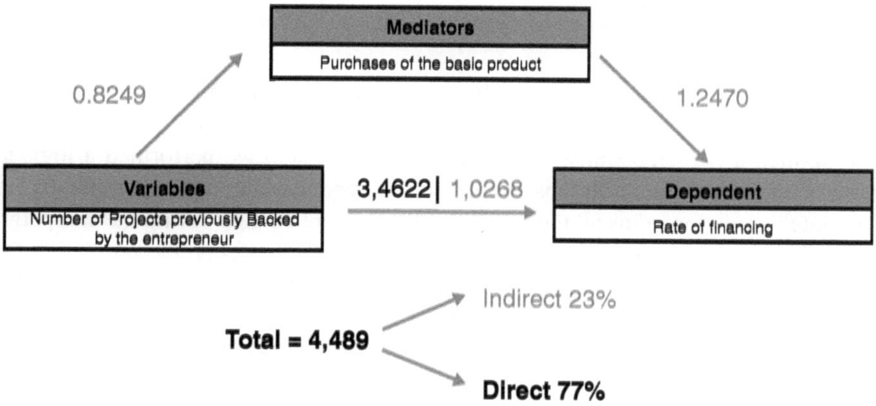

Fig. 3 The mediating role of the purchases of the basic product on the number of projects previously backed by the entrepreneur

the extent to which peer effects drive the demand for crowdfunding projects: they managed to isolate networking effects and concluded that peer effects do influence consumption.

In the case of the number of projects previously backed by the entrepreneur, Fig. 3 shows the results. In this case the direct effect is much stronger than the indirect one. This means that the mediator contributes partially to the relationship between the predictor and the dependent variable.

We have two different effects acting in this relationship: the first one is the confirmation of the *Patronage* effect, "the support, encouragement, and financial help that an individual bestows another" (Ordanini et al., 2011). The users see themselves as a community and this would make them more likely to help someone that shows commitment to the platform by backing others' projects. Also, some entrepreneurs use updates (internal messages to the backers) not only as their primary use of information, but also as a tool for sponsoring other projects: this means that an entrepreneur can "finance" a sponsorship inside the platform by backing other ongoing campaigns and asking them for a "shout out" at the bottom of an update.

The second effect and therefore another possible explanation can be "experience-based" creation of the campaign: it usually takes a little time on the platform to understand how it works plus some time dedicated to screening to find projects worth backing. Entrepreneurs with more than one backed project have definitely seen a lot of different projects, so they know how to tune a good campaign: what kind of ideas gets funding, what to say in the video, what and how to write the information that a potential backer looks for when he is making the pledging decision (for example, one of the classic tricks is to put an image showing precisely the pledge alongside with the rewards). Being able to fine-tune the campaign could help increase the number of people willing to buy the product.

6 Conclusions

The aim of this study was to analyse and find the determinants that make a crowdfunding campaign successful. We started with a database of 500 projects and applied a two-step statistical model: in the first step we performed a logistic regression on the predictors observable on the very first day of the campaign, the "ex-ante" predictors, thus all the variables that will not change during the campaign itself. The first step allowed us to spot some interesting effects: the presence of a video and of special offers for early backers are highly correlated with a higher odds ratio of success. In contrast, being too greedy when setting a goal or having a time to market too long will decrease the chances of getting funded. A stronger detrimental effect however occurs when the entrepreneur has less than 500 friends on Facebook: in this case the odds ratio is half that of not disclosing to the public his Facebook profile.

The second step of the analysis provides a new perspective to the relationship among the variables involved. Through a mediation model, we managed to point out how variables changing during the campaign affect the relationship between observable ex-ante predictors and the final rate of funding. All the studies carried out so far based their analysis on which variables were affecting the final result, but did not take into account the fact that a campaign has a time component that makes some variables interact with others. This means that with our analysis we managed not only to expose which variables affect the success rate, but also those predictors having a significant effect on others that will then lead to a higher success rate.

After running several tests we discovered that the only mediator showing a significant effect was the number of purchases of the basic product. By looking at the direct and the indirect effect we were able to conclude that this mediator was having a significant effect on the relationship of two predictors: the number of projects previously backed, and a stronger effect on the presence of a special offer for early backers.

The effect of the presence of discounts for early backers leads people to buy the product in the campaign's very early moments, giving it notoriety on the platform since the website has an algorithm that brings "popular" projects to the front page. The fact that other people decided to support a certain project also acts as a signal to potential backers that the product is of some value.

The mediator has a less strong carry over effect when we examine how it interferes in the relationship between the number of projects previously backed by the entrepreneur and the rate of financing. Displaying a community effort within the platform by backing other projects shows commitment and activates the effect known as *Patronage*.

Another possible explanation of this effect is given by mutual help among entrepreneurs with ongoing projects that usually back each other not only financially, but also by sponsoring other projects to their backers. A further possible explanation looks at the added value in the experience of the entrepreneur: since he has backed other projects, he has probably spent some time on the platform screening projects, thus acquiring experience on how to fine-tune the campaign.

Of course our study has limitations, and the most relevant ones may be addressed in future research. First of all it would be interesting to carry out a study on the behaviour of the rate of financing over time, to see if it is possible to identify useful marketing tools for entrepreneurs to get their projects viral and funded. It would also be interesting to narrow the field of study to certain specific categories, as we can expect that in the future, due to the increase in popularity of the platform, some categories will spin off in order to get visibility. In this analysis we handled all the effects together, but it would be interesting to see whether or not our findings will still hold when looking at each single category; certain effects could have been lost in the "noise" of all the other projects.

References

Agrawal, A., Catalini, C., & Goldfarb, A. (2011). *The geography of crowdfunding* (NBER Working Paper No. 16820). Retrieved from http://www.nber.org/papers/w16820

Baron, R. M., & Kenny, D. A. (1986). The moderator-mediator variable distinction in social psychological research—Conceptual, strategic, and statistical considerations. *Journal of Personality and Social Psychology, 51*(6), 1173–1182.

Belleflamme, P., Lambert, T., & Schwienbacher, A. (2013). Individual crowdfunding practices. *Venture Capital, 14*(4), 313–343.

Belleflamme, P., Lambert, T., & Schwienbacher, A. (2014). *Crowdfunding: Tapping the right crowd*. Manuscript submitted for publication.

Brabham, D. C. (2008). Crowdsourcing as a model for problem solving: An introduction and cases. *Convergence: The International Journal of Research into New Media Technologies, 14*, 75–90.

Burtch, G., Ghose, A., & Wattal, S. (2011). An empirical examination of the antecedents and consequences of investment patterns in crowd-funded markets. *SSRN Electronic Journal, 24*, 499–519. doi:10.2139/ssrn.1928168

Chitika. (2003). *The value of Google result positioning*. Retrieved from http://chitika.com/google-positioning-value

Gravitate Online. (2011). *2nd page rankings: You're the #1 loser*. Retrieved from http://www.gravitateonline.com/google-search/2nd-place-1st-place-loser-seriously

Iyengar, S. S., & Lepper, M. R. (2000). When choice is demotivating: Can one desire too much of a good thing? *Journal of Personality and Social Psychology, 79*(6), 995–1006.

Jennings, P. (2000). *New media arts, new funding models*. Creativity and Culture, The Rockefeller Foundation. Retrieved from http://www.pamelajennings.org/PDF/New_Media_Arts_New_Funding_Models.pdf

Kaplan, S. N., & Stromberg, P. (2000). *Financial contracting theory meets the real world: An empirical analysis of venture capital contract* (NBER Working Paper No. 7660). Retrieved from http://www.nber.org/papers/w7660

Kappel, T. (2009). Ex ante crowdfunding and the recording industry: A model for the U.S.? *Loyola of Los Angeles Entertainment Law Review, 29*(3), 375–385.

Kickstarter. (2015). Retrieved from https://www.kickstarter.com/learn?ref=nz_promo

Massolution. (2013). *Crowdfunding industry report 2013*. Retrieved from http://research.crowdsourcing.org/2013cf-crowdfunding-industry-report

Mollick, E. (2014). The dynamics of crowdfunding: An exploratory study. *Journal of Business Venturing, 29*(1), 1–16.
Ordanini, A., Miceli, L., Pizzetti, M., & Parasuraman, A. (2011). Crowd-funding: Transforming customers into investors through innovative service platforms. *Journal of Service Management, 22*(4), 443–470.
Preacher, K. J., & Hayes, A. F. (2004). SPSS and SAS procedures for estimating indirect effects in simple mediation models. *Behavior Research Methods, Instruments, and Computers, 36*(4), 717–731.
Wadhwa, V., Aggarwal, R., Holly, K. Z., & Salkever, A. (2009). *Anatomy of an entrepreneur: Family background and motivation.* Retrieved from http://www.kauffman.org/~/media/kauffman_org/research%20reports%20and%20covers/2009/07/anatomy_of_entre_071309_final.pdf
Ward, C., & Ramachandran, V. (2011). *Crowdfunding the next hit: Microfunding online experience goods.* Paper presented at annual meeting of INFORMS, Austin, TX.

Limitless Crowdfunding? The Effect of Scarcity Management

Dieter W. Joenssen and Thomas Müllerleile

Abstract Crowdfunding is a process by which enterprises or individuals seek to secure project funding by soliciting pledges from potential donors, usually via an Internet platform. These platforms offer project initiators the ability to limit the number of times a certain reward is claimed by supporters. This can be used to either offer a reward, which is naturally limited, or to induce an artificial scarcity for rewards without a natural limitation. The induction of such artificial limitations represents a signal which may, fundamentally, either have a positive or a negative effect on the crowdfunding project. To answer this question, this paper not only discusses the theoretical effects of scarcity management in the crowdfunding context, but also investigates this empirically. The analysis of 42,996 projects from Indiegogo.com indicates that current scarcity management is problematic at best and reduces the chances of projects to successfully achieve their target funding.

Keywords Crowdfunding • Pledge level design • Artificial scarcity

1 Introduction

The concept of crowdfunding has received much attention recently. Facilitated by telecommunication technologies, crowdfunding enables project initiators to integrate prospective customers or investors in the decision and funding process. Müllerleile and Joenssen (2015) define crowdfunding as "[. . .] a process where commercial or non-commercial projects are initiated in a public announcement by organisations or individuals to receive funding, assess the market potential, and build customer relationships. Pledgers may then contribute individual amounts of monetary or non-monetary resources, during a specified time-frame, using offline or online campaign platforms that utilise different pay-out schemes, in exchange for a product specific or unspecific, material or immaterial reward".

Normally, project initiators utilise crowdfunding in projects, for which they are either unable or unwilling to secure venture capital funding, traditionally a scarce

D.W. Joenssen (✉) • T. Müllerleile
Fakultät für Wirtschaftswissenschaften und Medien, Technische Universität Ilmenau, 10 05 65, 98684 Ilmenau, Germany
e-mail: Dieter.Joenssen@tu-ilmenau.de; Thomas.Muellerleile@tu-ilmenau.de

D. Brüntje, O. Gajda (eds.), *Crowdfunding in Europe*, FGF Studies in Small Business and Entrepreneurship, DOI 10.1007/978-3-319-18017-5_13

resource. Limited availability and the associated management of scarce resources trigger product and service innovation. This may be achieved by using the limiting factors more efficiently, which in turn increases competitiveness, e.g. through innovation or substitution (Cunha, Rego, Oliveira, Rosado, & Habib, 2014). In general, the concept of scarcity is at the heart of economics and management science. Research in these fields offers insights on how to manage scarce resources and their allocation. In terms of economic theory, crowdfunding is a service innovation to ameliorate a factor limitation, available venture capital funds. Thus, crowdfunding enables project initiators to tap into new financing streams and substitute traditional investors and intermediaries.

Other forms of scarcity exist within the context of crowdfunding. It can be observed empirically that some crowdfunding projects limit the availability of some forms of compensation. In reward-based crowdfunding projects, the number of available rewards that may be claimed by the pledgers is sometimes limited. Fundamentally, two limitations of the number of rewards may be observed. First, some rewards, which may be pledged for, have a natural limitation. These types of limitations are in place when the number of rewards offered on a pledge level may not be increased substantially, e.g. a night out with a musician seeking to finance a new album with crowdfunding (Kickstarter, 2012). In this case, the available time of the musician is finite. Second, some pledge levels are artificially scarce. Normally, these limited pledge levels offer the same reward as some other non-limited pledge levels, but with a lower minimum pledge amount. The project initiators seek to spark interest, increase media coverage, and trigger an early funding decision by the pledgers through these "early bird specials". Observations of crowdfunding platforms suggest that this type of scarcity management is widely used in projects. Thus, the effect of scarcity management, an available option for project initiators, on crowdfunding efforts may be of interest for researchers and practitioners.

The rest of this paper is organised as follows: Sect. 2 details the theoretical effects that scarcity management may have on crowdfunding project performance. Further, a research question is deduced. This question is answered empirically using data and analyses described in Sect. 3. Conclusions and future research directions are given in Sect. 4.

2 The Theoretical Effect

In behavioural economics and marketing, consumer decisions and valuations regarding the limited availability of resources are studied in depth. Several products, such as Apple's iPhone or Nintendo's N64, are known for their scarcity during launch. Other examples such as "Mighty Morphin Power Rangers" and "Tickle Me Elmo" have not only influenced Christmas time for anxious parents, but have also influenced popular culture substantially.[1]

[1] The attainment of the year's newest, hottest product is the main theme of the movie "Jingle all the way".

In economic theory high prices reflect the limited availability of a good. Thus, people tend to perceive scarce products as more desirable, because they normally express class, value, and a higher quality, which may not be achieved by all manufacturers. Lynn (1992) attributes this mindset to a naïve understanding of economics by customers. It is therefore understandable that researchers suggest scarcity strategies as marketing tools (Dye, 2000). Instead of catering to the customers' needs, scarcity management addresses the customers' primeval instincts, such as desire and fear of missing out (Brown, 2001). To a certain extent, addressing these instincts alleviates the burden of decision making from customers. In contrast, it can be argued that producers limiting availability contradicts economic theory in general. Economic theory dictates the existence of a supply-demand optimum. Rationing product availability, which increases deadweight loss or allocation inefficiency, results in a non-Pareto-optimal market equilibrium. Therefore, artificial scarcity prohibits achieving the total welfare maximum. However, customers may perceive goods as more valuable if the limited availability is caused by popularity and limited supply (Verhallen & Robben, 1994). Scarcity may also be used to generate a "hot product" by signalling a limited supply. Stock and Balachander (2005) conclude that a scarcity strategy may be useful as a signalling tool. They reason that new-to-the-world products are not likely to profit from scarcity strategies, because the number of experts who could evaluate such a new innovation is small. As a result, Stock and Balachander (2005) suggest favouring a pure price signalling strategy for innovative products. Further applications of scarcity management and its effect on clients' value appreciation can be observed in collectables and unique items (Lynn & Bogert, 1996).

Limiting the amount of possible slots per pledge level is quite common in crowdfunding projects.[2] However, as discussed, economic theory and scarcity management research contradict each other on this subject, and research in scarcity management is inconclusive.

Contrary to traditional sales channels, prospective pledgers can access information on the type of scarcity at the project's campaign site, if the crowdfunding effort is conducted online. Additionally, pledgers may simultaneously see the actual demand, supply, and prices for limited and non-limited reward levels. This is a big difference in comparison to traditional scarcity driven sales channels, e.g. telemarketing, which omit this information. Therefore, it is questionable, if scarcity in crowdfunding projects is communicated efficiently. Prospective pledgers may feel uncomfortable supporting a project if all "early bids" are sold out. They may feel that they are not getting a good deal. However, already claimed limited rewards may signal a high project success probability to prospective supporters, who have not yet pledged. This signalling may therefore incline others to jump on the proverbial bandwagon.

Problems arise in the context of flexible funding campaigns.[3] Pledgers bear the full risk in flexible funding campaigns, where the successful execution of the

[2] 23,341 of all projects analysed in this study make use of some type of limitation.

[3] In flexible funding schemes, funds are always paid out, even if the specified funding goal is not met.

crowdfunded project is more than questionable if a low proportion of required funds are collected. In this context, "early bird specials" may have an additional meaning for the pledgers. Depending on the pledgers' risk-averseness, a deferred funding decision is possible. In general, the pledger has to decide if the discount offered by the "early bird special" exceeds the additional risk.

Since these points may not be resolved by theoretical discussion, the empirical research in the next Section is guided by the following research question:

> Are crowdfunding projects, which use a scarcity strategy, more likely to secure the requested funding?

3 The Empirical Effect

The following Subsections detail an analysis performed on data collected to answer the previously defined research question. Sections 3.1 and 3.2, respectively, describe the sample and the logistic-regression-model. The final Sect. 3.3 discusses the results.

3.1 *Sample Description*

The crowdfunding platform Indiegogo.com was selected as a data source to answer the research question. Data on a total of 42,996 projects were collected between July 28 and August 2, 2013. A custom web crawler was created to systematically collect this publicly available data. Information collected included the project name, the amount of funding requested, the amount of funding obtained, project initialisation date, textual content of the reward levels, i.e. the reward itself, the maximum number of pledges that can be made for a certain reward level, and the number of pledges made for each reward level. Upon completion, variables were transformed to yield data suitable for statistical analysis. This included extracting required information from text and transforming strings to numerical values.

Table 1 shows descriptive statistics of the collected data. The first row indicates that project initiators have substantially different funding wishes. As is indicated by the discrepancy between the mean and median, most initiators seek small pledge sums, while some few request exorbitant amounts. Further, total pledged amounts are, on average, considerably lower than the requested amounts. This indicates that a substantial amount of projects are underfinanced. Indeed, only about 30.9 % of all projects receive pledges totalling more than the requested funding. Many projects feature a reward that may only be claimed a limited number of times. On average an Indiegogo.com project will feature 2.37 rewards that are constrained in this sense. One project even features 115 limited rewards.

Table 1 Descriptive statistics of the Indigogo.com data

	Min.	First Q.	Median	Mean	Third Q.	Max.
Funding goal	500	2,500	5,000	63,777	12,000	757 Mil.
Pledged amounts	0	845	1,590	4,180	3,444	6.9 Mil.
Funding percentage	0.00	14.33	40.82	63.68	101.10	140.60
Number of limited rewards	0	0	1	2.37	4	115

Table 2 Relative frequency of projects by the limited reward number

Number of limited rewards	0	1	2	3	4	5	6	≥7
Portion of projects (%)	45.7	9.1	8.3	8.3	6.8	5.7	4.5	11.6

Table 2 shows the percentage of projects within the data that feature a certain number of limited rewards. Approximately 54.3 %, constrain at least one reward to a maximum amount of pledges. 45.7 % of the projects do not use this option.

3.2 Analysis

Answering the chosen research question requires determining if limiting at least one pledge level influences the probability of successful project funding. This may be determined via logistic-regression-analysis. Logistic-regression was first developed and proposed by McFadden (1973). It can be used to determine the functional relationship between any number of independent variables and a single, binary dependent variable. This functional relationship may be written as follows:

$$P(success = 1|d) = \frac{e^{\beta_0+\beta_1 x_1}}{1 + e^{\beta_0+\beta_1 x_1}}.$$

Thus, the probability of success is dependent on a base success probability, determined through β_0, and the contribution of having a pledge level with limited availability, β_1. Again, a project is considered successfully funded if the sum of pledges exceeds the set funding goal.

3.3 Results

Results from a logistic-regression featuring one binary independent variable may be interpreted in a two-step approach. After the assessment of coefficient significance, the influence of the independent variable on the dependent variable must further be assessed. This is due to the non-linear functional relationship.

Table 3 Logistic regression results, estimates and bootstrap standard errors

	Coefficient	Wald z-statistic	Deviance statistic
(intercept)	−.703 (.015)	−46.42*** (.886)	–
x_1 ~ limited reward	−.182 (.020)	−8.71*** (.999)	75.748*** (17.504)

Significance codes: ***p < .001; **p < .01; *p < .05; p < 1

Table 4 Model predictions, estimates and bootstrap standard errors

Limited rewards	No	Yes
Project success probability	33.1 % (.3 %)	29.2 % (.3 %)

The parameter estimation results, given in Table 3, indicate that there is a significant base-success-probability ($p \approx 0$) and that limiting the availability of at least one reward level significantly influences the probability of successful project funding. These results hold, whether the Wald z-statistic is used or the deviance from the null-model is tested using a chi-squared test. Further, the standard errors, calculated via 10,000 bootstrap replicates and given in Table 3 beside the estimates, indicate that the estimates are robust.

The non-linear nature of the logistic-regression precludes direct interpretation of the coefficients. Solely the negative sign indicates can be directly interpreted. Having at least one limited reward level reduces the success probability. However, given that the independent variable is dichotomous, the results of the model prediction may readily be compared by applying the estimates from Table 3 to the formula from Sect. 3.2 (cf. Table 4). Model predictions indicate that including a limited reward reduces the project's probability of success by almost four percentage points. This equates to a reduction in success probability of almost 12 %, or an odds-ratio of .833. Again, the standard errors estimated via 10,000 bootstrap replicates indicate the robustness of the results.

4 Conclusions

This paper contributes to crowdfunding theory, by linking scarcity management to crowdfunding. Additionally, the effect of scarcity management is investigated empirically. The empirical investigation draws on a data set of 42,996 projects, collected from the Indiegogo.com website. Results indicate that scarcity management is used in more than half of all projects considered. Further, a logistic-regression-analysis shows that scarcity management, as currently performed, has an adverse effect on funding success, i.e. successfully achieving the set funding goal. This indicates that scarcity management is either used incorrectly or fundamentally not applicable in the context of crowdfunding.

This study offers first insights into the effects of tools at the disposal of project initiators, and lays the foundations for future crowdfunding research. Future research should differentiate between rewards with a natural limitation and rewards limited artificially. These investigations will no doubt be performed on smaller data sets, because the assessment of whether a pledge level is limited artificially or not needs to be performed manually. Further, it may be possible that scarcity management has different effects for different project types. Crowdfunding for music may need to be managed differently than video games. Differences in effects may also exist between crowdfunding projects having flexible or fixed funding goals. Since reactions to scarcity management are behaviouristic effects, pledger behaviour may also vary with cultural background.

Implications for project initiators include a rethinking of current scarcity management options. Crowdfunding, as a new phenomenon, requires new approaches. Not every type of project will profit from "early bird specials".

References

Brown, S. (2001). Torment your customers (they will love it). *Harvard Business Review, 79*(9), 82–88.

Cunha, M. P. E., Rego, A., Oliveira, P., Rosado, P., & Habib, N. (2014). Product innovation in resource-poor environments: Three research streams. *Journal of Product Innovation Management, 31*, 202–210.

Dye, R. (2000). The buzz on buzz. *Harvard Business Review, 78*(6), 139–146.

Kickstarter. (2012). *Amanda Palmer: The new RECORD, ART BOOK, and TOUR*. Retrieved from https://www.kickstarter.com/projects/amandapalmer/amanda-palmer-the-new-record-art-book-and-tour

Lynn, M. (1992). Scarcity's enhancement of desirability: The role of naive economic theories. *Basic and Applied Social Psychology, 13*(1), 67–78.

Lynn, M., & Bogert, P. (1996). The effect of scarcity on anticipated price appreciation. *Journal of Applied Social Psychology, 26*, 1978–1984.

McFadden, D. (1973). Conditional logit analysis of qualitative choice behavior. In P. Zarembka (Ed.), *Frontiers in econometrics* (pp. 105–142). New York: Academic.

Müllerleile, T., & Joenssen, D. W. (2015). Key success-determinants of crowdfunded projects: An exploratory analysis. In B. Lausen, S. Krolak-Schwerdt, & M. Boehmer (Eds.), *Data analysis, learning by latent structures and knowledge discovery* (pp. 271–281). Berlin: Springer.

Stock, A., & Balachander, S. (2005). The making of a "hot product": A signaling explanation of marketers' scarcity strategy. *Management Science, 51*(8), 118–1192.

Verhallen, T. M. M., & Robben, H. S. J. (1994). Scarcity and preference: An experiment on unavailability and product evaluation. *Journal of Economic Psychology, 15*, 315–331.

Equity Crowdfunding: Beyond Financial Innovation

Arash Gholamzadeh Nasrabadi

Abstract Often equity crowdfunding is just considered as a new viable method of financing beyond the traditional financial system. However, considering equity crowdfunding only within the financial sphere and as a financial innovation is very limiting and does not represent the reality. Equity crowdfunding innovation is not only a financial innovation; it encompasses many other features that make equity crowdfunding so innovative. The financial sphere is only a part of the innovation that interacts on different levels with other relevant features, thus creating synergies and a unique model.

The purpose of this article is to analyse the most relevant aspects of equity crowdfunding beyond the obvious financial sphere.

Keywords Equity crowdfunding • Innovation • Social community • Enterprise crowdfunding

1 Introduction

Equity crowdfunding is a new means of financing which differs from the traditional ways of obtaining funding. It has some characteristics that differentiate it from all the other crowdfunding models. One of the main characteristics of equity crowdfunding is that there is a different interaction with the investors. In fact, it issues equity which is distributed to the public. The result is that investors do not only finance a project to receive rewards, discounts or benefits; they own a small share of the company and then receive a portion of the profit, which is proportional to their investment. Another feature of equity is that on average there are more funds paid out per equity-based project than all other crowdfunding models; 42 % of the total projects in 2012 raised more than $100,000 (Crowdsourcing.org, 2012).

This characteristic, of course, attracted the interest of public institutions as they search for new viable ways to bring SMEs, which are suffering from a lack of funding after the credit crunch, back to life (De Buysere, Gajda, Kleverlaan, & Marom, 2012; Giudici, Nava, Lamastra, & Verecondo, 2012). The credit crunch has

A.G. Nasrabadi (✉)
Scuola Superiore Sant'Anna, Pisa, Italy
e-mail: arash.gn@gmail.com

D. Brüntje, O. Gajda (eds.), *Crowdfunding in Europe*, FGF Studies in Small Business and Entrepreneurship, DOI 10.1007/978-3-319-18017-5_14

worsened the scenario and small and micro-businesses have experienced great difficulties obtaining funds, in fact, macroeconomic conditions have a disproportionately high effect on small business finance (Berger & Udell, 1998). Market forecasts, stock market health, overall economic health, and monetary policy all have an effect on small business finance (Cumming, 2012). However, just analysing the financial sphere of equity crowdfunding and its ability to fund wider projects is limiting. In fact, the novelty and the potential of this model are intricately linked to the interaction of financial and social aspect. Equity crowdfunding is innovative in the way it interacts with the financial and social system. Issuing equity is nothing new as limited and public companies have long used this model of financing. The real novelty is separate from the financial sphere; it lies in the interaction of the model with the external environment and technologies that can create value in a transversal way, sometimes also limiting the financial sphere as an initial tool to benefit from all the other aspects that compose the overall phenomenon. Since crowdfunding is nothing new and has existed for centuries, what now makes it so unique and effective is its interaction with new technologies that were boosted by Web 2.0 and permit it to pursue value in many different ways (Danmayr, 2014; Ordanini, Miceli, Pizzetti, & Parasuraman, 2011).

The financial sphere can, in some cases, play a secondary role in the users' choice of crowdfunding forms, with it being used as a means to access other benefits. A clear example would be enterprise crowdfunding,[1] where crowdfunding is used solely to raise the participation, communication and entrepreneurial skills of the employees. Even if it cannot be classified as equity crowdfunding, it nonetheless demonstrates that the scope of crowdfunding goes beyond simply raising funds (Frick, 2013; Muller, Geyer, Soule, Daniells, & Cheng, 2013; Vogel & Fischler-Strasak, 2014).

Moreover, when users of crowdfunding are asked why they use it, it seems that they do not necessarily have any particular need for finance, but use equity crowdfunding in order to create something more participative and to gain support in the start-up phase of their business.

The aim of the next Section is to identify and analyse in greater depth the equity crowdfunding features that go beyond the financial sphere.

[1] Enterprise crowdfunding could be defined as an intranet venture application of crowdfunding aimed at reproducing the benefits of stimulation, participation and innovation inside the company, using unexpressed ideas, competencies and employee projects in order to improve the company's efficiency and entrepreneurial approach of employees.

2 Other Patterns Involved in Equity Crowdfunding

Equity crowdfunding, as general crowdfunding, is more than just an innovative financial tool designed to improve the possibility of financing for companies. In fact, many other facets demonstrate the multiple and complex roles that crowdfunding plays, such as involving the investor, searching for key co-operators, democratising entry and mitigating social discriminations and bias, validating the market, mitigating the risk, networking and stimulating innovation.

(1) Investor participation is a key aspect in the dynamicity of crowdfunding and for most of the companies it is an important aspect that helps them to find the best way of providing their service/product. In some cases the investors are also future customers and this is the reason for their strategic importance. Projects in which crowdfunding is used seem to benefit from the contribution and experience of the crowd known as the "Wisdom of the Crowd" (Surowiecki, 2005).[2] In fact, those who are willing to invest normally have some expertise and interest in the project and want to contribute not only their money, but also their knowledge. There is an auto-selective process that consists of investing in something the funders are able to manage or support via networks, knowledge or competencies which is often aimed at being useful to the community and to elevate their self-esteem while engaging and interacting within the community (Gerber & Hui, 2013; Gerber, Hui, & Kuo, 2011).[3]

    The financed venture will, of course, benefit from gaining information and support from these investors, especially if it is in the early stages. Sometimes the venture might also seek co-creators to fill the experience gap in a certain field and could have the chance to recruit them from within their investor group. In fact, finding the right employees is not one of the simplest stages in a start-up, and crowdfunding can help to make the process easier whether the theory of self-selection is valid (Cumming, 2012; De Luca, 2013).

(2) Entry democratisation is another important point supported by many scholars (e.g. Cumming, 2012; Mollick, 2013). Offering the company shares to the public reduces the risk of discrimination and hierarchy within the financing system and creates more opportunities for anyone who has an interesting project or idea for which to obtain funding.

    Even if many believe that crowdfunding creates opportunities for everyone, who wishes to run a business, in some cases this is not a realistic representation. One of the main limiting factors faced by investors in the initial phase is the sense of uncertainty which is caused by the prospect of investing in a complete stranger's company. Validation, in fact, is one the most critical aspects that an

[2] The wisdom of the crowd (or intelligence of the crowd) is a sociological theory according to which a mass of individuals would be able to provide a more adequate response to the problems than a small number of experts may be able to.

[3] The dynamics of crowdfunding are often linked to the interaction of very heterogeneous motivational factors, in part not related to economic rationality.

entrepreneur will face and it is important for the success of his/her campaign to be able to manage and convey a sense of reliability. Democratisation, in fact, could be undermined by famous venture capitalists, business angels, or famous people that could leverage on their advantaged position to obtain funding more easily, even if sometimes their projects may be less worthy than others (Blanding, 2013).

Such a result could lead to a completely different scenario, whereby democratisation is undermined, and a few big projects will end up with the lion's share of funding, while more experimental, unknown entrepreneurs will not be taken into consideration. However, this has always existed, and it is not anything new. It is hard to create something completely democratic. In part, it will depend on the crowdfunding corporate culture that could be interested in mitigating this issue. At the same time, the future widespread of crowdfunding will reduce certainly the risk perceived by investors, and it will induce a more democratic project-based selection rather than based on renowned initiators. Public institutions and researchers will play an important role in mitigating the perceived risk by producing more dedicated investor protection regulations and data publications (De Buysere et al., 2012).

Other research conducted by Mollick (2013) empirically demonstrates that equity crowdfunding presents less discriminatory biases by comparing it to venture capital financing operations.

The first is geographic concentration. Venture capitalists are principally concentrated in a few areas, where both entrepreneurs and venture capital firms are located. They usually create a cluster where it is easier to monitor, support and have face-to-face interaction, but they discriminate against any other deserving companies that are not within their area. Indeed, Sorenson and Stuart (2008) find that the average distance between a lead venture capitalist and their investment is 70 miles. In the case of early-stage ventures in particular, the cost of controlling activities is sensitive to distance (Ferryary & Mark, 2009).

The data presented by Mollick (2013) shows, instead, that on average equity crowdfunding is less geographically concentrated than venture capital funds, but the difference in magnitude is not great, especially for larger projects (more than $5,000).

Other studies conducted on the crowdfunding platform Sellaband (Agrawal, Catalini, & Goldfarb, 2011) found that online platforms are not influenced by spatial proximity. However, local investors, normally family and friends, are relevant as the first investors in the crowdfunding campaign, as they mitigate the asymmetry of information and reduce the risk perceived by other crowdfunders, thereby increasing their propensity to invest.

The findings highlighted two groups: the offline network and the online network. Offline networks are mostly local and, in part, made up of family and friends, whilst online networks can be made up of people from around the world. The particular finding that family and friends have a strategic importance in activating and increasing the likelihood of non-family and friends to invest deserves both interest and concern. The concern is that this would imply a new challenge to the widely held belief that crowdfunding represents "equal access for all" and "democratisation of selection".

However, the limits of these findings should be kept in mind. First of all, they are related to and were gathered in the music industry. Secondly, they were presumably collected more than 4 years ago, when the novelty of the phenomenon and the limited existence of crowdfunding could have raised the investment risk perceived by online users. Limited understanding of crowdfunding possessed by most people remains a very important limitation.

The second bias is related to the gender of entrepreneurs. In America, for example, 40 % of all business owners in the US are women, but historically less than 6 % of venture capital funding has historically gone to companies with female CEOs, and only 1.3 % of financed ventures have female founders. In crowdfunding, this bias is drastically reduced, in line with the principle of access for everyone without discrimination or prejudice. In fact, women were present in at least 21.1 % of funded projects. This is 15 times higher than in venture capital statistics (Mollick, 2013).

(3) Another consideration beyond financing is that ventures that use a crowdfunding platform also receive market validation which can reduce their activity risk in proportion to the success of their projects. The more enthusiastic the investors and the more successful the campaign, the higher the chance of it being a good idea. Last but not least is the importance of facing investors in the early stages of the project; in fact, it could be an effective way to gather information and validation from the potential consumers, named as pre-market analysis, with almost zero cost. It is also important to consider that a spontaneous social community will be created around the project which will be willing to contribute as much as possible, and their post-service/product feedback would probably be an important and valuable asset for driving the future product/service to be successful on the market (Martin, 2012).

(4) At the same time, crowdfunding could be used by the venture to mitigate the risk of investment in the business or just used to be able to exploit all the other beneficial aspects beyond the financial sphere. In the first case an entrepreneur could reduce the risk of his/her company even if they do not lack the financial resources, on the basis of reducing the risk of losing a lot of money as well as gaining the experience, competencies, validation and expertise of external investors (Cumming, 2012; Martin, 2012).

(5) Crowdfunding could be a very effective tool to create an active network made up of evangelist investors willing to employ significant efforts in promoting and supporting the project. This could be extremely useful if there is a lack of resources. Investors who are interested in the product/service are willing to promote the fund-raising campaign within their network for two reasons. Firstly, to ensure that it achieves the funding goal and secondly, because they have a part of the equity share of the company and an economic interest in promoting and using that product/service, rather than a competitor service due to the fact that they receive a share of the revenues (Cumming, 2012; Martin,

2012).[4] The crowdfunding campaign, stimulated by the investor's word of mouth, could create a synergy and a buzz effect that could positively affect the future success of the crowdfunded company.

(6) Crowdfunding is also a stimulator of innovation. Innovation is boosted by the interaction between different users. One of the most important characteristics involved in innovation is the diversity that can be derived from different cultures, ethnicities, types of knowledge, and points of view that can stimulate the "cross-pollination of ideas" (Fleming, 2004; Hewlett, Marshall, & Sherbin, 2013).

Fleming (2004) identified the fact that diversity boosts innovation, and is particularly significant in boosting high value innovation. Diversity is necessary to create dynamicity within the market and to foster an "open mind" culture within the company which enables proactivity and efficiency.

In crowdfunding, all this happens to a greater or lesser extent through the contribution of investors. Investors come from different regions of the world and have a totally different background and culture that could positively affect the value creation and could intensify the innovativeness of the project.

This was the aim of IBM during their "enterprise crowdfunding" trials which aimed to raise participation within different departments of different fields around the world in order to create multidisciplinary synergies to increase the chance of producing breakthrough innovations (Muller et al., 2013).

3 Conclusion

Equity crowdfunding is not only a financial innovation, many other aspects such as risk mitigation, marketing tools, social community, investor and non-investor participation are the "ingredients" that interact with the environment and the financial sphere in order to make it an innovative and promising model.

Looking solely at the financial innovation is limiting and does not represent the reality. In fact, as described above the financial part is just a small part of the phenomenon and in some cases, projects initiators are more interested in looking for other aspects such as involving the investor, searching for key co-operators, democratising entry and mitigating social discriminations and bias, validating the market, mitigating the risk, networking and stimulating innovation rather than the purely financial aspect.

[4] There is a trade-off between the number of shareholders and the commitment to promotion. The greater the dilution of ownership, the lower the commitment to promoting the product, because the direct benefit is lower. Vice versa, the lesser the dilution of ownership, the higher the commitment to promotion, which also leads to lesser exploitation of the network due to less investors. There is a mid-point at which the promotion benefit will be maximised.

The innovative aspects of equity crowdfunding lie in the interaction of the financial sphere with the social one, which is why equity crowdfunding should be considered as multilevel innovation combing different spheres in the same model.

Crowdfunding stimulates innovative projects due to its interactive nature and at the same time it is using innovation to fill the financial gap that traditional financial systems are unable to.

The novelty, the high risk rate and the lack of collateral drastically reduce the propensity of traditional financing actors to invest in innovative and high-tech projects. The intrinsic characteristics of equity crowdfunding as a stimulator of innovation and the financial shortage of innovative ideas/firms will definitively raise the chance of an even stronger relationship with innovation in the future. This has already happened in the Italian case that has expressly regulated equity crowdfunding solely for innovative start-ups (Paglietti, 2013; Pais & Castrataro, 2012).

The link between equity crowdfunding and innovation is a promising starting point for future empirical academic research.

References

Agrawal, A., Catalini, C., & Goldfarb, A. (2011). *Friends, family and the flat world: The geography of crowdfunding* (NET Institute Report). Retrieved from https://www.law.northwestern.edu/research-faculty/searlecenter/workingpapers/documents/AgrawalCataliniGoldfarb.pdf

Berger, A. N., & Udell, G. F. (1998). The economics of small business finance: The role of private equity and debt markets in the financial growth cycle. *Journal of Banking and Finance, 22* (6–8), 613–673.

Blanding, M. (2013, July). Crowdfunding a poor investment? *Harvard Business School, Research and Ideas*. Retrieved from http://hbswk.hbs.edu/item/7249.html

Crowdsourcing.org. (2012). *Crowdfunding industry report: Market trends, composition and crowdfunding platforms*. Retrieved from http://www.crowdfunding.nl/wp-content/uploads/2012/05/92834651-Massolution-abridged-Crowd-Funding-Industry-Report1.pdf

Cumming, D. (2012). *The Oxford handbook of entrepreneurial finance*. New York: Oxford University Press.

Danmayr, F. (2014). *Archetypes of crowdfunding platform: A multidimensional comparison*. Wiesbaden: Springer Gabler.

De Buysere, K., Gajda, O., Kleverlaan, R., & Marom, D. (2012). *A framework for European crowdfunding*. Retrieved from http://www.europecrowdfunding.org/files/2013/06/FRAMEWORK_EU_CROWDFUNDING.pdf

De Luca, A. (2013). Accesso al capitale di rischio delle PMI innovative. *PMI, 19*(10), 31–35.

Ferryary, M., & Mark, G. (2009). The role of venture capital firms in Silicon Valley's complex innovation network. *Economy and Society, 38*(2), 326–359.

Fleming, L. (2004, September). Perfecting cross-pollination. *Harvard Business Review*. Retrieved from https://hbr.org/2004/09/perfecting-cross-pollination

Frick, W. (2013, September). Can internal crowdfunding help companies surface their best ideas? *Harvard Business Review*. Retrieved from https://hbr.org/2013/09/can-internal-crowdfunding-help-companies-surface-their-best-ideas/

Gerber, E., & Hui, J. (2013). Crowdfunding: Motivations and deterrents for participation. *ACM Transactions on Computer-Human Interaction, 20*(6). doi: 10.1145/2530540

Gerber, E., Hui, J. S., & Kuo, P. Y. (2011). *Crowdfunding: Why people are motivated to post and fund projects on crowdfunding platforms*. Retrieved from http://www.juliehui.org/wp-content/uploads/2013/04/CSCW_Crowdfunding_Final.pdf

Giudici, G., Nava, R., Lamastra, C. R., & Verecondo, C. (2012). *Crowdfunding: The new frontier for financing entrepreneurship?* (SSRN Working Paper). Retrieved from http://papers.ssrn.com/sol3/papers.cfm?abstract_id=2157429

Hewlett, S. A., Marshall, M., & Sherbin, L. (2013). How diversity can drive innovation. *Harvard Business Review*. Retrieved from https://hbr.org/2013/12/how-diversity-can-drive-innovation

Martin, T. A. (2012). *The JOBS act of 2012: Balancing fundamental securities law principles with the demands of the crowd*. Retrieved from https://web.law.columbia.edu/sites/default/files/microsites/capital-markets/files/JOBS%20Act%20Fundamental.pdf

Mollick, E. (2013). *Swept away by the crowd? Crowdfunding, venture capital, and the selection of entrepreneurs*. Retrieved from https://www.business.utah.edu/sites/default/files/media/mollick_swept_away_byu_utah3-5.pdf

Muller, M., Geyer, W., Soule, T., Daniells, S., & Cheng, L.-T. (2013). Crowdfunding inside the enterprise: Employee-initiatives for innovation and collaboration. In *Proceedings of the SIGCHI Conference on Human Factors in Computing Systems* (pp. 503–512).

Ordanini, A., Miceli, L., Pizzetti, M., & Parasuraman, A. (2011). Crowdfunding: Transforming customers into investors through innovative service platforms. *Journal of Service Management, 22*(4), 443–470.

Paglietti, G. (2013). Il Regolamento sull'equity crowdfunding. *Dossier del Consorzio camerale per il credito e la finanza, 4*(4), 1–18.

Pais, I., & Castrataro, D. (2012). *Analisi delle Piattaforme di Crowdfunding Italiane*. Retrieved from http://www.consorziocamerale.eu/writable/documenti/DOC_20130424091055.pdf

Sorenson, O., & Stuart, T. E. (2008). The evolution of venture capital investment networks. *Administrative Science Quarterly*.

Surowiecki, J. (2005). *The wisdom of the crowd*. New York: Anchor Books.

Vogel, P., & Fischler-Strasak, U. (2014). Fostering sustainable innovation inside organizations by adopting entrepreneurial ecosystems. In C. Weidinger, F. Fischler, & R. Schmidpeter (Eds.), *Sustainable entrepreneurship: Business success through sustanability (CSR, sustainability, ethics and governance)* (pp. 191–205). Berlin: Springer.

Part IV
Selected Case Studies on Crowdfunding Practice

The *Crowdpower 2.0* Concept: An Integrated Approach to Innovation That Goes Beyond Crowdfunding

Reinhard Willfort and Conny Weber

Abstract Many entrepreneurs or small and medium-sized enterprises (SMEs) are really dynamic, highly innovative and willing to bear the risk of innovative projects. However, a bottleneck for realising such projects is often both the lack of support from relevant know-how (could be solved by crowdsourcing), and risk capital (could be provided by crowdfunding). After introducing some aspects of innovation the *crowdpower 2.0 concept* will be explained, and insights and best practices of practical experience in Austria of a crowdsourcing and a crowdfunding platform will be presented. The overall aim of the *crowdpower 2.0 concept* is to foster the evolution of a new ecosystem for innovative SMEs and entrepreneurs by combining open innovation approaches with the latest crowd technologies.

Keywords Innovation management • Crowdsourcing • Crowdfunding platform • Austria

1 Introduction

In the last few years crowdfunding has become a promising tool for leveraging funds not only for private projects, public organisations or start-ups, but also for established organisations. Besides the acquisition of financial resources, crowd-related activities offer several added values regarding innovation aspects and risk management.

The objective of the *crowdpower 2.0 concept* is to take advantage of these added values by systematically exploiting open innovation concepts such as crowdsourcing and crowdfunding in order to engage the crowd to develop and realise sustainable innovations. Independently of the organisation or project type, the crowd is activated throughout the whole innovation management process (Fig. 1). In the early stages of the innovation process, such as the idea-finding phase, the *crowdpower 2.0 concept* allows for example the management of crowdsourcing campaigns by inviting a wide target group to submit their ideas in

R. Willfort • C. Weber (✉)
ISN – Innovation Service Network GmbH, Graz, Austria
e-mail: conny.weber@innovation.at

D. Brüntje, O. Gajda (eds.), *Crowdfunding in Europe*, FGF Studies in Small Business and Entrepreneurship, DOI 10.1007/978-3-319-18017-5_15

Fig. 1 The innovation management process. *Source*: Author's own elaboration

response to a defined challenge, to provide feedback on project ideas, or to vote for the best ones. Ideas that have been evaluated successfully in the first phase are further supported for promotion on an appropriate crowdfunding platform. Thus, the realisation of a collaboratively developed new project, product or service is supported by the crowd both by gathering the relevant know-how and raising funds.

From a management perspective, the *crowdpower 2.0 concept* can be seen as an innovation management tool, which involves the crowd in all phases of innovation. In doing so, the most important aspects are to make use of crowd evaluation principles and to receive early feedback from the crowd, and thus to minimise the innovation risk and leverage market success.

2 Crowd Innovation Basics

The need for innovation is obvious, as the lifetime of new products and services is steadily getting shorter, and increased competition forces the founders of ventures or companies to surprise their customers with new products and services. Innovation management aims to systematically implement innovation in organisations. More specifically, innovation management focuses on how to derive profitable products and services from creative outputs within an organisation. Innovation management has significantly changed, especially with respect to approaches for supporting the innovation process and gathering ideas from outside the organisation. With the advent of Web 2.0 these approaches have become increasingly computer-based while enabling access to large user communities. This phenomenon is summarised under the term open innovation (Chesbrough, 2003) and goes one step further by including external resources, i.e. stakeholders, end-users or communities in the innovation process. According to Chesbrough (2003, p. 24) open innovation "is a paradigm that assumes that firms can and should use external ideas as well as internal ideas, and internal and external paths to market, as the firms look to advance their technology". Even more precise is the term crowdsourcing, which was coined in 2006 by Jeff Howe, and describes an organisation leveraging the power of crowds for generating and assessing new ideas as well as for developing and marketing new products and services.

Crowdfunding is a special form of crowdsourcing. The idea of crowdfunding is to collect many small amounts from a community in order to support and realise a certain project, thereby to provide a new dimension of venture capital financing. Similar to crowdsourcing, all stakeholders interested in a project idea can support the realisation of the project with their funds. Recognition of the funders ranges from a "thank you" to a prize or other rewards.

In a nutshell, crowdfunding is when *co-thinking* micro-investors provide small amounts for big ideas. Combined with the intelligent use of *crowd-technologies*, crowdfunding shapes new ways of entrepreneurship. The difference from traditional ways of financing such as credits or individual investors is mainly that a larger group of investors raises smaller amounts to realise a project. By spreading the investments across different projects the risk for an individual investor is lower, and investors can build up a portfolio with different crowdfunding allocations. The necessity of alternative ways of financing is obvious due to the hard restrictions of many banks caused by the ailing financial system.

A new stage of crowdfunding has been reached with the phenomenon of equity-based crowdfunding, called crowdinvesting for short. This form of crowdfunding is very interesting as it delivers financial returns on investments. While crowdfunding is frequently used for financing smaller projects in the culture and arts scene, crowdinvesting additionally provides equity financing for the innovation projects of small and medium sized enterprises (SMEs) or start-ups.

3 The Crowdpower 2.0 Concept

The *crowdpower 2.0 concept* (Fig. 2) presented in this Section describes a theoretical framework supporting the innovation process for crowdfunding projects. A traditional innovation process (see Fig. 1) starts with the (creative) finding of ideas, evaluating these ideas, realising an idea i.e. a new product or service, and finally marketing the idea. Basically, the *crowdpower 2.0 concept* also follows this process; however, it includes the "wisdom of crowds" (Surowiecki, 2005) in all stages.

In the first crowdcreativity phase an organisation, entrepreneur or any other individual can describe a challenge and start an open ideas contest for gathering ideas from the crowd. In the next step, these ideas are evaluated and commented on by the community. This community is open to anyone and consists ideally of very heterogeneous individuals, including creatives, potential stakeholders, and experts

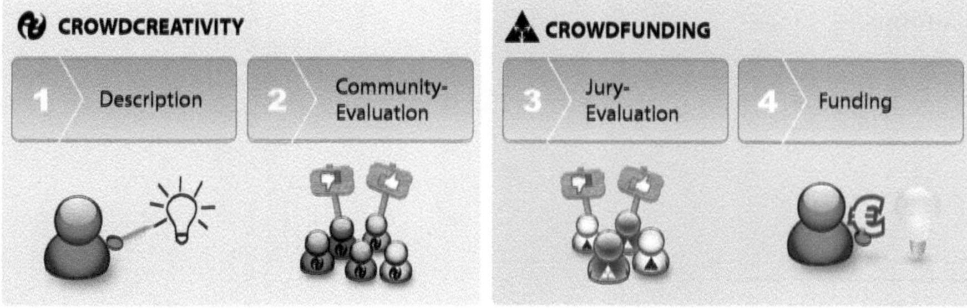

Fig. 2 The crowdpower 2.0 concept. *Source*: Author's own elaboration

on selected topics. The aim of the crowdcreativity phase is to take advantage of a network consisting of *co-thinkers*, creatives, entrepreneurs and organisations that collaboratively submits ideas, evaluates the ideas, and shapes them into a final concept for a new product, service or start-up. Thus, entrepreneurs or SMEs can collect feedback and reduce the innovation risk at a very early stage, and at the same time leverage the chance for a successful crowdfunding or marketing campaign.

The second crowdfunding phase aims to support the realisation of a promising project idea by providing both the know-how of experienced innovation experts, investors and multipliers, and financial support. Within this phase, a jury, e.g. from a crowdfunding platform, selects the most promising ideas from the crowdcreativity phase and supports the entrepreneur to promote it on an appropriate crowdfunding platform. Crowdfunding provides a valuable means for the realisation of projects; however factors associated with success and failure among crowdfunded projects are very diverse and may depend not only on the project's quality, but also, for example on the number of friends in social networks, geographical aspects, the duration, domain or the funding goal etc. (for details refer to Mollick, 2014).

The *crowdpower 2.0 concept* proposes a tool for increasing the quality of a project through early crowd involvement. This may be a relevant success factor for a crowdfunding campaign. The concept supports the idea-finding and evaluation phase by involving the crowd, and supports the idea-realisation phase by involving potential investors. Finally, the best marketing for innovations is to involve the users in the innovation process and to encourage them to actively communicate the idea and to contribute in terms of ideas or financial support.

4 Crowdpower 2.0 in Practice

A pilot of the *crowdpower 2.0 concept* has been initiated in Austria by interlinking a crowdsourcing and a crowdfunding platform. In the following, these two initiatives, which support the *crowdpower 2.0 concept* are briefly presented. The crowdcreativity phase (see Fig. 2) is covered by the Neurovation[1] platform, an open innovation and idea management platform. For supporting the crowdfunding phase (see Fig. 2) the 1000x1000[2] platform has been developed. Future development plans foresee the continuous strengthening of the relationship between these platforms.

---

[1] www.neurovation.net

[2] www.1000x1000.at

4.1 An Example of a Crowdsourcing Platform Supporting the Crowdcreativity Phase

The open innovation and idea platform Neurovation is a result of a research project aimed at enhancing creativity in the workplace, and supports the collaborative idea finding and evaluation process (Willfort, Tochtermann, & Neubauer, 2007). Neurovation is closely linked to the crowdfunding platform www.1000x1000.at, i.e. ideas for projects to be crowdfunded are first evaluated by a community and jury. Besides Neurovation.net, there are similar German platforms supporting early stages of an innovation process e.g. Hyve[3] and Atizo,[4] however these platforms are not linked to crowdfunding.

At Neurovation, any organisation or individual can post a challenge and start an open idea-finding contest with the community or only a selected group. At the same time, anyone who has an idea can submit it here, can contribute to idea contests or start a first market test in the form of a community assessment. The aim of this platform is to take advantage of the *wisdom of crowds* and to receive new ideas, improve existing ones, validate and select ideas, or get feedback on a new product or service. The most promising ideas are evaluated by community voting and are invited to submit further documents, such as a business plan. After this detailed assessment of the concept, the final selection is made by an expert jury, e.g. from the www.1000x1000.at platform, who examine the idea and select the most promising projects from the evaluated ideas. The individual steps of the crowdcreativity process supported by the Neurovation platform are depicted in Fig. 3.

Currently, the platform counts a community with more than 6,000 users who actively contribute to open-innovation challenges, submit ideas and vote for ideas. Since the platform went online in 2010, approximately 60 crowdsourcing contests took place online, ranging from a logo contest for an e-mobility platform, to an idea

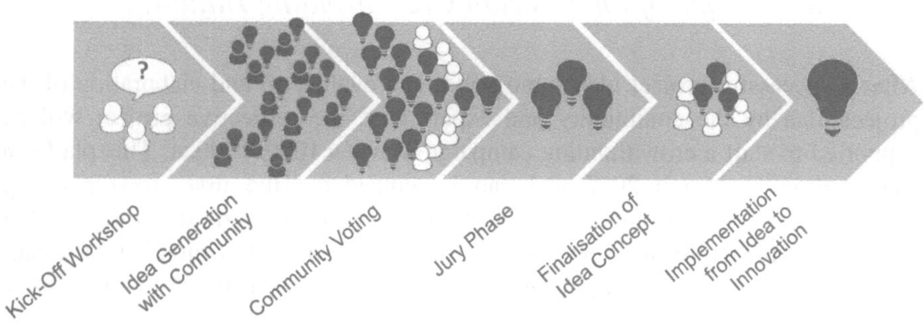

Fig. 3 The crowdcreativity process supported by Neurovation. *Source*: Author's own elaboration

[3] www.hyve.de

[4] www.atizo.com

Fig. 4 Screenshot showing some ideas for crowdfunding on Neurovation

contest for innovative services for a library, to design proposals for a wooden bench, etc. The duration of the different phases varies between 6–8 weeks for the idea finding and submission phase, and 2–4 weeks for the community evaluation phase. On average 60 ideas are submitted to a crowdsourcing challenge, however the quantity varies from 20 ideas up to 300. Since the beginning of 2014, one idea contest is dedicated to idea proposals for crowdfunding campaigns (Fig. 4). Entrepreneurs or SMEs can sketch out their ideas and receive feedback from the community. By the end of 2014, the first winning project will be promoted for crowdfunding.

4.2 An Example of an Austrian Crowdfunding Initiative

After a successful project idea submission, and evaluation and elaboration of the project idea by the community and expert jury, the respective project will be supported to start a crowdfunding campaign at www.1000x1000.at. This platform went online in March 2012 and can be considered the first crowdinvesting platform in Austria. Besides the 1000x1000 platform, by mid-2014 three further crowdinvesting platforms were online in Austria, namely Greenrocket,[5] Conda,[6] and Crowdcapital.[7] All these platforms provide equity-based crowdfunding. Unlike

[5] www.greenrocket.com

[6] www.conda.at

[7] www.crowdcapital.at

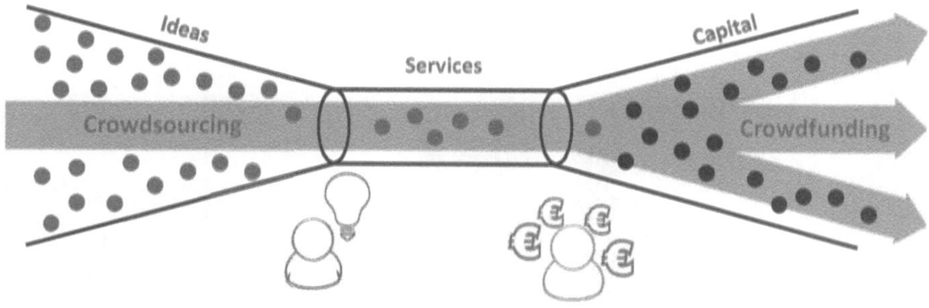

Fig. 5 The three pillars of the 1000x1000 platform. *Source*: Author's own elaboration

platforms like Kickstarter and Indiegogo, which act only in reward-based crowdfunding mode, the equity-based crowdfunding investors receive an entitlement to participate in the profits and asset value of the company. However, the invested funds are venture capital and investors lose if a project fails.

The 1000x1000 platform is based on three main pillars (Fig. 5): *ideas* for new projects or companies applying for crowdfunding. *Services,* which cover the assessment of new projects or support for realising mature ideas. And *capital,* where the basis for successful crowdfunding comes from interested investors.

Anyone who wants to be an investor on 1000x1000 must first register with the platform. Depending on the project, people can invest between 250 and 5,000 € in equity-based crowdfunding mode. Investors receive participation certificates in accordance with their investment. These certificates allow investors to participate in the annual profits of their supported company and to receive a proportionate holding in the assets of the company in the event that the company is sold. The maximum financial support a project idea can receive in Austria through crowdinvesting is limited to 250,000 € since July 2013.

Business ideas that are not suitable for crowdfunding are proposed to interested partners, usually VIP members of the 1000x1000 investor network or other partners, and thus also have the chance to get support and further funding. Business ideas that are already sufficiently developed can go straight to the jury phase. Projects are continuously selected and proposed to all investors for funding. Mostly, the project idea and the people behind it present themselves in a short video (for example Fig. 6), enriched with detailed further information about motivation, USP, business model and goal, market etc. Basically, everyone can invest in every project. However, it is not recommended to invest all one's capital in only one project. By building a portfolio of different projects the risk can be reduced significantly, as it is not likely that all projects will fail.

Fig. 6 Project presentation on the 1000x1000 platform

One of the most important aspects regarding the realisation of crowdfunding is the security aspect and transparency. Before a new crowdfunding project starts at 1000x1000, the maximum target amount and the fundraising period are defined. The investors then transfer the funds to an escrow account where the capital is held temporarily. Once the minimum amount specified by the crowdfunding project is reached, the overall investment is considered to have been successful. If the minimum amount is not reached within the specified fundraising period, all provided capital is returned to the participating investors.

The platform itself generates income by collecting a fee for acting as a broker between investors and companies. In any case, the platform operator only gets earnings for its services when the funding has been arranged successfully. Further services offered by the platform are support services for the realisation of a project by experienced innovation experts. This service takes over a part of the risk and at the same time ensures a high probability of project success.

Since the platform went online ten projects have been selected for funding out of which four have not reached the funding goal. Table 1 shows details about the projects, the funding goal, the funding amount and the number of investors.

An interesting aspect to observe in the next few years will be whether projects submitted and evaluated first by a crowdsourcing platform have better chances to succeed with crowdfunding due to their high quality, or if in the end a large number of friends on online social networks, or the geographic component (Mollick, 2014) have more effect on succeeding.

Table 1 Details on crowdfunding projects on the 1000x1000 platform

	Project	Description	Funding goal (€)	Funded (€)	Investors
1	Alm Resort Nassfeld (lending-based crowdfunding project)	Real Estate project in Carinthia	300,000	450,121	99
2	IBIOLA Mobility Solutions	Private carsharing	25,000	31,250	23
3	Neurovation GmbH	Crowdsourcing platform	50,000	75,100	84
4	Woodero GmbH	Wooden tablet cases	20,000	166,950	177
5	Schneerlebniswelt Wien	Snow park Vienna	40,000	93.601	94
6	1000x1000 Crowdbusiness GmbH	Crowdbusiness company	25,000	51,660	135
7	Darling 4 me	Mobile video dating agency	25,000 (not reached)	5,300	7
8	geschichtenbox.com	Personalised stories for children	50,000 (not reached)	12,350	16
9	Panna-KO	Street soccer	50,000 (not reached)	14,000	15
10	Das Buch-Café	Book coffee shop	50,000 (not reached)	8,350	22

5 *Crowdpower 2.0*: Best Practices

Crowdsourcing and crowdfunding can provide much added value for organisations. However, such a campaign has to be planned very carefully. Due to the rapid rise of crowdfunding, there are few guidelines in literature examining the factors for failure or success, e.g. Mollick (2014) analyses the underlying dynamics of success and failure among crowdfunded ventures based on data from Kickstarter, the largest crowdfunding site in the US. Nevertheless, when looking for a successful integrated approach to innovations, a collection of some best practices based on practical experience from crowdsourcing (neurovation.net) and crowdfunding (www.1000x1000.at) platforms, as well as from discussions with other similar platforms can be summarised as follows:

1. **Elaborate a communication and marketing plan.**
   In order to reach a wide audience and to convince them to support a project it is important to define which target group should be addressed when, and with which instruments.

2. **Establish personal communication with potential investors.**
   Primarily, investors fund the person behind an idea. Therefore, it is important to allow personal communication, e.g. by providing a phone number or visiting events for getting in touch with potential investors or allowing face to face communication.
3. **Investors are more than investors.**
   For sustainable innovation it is important to take advantage of crowd side effects. Very good personal communication allows the involvement of investors in the project. Thus, investors become multipliers, co-thinkers and partners at the same time.
4. **The team behind the idea.**
   Usually, successful start-ups are founded by more than one person, complementing each other's competences and knowledge. For successful crowd campaigns it is important to present the whole team, as heterogeneous teams promise success.
5. **Reporting the project's progress.**
   Social media allows continuous reporting of the project's progress. By involving the crowd in the discussion more people get involved in the project idea. The crowd wants to see persons moving things forward. This is supported by authentic communication, including reports about setbacks.
6. **Clear presentation of how the funds will be used.**
   A clear presentation of how the collected funds will be used is essential. It is recommended also to indicate potential for further investments, in case more funds than planned are raised.
7. **Enough time for the preparation of a crowd campaign.**
   To ensure a good preparation for telling the story and activating the crowd during the idea finding or the funding process it is important to have enough time.
8. **Crowd campaigns are a time consuming task.**
   Promoting a crowd campaign requires a very engaged team who spend much of their time in moderating the crowdsourcing or crowdfunding process, and being visible in discussions.
9. **Involve cooperation partners.**
   It is very helpful to involve further cooperation partners who support the promotion of the project idea, or are willing to further elaborate the project idea.
10. **Start the campaign by activating family, friends and fans.**
    Attracting much funding at the beginning seems to be a success indicator and motivates people who usually prefer waiting. This can be achieved by making sure that friends and families are aware of the project and support it at an early stage. Moreover, many crowd members tend to wait for a certain dynamic until they start their investment.
11. **After successful funding, stay in touch with your supporters.**
    Provide regular updates to keep your supporters informed about the realization of your project. Let people know how you proceed and highlight milestones

you have reached. This may encourage people to share it with their networks and at the same time promote your project results in advance.

However, probably the most important and interesting aspect regarding the *crowdpower 2.0 concept* presented here, i.e. the combination of crowdsourcing and crowdfunding, is provided by the fan community, consisting of the *co-thinkers* of a project, who are emotionally and personally motivated and deal in trustful relationships.

References

Chesbrough, H. W. (2003). *Open innovation. The new imperative for creating and profiting from technology*. Boston: Harvard Business School Press.

Howe, J. (2006, July). The rise of crowdsourcing. *WIRED 14.06*. Retrieved from http://archive.wired.com/wired/archive/14.06/crowds.html

Mollick, E. (2014). The dynamics of crowdfunding: An exploratory study. *Journal of Business Venturing, 29*(2014), 1–16.

Surowiecki, J. (2005). *The wisdom of crowds*. New York: Anchor Books.

Willfort, R., Tochtermann, K., & Neubauer, A. (2007). *Creativity@Work für Wissensarbeit. Kreative Höchstleistungen am Wissensarbeitsplatz auf Basis neuester Erkenntnisse der Gehirnforschung*. Aachen: Shaker Verlag.

Crowdfunding of a Social Enterprise: The GloW Project as a Case Study

Radha D. Banhatti

Abstract Crowdfunding (CF) is emerging as a fairly potent tool of civil society by providing an alternative mode of financing outside traditional and formal systems for creative and innovative projects. In this article, the focus is on using CF for financing initial phases of a social enterprise (SE). The first part begins with a brief description of the CF phenomenon and its characteristics. Then, the positioning of CF in the context of traditional financing is discussed. Further, various factors that make CF a particularly relevant tool for providing the much needed start-up capital for an SE are enumerated. The first part ends with a short discussion on current regulatory issues for the CF industry in Germany and its implications for SEs. In the second part, a case study of the recently concluded CF campaign of the "GloW project" is taken up. This is a pilot phase of an SE called GloW Energy. The vision and the business model of this SE, which aims to pre-assemble energy-saving stoves locally and supply them to well-identified partners in developing countries, is presented. Details of the CF campaign and strategies employed are then given. Analysis of data from this CF campaign reveals a number of insights which are presented in detail. The positive role played by the coverage of the project both in traditional and social media is briefly discussed. Inferences from this study that indicate aspects, which might make CF a sustainable option for both SEs and the CF industry, are given.

Keywords Crowdfunding • Social enterprise • Social return on investment • SROI • Civil society

R.D. Banhatti (✉)
Department of Political Sciences, University of Muenster, Scharnhorststrasse 100, Muenster D-48151, Germany
e-mail: r_banh02@uni-muenster.de; radhadilip@gmail.com

D. Brüntje, O. Gajda (eds.), *Crowdfunding in Europe*, FGF Studies in Small Business and Entrepreneurship, DOI 10.1007/978-3-319-18017-5_16

1 Introduction

1.1 Definitions, Models and Facts

"Crowdfunding involves an open call, mostly through the Internet, for the provision of financial resources either in the form of donation or in exchange for the future product or some form of reward to support initiatives for specific purposes" (Belleflamme, Lambert, & Schwienbacher, 2014, p. 588). CF platforms enable creators to present their project, idea or concept online, enable funders to invest in projects of their choice and facilitate interaction.

Four major models are in vogue: (i) *Debt Crowdfunding:* peer-to-peer lending to individuals or companies; (ii) *Equity Crowdfunding*: both primary and secondary funding for start-ups; (iii) *Reward Crowdfunding:* funding of designs/products, services or creative projects, with a token or a real *reward* in return; (iv) *Donation Crowdfunding*: funding without expecting any returns for a social project or undertaking. Several hybrid models, which are a variation and/or a combination of these four basic models, are possible and are, indeed, in vogue (De Buysere, Gajda, Kleverlaan, & Marom, 2012; Hemer, 2011).

Although about 15 years old, CF has become operative and visible on a wide scale only in the last 5 years, and is growing explosively. Though the volume of CF in Germany was only about 200,000 € in 2012—a small fraction of the volume of bank loans—what is significant is its growth by 320 % from 2011 (Dapp, 2013). Until the third quarter of 2014, the volume of crowdfunding in Germany has risen to about 14 million euros (Für-Gründer.de, 2014). In North America, the volume was $1.6 billion in 2012, showing a 105 % rise from 2011. Global CF volume was about $5.1 billion in 2013 (Massolution, 2013).

To understand the potential and the characteristics of the crowdfunding phenomenon, a second definition from the perspective of the funder is essential: "Crowdfunding systems enable users to make investments in various types of projects and ventures, often in small amounts, outside a regulated exchange, using online social media platforms that facilitate direct interaction between investors as well as with the individual(s) raising funds" (Agrawal, Catalini, & Goldfarb, 2011, p. 3).

While the first definition gives us rather a clear indication that this innovative phenomenon might have been ushered in as an alternative to the currently prevailing overly stringent conditions in traditional financing, namely, a hierarchical decision-making process and a lack of a broader funding framework, the second definition highlights an emergence of civic participation of funders in the otherwise traditional set-up of the financing sector. Furthermore, from the second definition one can note that (i) funding is "often in small amounts", (ii) that projects are searched for actively by potential funders on online social media or directly on crowdfunding platforms, and (iii) that there is a keen interest in direct interaction.

1.2 *Crowdfunding and Traditional Financing*

It is reasonable to assume that in the early days, as societies emerged, offline CF would have been an ever-present phenomenon across all cultures and communities. Resources were readily shared since progress and common conveniences were a priority. However, as the structural set-up of societies and their governance hierarchies began slowly emerging, followed by the concrete value attached to money, any funding might have been viewed as a donation, sponsorship, an investment or a loan, and informal crowdfunding became a minor component of the bigger picture of financing. Thus, from the tenth to the eighteenth century, rulers and rich patrons were the major funders of many human endeavours in the field of trade and exploration, science and technology, and various kinds of arts.

The formal banking system was established in Siena, Italy around the mid-twelfth century. The central banking system began with the bank charter in 1844 (Hoggson, 1926). It was in the nineteenth and twentieth centuries that banking institutions grew in stature and power (Grossman, 2010) and made access to funding and investment even more formal and regulated. In the last three decades, many proposed new and small and medium-sized enterprises (SMEs) have been subject to stringent rules and have had difficulties in overcoming the barriers stipulated by the banks for funding.

SMEs typically require funding below the 100,000 € limit for their project or enterprise. Bank and credit institutions would be one possibility. However, in the case that a much smaller volume of credit is needed, for example, less than 30,000 €, bank credits are unattractive as their administrative costs are high. Further, they require a detailed risk-analysis (SWOT) and a guarantee for the credit sum. Venture capital is an alternative avenue of funding, but this has been on a fairly steady decline in the last decade in Germany due to crisis in the periphery of the euro zone, and economic slowdown. A recent report states that German start-ups received only 2 billion euros ($2.2 billion) in venture capital in the past three years, against 64 billion euros for US companies (Ernst & Young, 2014). Furthermore, companies engaged in information and telecommunication technology or life sciences stand a higher chance of their endeavour being funded by venture capital in comparison to others. In addition, statistics show that venture capital is more widely used in financing companies in their secondary stages (Dapp, 2013). In contrast, 'business angels' (individual investors) stake their capital and acquire equities in start-ups looking for finances, also providing networking or other strategies needed for the growth of the company they now have a stake in. Microfinancing, which is a real option for alternative financing in developing countries, has not really caught on in Germany. Thus, SMEs and SEs do not always have easy and promising financing possibilities available.

Returning to the chronology of the earlier paragraph, two major sets of events unfolded in the first decade of the twenty-first century. *The first was a negative but high-impact event:* the financial crisis in 2008 whose repercussions were felt up until 2012 as worldwide negative economic growth and resulted in the increased disillusionment of individuals with the banking system. The Occupy movement of

2011 is a social manifestation of this frustration, voicing wider concerns about social and economic inequality resulting from the global financial system (Chomsky, 2012). Secondly, the advent of the World Wide Web in the 1990s, which facilitated and enabled the individual to connect and communicate via blogs and social media, *led to the emergence of the individual as an active prosumer* (Toffler, 1980) rather than the passive role of a consumer.

Online CF, since the time was ripe, thus emerged tentatively around the turn of the twenty-first century, and during its gestation period was reasonably successful in financing artistic projects (film production, music/dance shows for social benefits etc.) by way of normal online fundraising channels or on crowdfunding platforms (CF-early campaigns, 1997). However, it shows signs of establishing itself as a stable phenomenon, as evidenced by its explosive growth in the last 15 years. CF is thus starting to be used as a source of financing for mainstream markets as well as for social projects and creative enterprises.

1.3 Crowdfunding: A New Hope for Social Enterprises

A social enterprise (SE) is an undertaking with a social or environmental mission as its primary goal, with profit having a lower rank and value than the success, effectiveness and impact of the mission itself. SEs usually start projects or a business in areas which are of public importance, areas where governments and their public policies have been inadequate and where markets/industries operate only with short-term gain or profit as their aim (Dart, 2004).

While SEs do aim to become self-sufficient and sustainable in the long run, they are more often focussed on their aims and visions rather than on astute planning and management. When it comes to being a candidate for funding, SEs present peculiarities for the traditional financing world—their entrepreneurs often have a non-business background, their aims and visions are not supported sufficiently by a promise of effective management, their communication is not easily understood by financiers or their intermediaries and their resolve to become financially sustainable is not backed with a knowledge of cash-flow liquidity, of long-term financial return or of planning and forecasting (Lehner, 2013). In short, for traditional financiers, it is not an easy task to see how their expected Return on Investment (ROI) ensues from a projected Social Return on Investment (SROI) offered by the proposed social venture.

The other option open to SEs is to seek the backing of business angels, social-business investors or large companies which are prepared to fund a particular SE because it might boost their Corporate Social Responsibility image (Baron, 2007; Cornelius, Todres, Janjuha-Jivraj, Woods, & Wallace, 2008). Normal avenues of donations or public grants are getting increasingly competitive, and hence it is not always easy for an SE to get a piece of that pie. With this backdrop and with the concise basis established in the earlier two Subsections, we are in a position to enumerate those factors of CF which are attractive, relevant and favourable for SE:

i. *Funders are not passive individuals or mere donors*, since they actively search out projects which match their interest and fund only those which they feel have a greater chance of making an impact (social projects or enterprises). Thus CF and SE, both being democratic per se, should be well-matched.
ii. In CF *funding is based on trust* (Dapp, 2013). The funding follows from the crowd when their interests are awakened in a particular project or an idea without it having been verified for its viability elsewhere. Also, funders being many and contributions being small amounts, the high stakes for returns expected by venture capitalists or business angels becomes a non-issue.
iii. CF *empowers the people* to choose or reject a creative idea for itself. To quote one of the founders of the crowdfunding platform Indiegogo, "the meritocracy and relevancy of a project has no central assessing unit" (Ringelmann, 2013).
iv. *The ease and transparency* offered by CF in contrast to the formidable and obscure formalities of traditional funding add to a general motivation to the human impulse to actively participate for a cause or change.
v. Most importantly, *the individual can comfortably change his/her role*. He or she can be a creator, co-creator, funder or an observer or supporter of any project. This unrestrictive freedom facilitated by CF makes the individual active and engaged in local and global projects, thereby making him/her a true part of civil society.

1.4 Regulations of CF Industry Favourable for SEs

Whether for commercial or social projects, CF, apart from functioning as a revolutionary/innovative phenomenon, also needs to be a sustainable one. The dynamics of the CF industry is not only dependent on the role played by individuals who participate in crowdfunding as a creator or funder, but also on the role played by the CF platforms themselves. Of the hundreds of CF platforms that are available, only a minority are run by professional undertakings, the majority being the passionate work of enthusiastic and able amateurs (Gajda, Personal Communication, 2013). Further, the role played by the financial instruments of the state and the regulations placed by them on these platforms are crucial for enabling the industry to grow [e.g. for an overview of regulations and restrictions in the German context see Müller-Schmale (2014)]. Given that it can be a win-win situation for all, everything depends on how proper and effective the self- and enforced regulatory measures are. Such measures are usually a joint undertaking between the state and the CF industry, typically mediated by a third-sector (non-profit) organisation. This role is being played by the European Crowdfunding Network (ECN, 2014), which is a voluntary standard-setting association for CF platform members and is an effective partner in dialogue with the regulatory body of the EU. In this context, they are championing the cause of this industry for long-term stability.

In the European context, regulations are in their initial stages, especially as the volume of CF is not yet close to the threshold where special regulations are needed (Dapp, 2013). However, in October 2012, a framework for crowdfunding (De Buysere et al., 2012) was published as a position and white paper by the

ECN. Recently, a CF regulation in selected EU countries (Aschenbeck-Florange et al., 2013), as well as an exhaustive review of CF regulations comprising interpretations of existing regulations in Europe, North America and Israel have also been compiled (Tax and Legal Working Group of ECN, 2013). *One positive aspect of the above is that social projects and social enterprises are and will be least affected by various regulatory processes.* However, if additional EU regulations are superimposed on national level regulations, it might cripple the commercial CF industry (Aschenbeck-Florange et al., 2013). What is of current relevance is that as late as in the third week of April 2015, the German government adopted a new CF law for the equity model, which (according to CF industry struck the right balance) while protecting small investors (1,000 €, or up to 10,000 € if they have assets to cover for losses, if any) from risks, at the same time supports innovative start-ups–for example has relaxed the limit where no prospectus is needed to up to 2.5 billion euros, and allowed advertising on social media and networks, if factors of risks are adequately mentioned (Nienaber, 2015).

Thus, the prognosis that CF can and will be used for funding SEs is quite good. In the following, we use a simple case study to explore how CF works in practice for an SE.

2 The GloW Project and Crowdfunding

We chose the example of a pilot phase, namely the GloW project, of an SE called GloW Energy which needed financing. *The motivation for starting this SE came from two of the four entrepreneurs* during a year of social work in Africa. They had discovered an unaddressed requirement in the project that they were involved in, and on return to Germany for their studies, they evolved a way to address it. Thus, along with two other students, they planned and launched the pilot phase of their SE. Further, the *mission* of this SE addresses both socioeconomic and environmental aspects. The *modus operandi*of this venture is: "*act locally, yet reach out globally*". The entrepreneurs also developed a solid business strategy before starting a CF campaign. Thus, it is a visionary and a young SE in every sense of the word. All these aspects influenced our choice of a suitable CF campaign of an SE for a detailed case study. Details of the GloW project are presented below.

2.1 The GloW Project

The GloW project is the *pilot phase* of an upcoming SE, in which energy-saving stoves will be pre-fabricated here in Germany and distributed through the organisation Joint Energy and Environmental Projects (JEEP) in Uganda (and later in many developing countries) as a simple-to-assemble set.

The GloW project covers two issues simultaneously: *energy and utility* (GloW Energy, 2014a). Its three main features are efficiency, sustainability and lower emission.

The project is *innovative* since it integrates two techniques in one: the stove has charcoal in the bottom chamber; the upper chamber has wood, which is tightly packed, and it functions as a micro-gasifier. When the stove is lit, the fire goes below; air circulation is reduced and gasification starts. This gasification allows a more efficient combustion compared to a conventional fire and additionally it produces charcoal and *low emissions* instead of ash and a lot of smoke.

The stove is *efficient*, since the cooking time, air pollution and toxic effects for the person who does the cooking are minimised. In addition, the stove is environmentally friendly, since wood is converted to coal, which can either be recycled or becomes *terra preta*—a fertile soil form.

Another attractive feature of the project is that it is *sustainable*. The energy-saving stove is sold as an assembly set for the masses in various developing countries. The SE wishes to do the pre-fabrication in Germany, for which they will use an existing workforce or create one, and at the same time, create job opportunities for the assemblers and distributors of the stoves in the country of distribution, as well as encourage the buying and selling of recycled coal/soil for future use.

There is also a *transfer of technology*, although the high-technology aspect is retained in Germany, as partner countries are given an insight into this while only being required to use basic (and hence cost-effective) technology. Thus, the GloW value chain is both technically and business strategy wise, well-placed. The technical innovation has also been recognized by grant of a research patent by University of Kassel, Germany.

This project is the brain child of a team of four young graduate students. When they started the SE and realized the crowdfunding campaign, three were students at the University of Kassel and the fourth was a student at the University of Leipzig. Detailed information about them and how and why they came up with this idea and how they took it forward can be found on the GloW project website (GloW Energy, 2014a).

2.2 *Crowdfunding of the GloW Project*

For the pilot phase, the team wished to raise money for the building of 100 assembled sets and for shipping them to Uganda, where they would then be handed over to the JEEP Organisation. No sale of these stoves is planned in the pilot phase as the focus is to set the chain in motion and have reliable partnerships. Instead of either bootstrapping or borrowing, or seeking business angels, the team decided to use CF. The strategies for the CF project are reviewed below:

1. **Choice of a CF platform**. Normally, creators need to deliberate on the transaction modalities and fee structure, which depends on the model ("keep what you collect" or "all-or-nothing") supported by the platforms; they also need to review the kind of interaction allowed between the creators and funders by the

CF platforms, and choose one which best suits their enterprise. However, three of the four-member team of the GloW project had the advantage that their parent university supports entrepreneurs in dealing with various issues and offered not only support in strategy planning, but also recommended the university's CF platform Unikat Crowdfunding (2015) which is appended to the German crowdfunding platform Startnext. Hence, they did not give this aspect any further thought.

2. **Video presentation of the venture**. The team presented their project as a 2 minute video on Unikat Crowdfunding (GloW Energy, 2014b). The video was shot by the team with the help of two art students from their parent university. In the first minute of the video one gets to see all the four members of the team, each introducing themselves, saying what inspired them to start this SE and clearly stating the roles they have assigned for themselves in the SE. In the next 40 seconds, we see the product—the prototype of the energy-saving stove, a description of the innovation that they made in Kassel, the demand for such stoves in Uganda in general, and how they would conduct their SE. *One sees not only the viability and market demand of the product, but also the business strategy that would make this enterprise sustainable and the innovation scalable*. In the last 20 seconds, the request for funding for the pilot phase is made by two members of the team.
3. **Target sum and time**. The CF campaign ran from the middle of the 8th week of 2014 (20 February) until end of the 20th week of 2014 (18 May), spanning a period of about 90 days which is a fairly typical time span for a CF campaign. The target sum was fixed at a modest sum of about 10,000 €, which would *only* cover the material, assembly and shipping costs of the 100 assembled sets as well as the purchase and shipping of low-technology equipment (such as hammers and spanners) which would be made available at the distribution centre in Uganda. *Restricting the* CF *campaign to cover just these costs and avoiding asking for additional working capital was a tough decision made by the creators, but it was an astute business strategy as it inculcates trust*. Funders know that each cent of the sum they donate goes towards getting the project and its value chain on its feet.
4. **Choice of a CF model best-suited to their venture**. An interesting aspect of this CF campaign was the strategy employed. It was a typical *reward or donation model, but with an incremental increase of rewards in return for the money contributed*. One was allowed to contribute any amount from 1 € to 2,500 €, and receive suitable rewards in return; or the funder could state that the contribution is a pure donation. A complete list of these rewards is available in Table 1 and also on the Unikat CF platform.
5. **Maintenance of interaction on various online social network pages**. The GloW project team naturally also set up *various forums for online interactions*. On their own website, they had (i) three short, concise write-ups about GloW, (ii) a team description (where each of the members was accessible through their Facebook and Xing profiles, and one of them also on Twitter, as well as via e-mail), (iii) Frequently Asked Questions (FAQs) and (iv) blogs (which gave

Table 1 Range of contributions and rewards announced on the Unikat CF platform

Amount in euros	Rewards	Upper limit for number of sponsors
1	The GloW team thanks you for your kindness	
5	Thanks with your name mentioned on the GloW website	
10	GloW sticker; your name mentioned on the GloW website	1,000
20	Easter special key chain made of the prototype material used for the stove; your photo and name on the GloW website	20
50	Gift from Uganda; your name mentioned on the GloW website	100
100	Cookbook from Africa; your name and photo on the GloW website	
300	A GloW stove presented; your name and photo on the GloW website	
500	You are invited to participate in a workshop where a GloW stove will be put together; a social evening; a GloW stove presented; your name and photo on the GloW website	
900	A combined gift package with all above mentioned rewards	
2,500	You can work with us in naming the product; you are presented with a GloW assembly set; your name and photo on the GloW website	2

various links to articles and their own description of how the SE proposes to proceed).

The CF *project website was very informative*, containing various details about the category of the project (technology) and about target groups, the business model, actual use of the money; it also had FAQs.

Further, *the GloW project team also set up a Facebook page* (GloW Energy, 2014c) where they presented in their timeline various information on the activities and events related to the GloW project, such as entering their vision and idea in "yooweedoo Ideenwettbewerb" and Famelab event, both of which they subsequently won. These posts, prior and after the events, helped in disseminating information about various recognitions that the GloW project got. Links to articles on the GloW project as and when they appeared in print media, as well as links to videos and articles relevant to the GloW project (JEEP, UN-climate, WHO study links etc.) were provided. From the GloW Facebook page one could also learn which projects and actions other than their own the team follows and encourages, which also demonstrates networking among their age group and peers.

6. **Returns made diligently**. Rewards were carefully planned and resources were carefully allotted (see again Table 1), with a limit to the number of sponsors in some contribution ranges (indicated in the third column). This is also seen from the CF website—rewards for various categories were limited and no over-commitments were made. Currently, names and photos of all funders, who have requested it, are already published on the GloW Energy website, and rewards were delivered as promised.

2.3 Analysis of the Crowdfunding Campaign

Using the database kindly provided by the GloW project team, several interesting aspects of this CF campaign are presented below. We start by stating the essential fact that a total of 118 funders contributed a total sum of about 10,338 €.

The first aspect we look at is the *geographical distribution* of those who contributed various amounts. The funders, apart from a person from Vienna, were all from Germany. Figure 1 shows the geographical distribution of these national-level funders. Each pin mark in the figure represents the location of one funder. As we will see later (Fig. 4 and the related text), only those funders who opted for the 20 € and more (Table 1) provided a postal address. Sometimes, these funders financed more number of units in the particular range of contribution they chose. Hence, there are about 50 pin marks, although the total number of funders is 118. Contrary to what one might expect, donors and sponsors are distributed, and are not just close to Kassel.

The geographical distribution of funders, as shown in Fig. 1, is surprisingly similar to the population density of Germany. If we do not attribute to the GloW project an extra special status as an SE in comparison to various other SEs looking for start-up finance, then this similarity seems to confirm the potential of crowdfunding has in reaching out to active individuals regardless of where they may be geographically located.

Figure 2 shows *the breakdown of the contributions*. Again, we encounter features that are unique to crowdfunding. Nearly half of all contributions correspond to the higher bracket of 500–2,500 €. It is evident that the number of contributors in this regime is fewer than in other ranges. The remaining greater half can be further broken down into three roughly equal parts of 1–99 €, 100–199 € and 200–499 €. Figure 2 shows a further breakdown in the first one-sixth. The average contribution per person is 88 €. Such a high average is also typical for crowdfunding (Massolution, 2013).

What enables a CF campaign to reach its target sum and thus helps a project come alive is the possibility that funders can contribute in various ranges. While funders of the bigger contributions might evaluate the tangibility of a project before contributing, the smaller contributions can come from friends, well-wishers and the general crowd who contribute little to assist a good idea to take off. That CF allows for participation with varying motives is another reason why this phenomenon can be a sustainable one.

The following typical occurrence is a practical illustration of active searches of projects on CF portals by potential funders: In trying to access any of the bigger platforms, one will sooner or later temporarily be denied entry because the site's reloading and transaction threshold have been reached, as many potential funders are already browsing various projects on the CF portal. In Fig. 3, we consider *the collection as a function of time*. In fact, the CF campaign began in the middle of the 8th calendar week of the year and lasted until end of the 20th week. From the total sum collected, one deduces the average sum collected per week to be about 800 €.

Fig. 1 Geographical distribution of funders (own illustration)

As is to be expected, Fig. 3 shows that the variations from this average are considerable. Especially in the first phase of the CF campaign, that is, after the end of the first week's collection of about 645 €, the collection went continuously down to about 120 € at the end of the fourth week and picked up thereafter. It does not go much below 500 € in later weeks.

If the CF campaign were an isolated effort, it is possible that the definite upward turn in the graph may never have happened, leading to the possibility that the CF

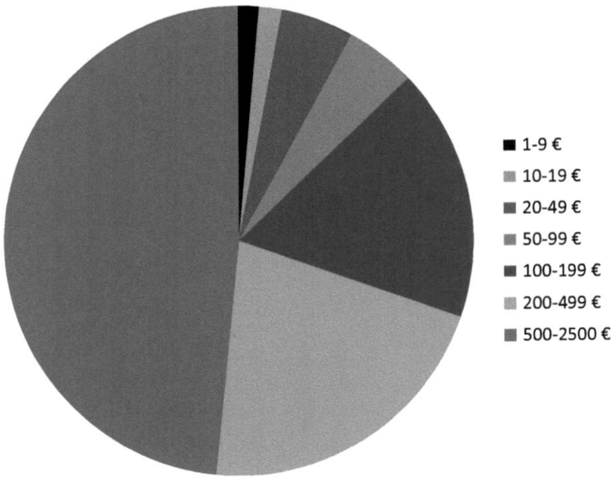

Fig. 2 Breakdown of contributed amounts

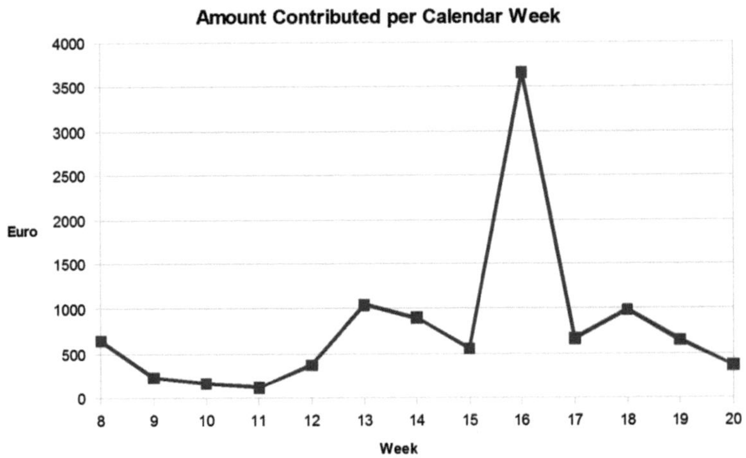

Fig. 3 Timeline of the CF campaign

campaign fails. We attribute the upward turn to the awareness generated via social media such as Facebook, Twitter and blogs.

For example, there seems to be a direct correlation between the events posted on the GloW Facebook page and the pick-up of contributions. The Facebook timeline starts in January 2014 (GloW Energy, 2014c). In mid-February, the launch of the CF campaign was also announced on Facebook. Alternative funding possibilities and competitions were announced as and when they arise. The organisation JEEP, which will be the partner NGO organisation in Uganda, was introduced. Votes for the project were sought in other competitions. The fact that the Startnext CF platform chose the GloW project as "Project of the Day" on 11 March, 2014 was also published. This was followed by promotion of the Famelab event in Kassel, videos of which were posted online immediately, and then immediately followed by the announcement that yooweedoo has chosen the GloW project for part-sponsoring of its pilot phase. At the end of the sixth week the amount collected per week went up to 1,000 €. Parallel to this, traditional print media and television and radio programmes in the states of Hesse and North Rhine-Westphalia also brought this project to the public's attention. The peak corresponds to one contribution of 2,500 € in the 9th week of the campaign (16th calendar week in Fig. 3).

Thus, throughout the entire campaign, social media played an active role in informing the fans and followers of the amounts collected and other environmentally relevant aspects of the project, and also congratulating or mentioning other recent CF projects. It is not clear what percentage of the social network followers were also funders, but this aspect is not easy to investigate. At the moment one can only assume definite and positive correlations. Another minor but important fact is that a few funders contributed more than once, probably motivated by new postings on social media and possibly by following the CF campaign and seeing the sum grow.

We now consider the next question, what drove the CF campaign to its success: *reward or donation?* The distribution of the crowd's choice of contribution is plotted versus the same breakdown ranges as in Fig. 2 and is shown in Fig. 4.

Although for the amounts in the range from 50 € to 199 € rewards and donation are comparable, it is clear that rewards were a real draw for the funders. About 68 % of all contributions fell into a reward category as per Table 1, while the remaining 32 % of contributions were free donations or were 1 € contributions. Interestingly, experiments on charitable giving, with and without gifts, for offline fundraising

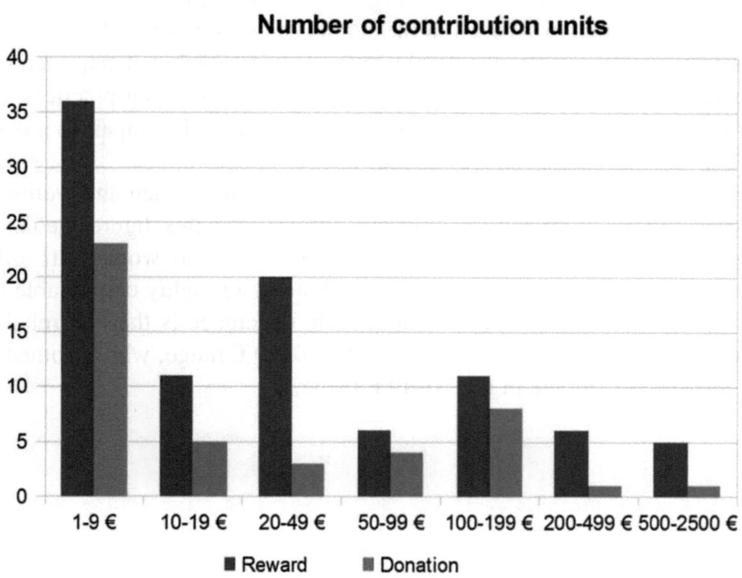

Fig. 4 Distribution of reward versus donation choice for the same breakdown ranges as in Fig. 2

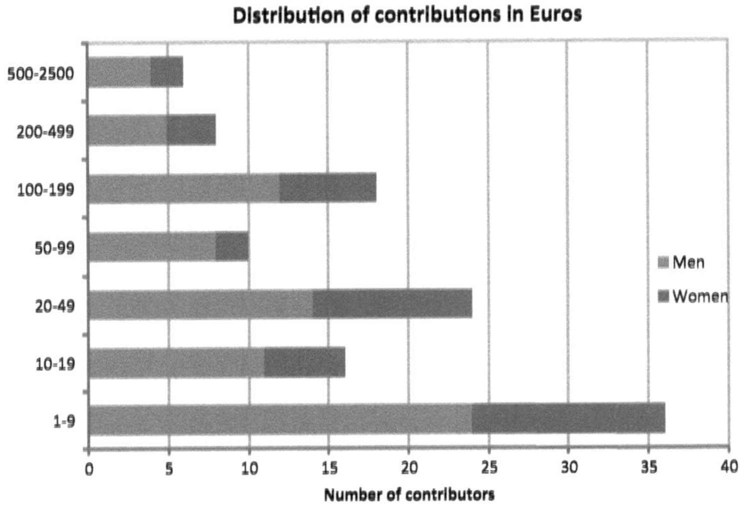

Fig. 5 Gender distribution for the breakdown ranges as in Fig. 2

have shown that offering reward triggers "crowding-out effect" of altruistic donors thereby reducing average donations (Newman & Shen, 2012). However, it is a common practice in various CF campaigns to use a combination of reward and donation models to ensure success. Although research on this aspect is yet to emerge for CF campaigns, the current study confirms its effectivity.

We next consider *the gender distribution* of the funders. Of the 118 supporters, 70 were men and 48 were women. In Fig. 5, the contribution breakdown ranges of Fig. 2 are now plotted as a function of number of contributors. The first feature is that not only overall are men the dominant funders (59 %), but also in each range of contributions. A detailed profile of funders of traditional giving practices is available (Fidelity Charitable Gift Fund, 2009). However, for CF campaigns it is still too early days for obtaining such typical profiles.

In Fig. 6, we plot the relative percentage of funding by men and women in the breakdown ranges as in Fig. 2. The new information this figure yields is that, although the total percentages of funding from men and women are different, when seen relatively, men and women contribute in a roughly comparable manner in various brackets. Of course, one noticeable difference is that the relative percentage of men contributing is greater in the 50–99 € range, while women have a higher relative percentage in the 20–49 € range.

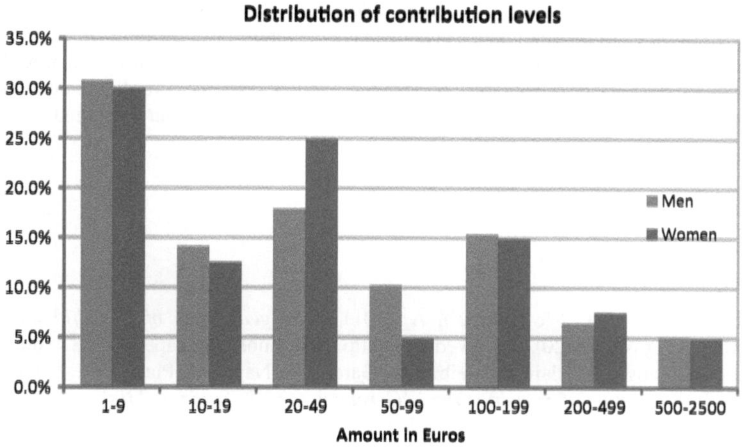

Fig. 6 Contribution from men and women in relative percentages for the breakdown ranges as in Fig. 2

3 Conclusions

We have attempted to describe in detail the relevance of crowdfunding for providing start-up capital for an SE. The study analysed the CF campaign of one representative project of such an upcoming SE, called GloW, picking out features which are interesting for academic research, social entrepreneurs and the CF industry itself.

While talking with a member of the entrepreneurial team, it emerged that since they found a good resonance from the crowd in their first attempt, next time they would take the CF campaign to an international platform and also set a higher target sum. Positive correlations between the CF campaign and engagement in social media networking seem to be clearly present. However, it may not be easy to quantify this. To do this, information needs to be specifically sought. This may not be of immediate interest to the entrepreneurs or the CF industry, but is an important aspect of academic and applied research.

German CF platforms and policy makers need to make equity crowdfunding attractive for a CF campaign by SEs. For example, following a successfully completed funding of the pilot phase of an SE project such as GloW, entrepreneurs might consider a second-phase CF campaign with equity crowdfunding. This, however, can become a possibility or a reality only if an effort is made by the SE to understand how best to match their interests with the expectation of investors. Both the CF industry and representatives of policy makers, such as ECN or other governmental finance institutions, can help in this process. This calls for an active engagement in researching the existing database for understanding various facets of the CF phenomenon.

Acknowledgements It is a pleasure to thank Alexander Raguet and Oliver Gajda who got me interested in this area of research. I also acknowledge the interest and encouragement provided by Annette Zimmer. My sincere thanks to Markus Espeter, a member of the GloW team, for his time, and for making the datasheet from the CF campaign readily available. I further thank him and the GloW Energy team for their permission to use their data for carrying out a detailed analysis.

References

Agrawal, A., Catalini, C., & Goldfarb, A. (2011). *The geography of crowdfunding* (NBER Working paper No. 16820). Retrieved from http://www.nber.org/papers/w16820.pdf

Aschenbeck-Florange, T., Blair, D., Beltran, J., Garcia, A., Nagel, T., Piatelli, U., & Quintavalla, L. (2013). *Regulation of crowdfunding in Germany, the UK, Spain and Italy and the impact of the European single market*. Retrieved from http://www.osborneclarke.com/media/filer_public/51/b3/51b3007b-73aa-4b9a-a19d-380fc1d6ff35/regulation_of_crowdfunding_ecn_oc.pdf

Baron, D. P. (2007). Corporate social responsibility and social entrepreneurship. *Journal of Economics and Management Strategy, 16*(3), 683–717.

Belleflamme, P., Lambert, T., & Schwienbacher, A. (2014). Crowdfunding: Tapping the right crowd. *Journal of Business Venturing, 29*, 585–609.

CF-early campaigns. (1997). Retrieved from i) http://artistshare.com/v4/About; ii) Golemis, D. (1997, September 23). British band's US tour is computer-generated. *Chicago Tribune*. Retrieved from http://articles.chicagotribune.com/1997-09-23/features/9709230071_1_music-fans-newsgroup-marillion; iii) Andrew, R. (1999, July 11). Filmmaker uses web to help finance, cast movie. *Chicago Tribune*. Retrieved from http://articles.chicagotribune.com/1999-06-11/features/9906110076_1_kines-investing-film

Chomsky, N. (2012). *Occupy*. New York: Penguin.

Cornelius, N., Todres, M., Janjuha-Jivraj, S., Woods, A., & Wallace, J. (2008). Corporate social responsibility and the social enterprise. *Journal of Business Ethics, 81*(2), 355–370.

Dapp, T. F. (2013). *Crowdfunding, an alternative source of funding with potential* (DB Research Report). Retrieved from http://www.dbresearch.com/PROD/DBR_INTERNET_EN-PROD/PROD0000000000303056/Crowdfunding%3A+An+alternative+source+of+funding+wit.pdf

Dart, R. (2004). The legitimacy of social enterprise. *Nonprofit Management and Leadership, 14*(4), 411–424.

De Buysere, K., Gajda, O., Kleverlaan, R., & Marom, D. (2012). *A framework for European crowdfunding*. Retrieved from http://www.eurocrowd.org/files/2013/06/FRAMEWORK_EU_CROWDFUNDING.pdf

ECN. (2014). Retrieved from http://www.eurocrowd.org

Ernst & Young. (2014). *Venture capital and start-ups in Germany 2014*. Retrieved from http://de.slideshare.net/szasz1/ernst-young-venture-capital-and-startups-in-germany-2014

Fidelity Charitable Gift Fund. (2009). *Gender differences in charitable giving 2009—Executive Summary*. Retrieved from http://www.fidelitycharitable.org/docs/Gender-Study-Executive-Summary.pdf

Für-Gründer.de. (2014). *Gesamtvolumen des durch Crowdfunding eingesammelten Kapitals in Deutschland vom 1. Quartal 2011 bis zum 3. Quartal 2014 (in Millionen Euro)*. Retrieved from http://de.statista.com/statistik/daten/studie/252385/umfrage/volumen-des-durch-crowdfunding-eingesammelten-kapitals-in-deutschland/

GloW Energy. (2014a). Retrieved from http://glow-energy.de/

GloW Energy. (2014b). *GloW—Energiesparherde als Bausatz für Entwicklungsländer*. Retrieved from https://www.startnext.de/glow-energy/

GloW Energy. (2014c). Retrieved from https://www.facebook.com/glow.nrj

Grossman, R. S. (2010). *Unsettled account: The evolution of banking in the industrialized world since 1800*. Princeton, NJ: Princeton University Press.

Hemer, J. (2011). *A snapshot on crowdfunding* (Working Papers firms and region No. R2/2011). Retrieved from http://www.isi.fraunhofer.de/isi-wAssets/docs/p/de/arbpap_unternehmen_region/ap_r2_2011.pdf

Hoggson, N. F. (1926). *Banking through the ages*. New York: Dodd, Mead and Company.

Lehner, O. M. (2013). Crowdfunding social ventures: A model and research agenda. *Venture Capital, 15*(3), 289–311. doi:10.1080/13691066.2013.782624

Massolution. (2013). *2013CF—The crowdfunding industry report*. Retrieved from http://research.crowdsourcing.org/2013cf-crowdfunding-industry-report

Müller-Schmale, V. (2014). *Crowdfunding: Supervisory requirements and investor responsibility*. Retrieved from http://www.bafin.de/SharedDocs/Veroeffentlichungen/EN/Fachartikel/2014/fa_bj_1406_crowdfunding_en.html

Newman, G. E., & Shen, Y. J. (2012). The counterintuitive effects of thank-you gifts on charitable giving. *Journal of Economic Psychology, 33*, 973–983.

Nienaber, M. (2015, April 23). Germany approves new rules to protect small investors. *Reuters*. Retrieved from http://www.reuters.com/article/2015/04/23/germany-crowdfunding-idUSL5N0XJ2JB20150423

Ringelmann, D. (2013, April 10). Why crowdfunding is world's incubation platform. *Guardian*. Retrieved from http://www.theguardian.com/media-network/media-network-blog/2013/apr/10/crowdfunding-businesses-social-projects

Tax and Legal Working Group of ECN. (2013). *Review of crowdfunding regulation. Interpretations of existing regulation concerning crowdfunding in Europe, North America and Israel*. Retrieved from http://www.eurocrowd.org/wp-content/blogs.dir/12/files/2013/12/ECN-Review-of-Crowdfunding-Regulation-2013.pdf

Toffler, A. (1980). *The third wave*. New York: Bantam Books.

Unikat Crowdfunding. (2015). Retrieved from http://www.unikat-crowdfunding.de

The Ten Commandments of Crowdfunding

Fabien Risterucci

Abstract Crowdfunding is changing the way we think about finance. It is becoming a real alternative for financing creative projects, for start-ups and as seed capital. To date, an extended number of Internet crowdfunding platforms are operational across all continents and have allowed leaders of creative, entrepreneurial and/or social projects, to raise, in aggregate, billions of euros in various forms, e.g. donations, subscriptions, equity stakes, or financial loans. The involvement of project leaders is key to the success of a crowdfunding campaign both in the crucial phase of preparation, and in the course of the campaign. However, the decision to use crowdfunding is at times problematic for potential project leaders. Limited knowledge, lack of time to dedicate to a potential campaign project or uncertainties on how to use the tool may represent barriers. Before even reaching the crucial campaign preparation phase, potential project leaders have to clearly understand the pre-requisites of the crowdfunding concept and evaluate whether it is suitable for their project, personality and interests. For that purpose, *The Ten Commandments of Crowdfunding* has been developed for potential project leaders to complete. This self-assessment approach includes essential rules to take into account when considering whether to use crowdfunding as a marketing and funding tool.

Keywords Crowdfunding • Financial innovation • Self-assessment • Recommendations • Collaborative finance • Community

1 How to Determine if Crowdfunding Matches Potential Project Leaders' Interests

Crowdfunding is increasingly becoming an alternative (Risterucci, 2013a) to project financing, due to an evangelisation effort and measures introduced by decision makers in some countries to professionalise this emerging industry.

F. Risterucci (✉)
FR Prospektiv, Paris, France
e-mail: contact@frprospektiv.com

D. Brüntje, O. Gajda (eds.), *Crowdfunding in Europe*, FGF Studies in Small Business and Entrepreneurship, DOI 10.1007/978-3-319-18017-5_17

Crowdfunding allows many financial contributors to invest small amounts in projects listed on innovative Internet platforms. These contributors then have the option of choosing the final destination of their money (creative, entrepreneurial and/or social projects) in various forms: donations or subscriptions with financial compensation or compensation in kind called "rewards" or "production" (crowdfunding), equity with stakes in the company's capital (crowdinvesting), interest-bearing personal or business loans (peer-to-peer lending), or interest-free solidarity loans (social lending). Generally speaking, the term crowdfunding is used to refer to all categories of offers presented above, and also in this paper.

Each category requires a specific positioning, so campaigns need to be adapted according to the nature of the operation (donation, reward or production, equity, lending with interest or social lending).

For equity platforms, the project needs to be attractive from a financial point of view. But beyond the financial aspect, crowdfunding is in essence a marketing operation. For donations or subscription platforms, it is the nature of the project itself that is most important. It is the same for social lending platforms, whose model is not necessarily based on the circles of supporters principle, whereby the first circle of support (family, friends, or professional acquaintances) attracts a second circle of support (friends of friends), eventually reaching a third circle of more widespread support, the "Target Group".

To be successful, the involvement of the project leader is essential (Risterucci, 2013b) when preparing the fundraising campaign. The *Crowdfunding Campaign Planification Dashboard* (Risterucci, 2014a) and the *Crowdfunding Collection Tool* (Risterucci, 2014b) have been developed by FR Prospektiv to contribute to the project leader's preparation and management of a successful crowdfunding campaign. Since this paper does not intend to demonstrate how to design a crowdfunding campaign, it will be briefly referred to without details.

This is to say that before reaching the crucial campaign preparation phase it appears that potential project leaders sometimes find it difficult to understand the pre-requisites of the concept and determine whether the use of crowdfunding is fully appropriate and acceptable in relation to their interests, capabilities and own attitude.

Limited knowledge, lack of time to dedicate to a potential campaign project or uncertainties regarding how to use the tool can sometimes impede progress.

Therefore, to facilitate the decision to use crowdfunding *The Ten Commandments of Crowdfunding,* a self-assessment approach, has been created. It is designed to be completed as a form of self-assessment, in order for the project leader to prepare and equip oneself for using crowdfunding.

The 10 recommendations have been selected by the author of this paper following an in-depth analysis of the crowdfunding ecosystem at an international level over 3 years. It has been made possible through the monitoring of the different stakeholders, meetings, publication work,[1] and support activities for entrepreneurs and platforms.

[1] For further publications refer to www.frprospektiv.com/crowdfunding-competitiveness-resources

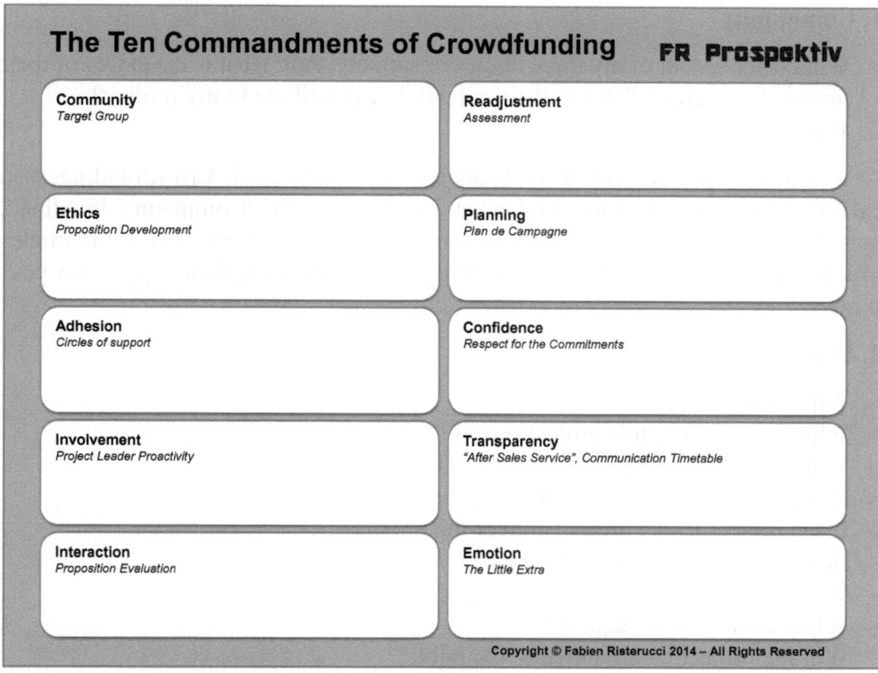

Fig. 1 The Ten Commandments of Crowdfunding. © Fabien Risterucci

Above is a table to complete (Fig. 1) of the 10 key recommendations necessary to consider in order to use crowdfunding successfully. For clarity, points are listed as single words instead of sentences, with a brief explanation in italics. Below the table, the author develops the ideas relative to each recommendation, in the form of self-assessment and an optional brief comment that should not influence the reader's personal views.

Again, since the question addressed is not about best practice in crowdfunding campaigns, there is no specific process or order for the commandments. Some pre-requisites are more fundamental than others and are therefore listed first. However, each commandment is equally important in determining the suitability of the use of crowdfunding.

2 The Self-Assessment Approach of *The Ten Commandments of Crowdfunding*

Is crowdfunding a tool within reach? Is it made for me? Is it in tune with my working philosophy? *The Ten Commandments of Crowdfunding* and the elements that should be taken into account when considering a crowdfunding campaign are explored in more detail below.

1. Community

- What is the extent of my three circles of support? And what is the extent of their financial potential? What is their potential to contribute to my project?
- What is my target group?

It is not simply an appeal for financing from the crowd. Crowdfunding, also called collaborative finance, and what I prefer to call "Community Funding", appeals more to a "Target Group" that stems from your networks, from your circles of support, which you will need to identify before soliciting their support for your project.

2. Ethics

- What is my project?
- Why am I starting this project?
- What are my values?
- Does the proposal meet an ethical promise?
- Is the project leader able to deliver the project?
- How will the funds raised be used?
- What can contributors/investors expect in return?
- Is this a reasonable request?
- Will the project be attractive to the public?

While drawing up a proposal, the project leader must ensure that the ethical dimension of the project is presented to the public. Obviously, the minimum prerequisite is that the purpose is real, fulfilling a clearly identified need. It can be difficult for the project leader to relay the project's financial or technical characteristics to members of their inner circle of supporters. They must however maintain trust and always ensure a fair approach by putting forward the unique value proposition of the project and by clearly demonstrating to potential contributors what they can specifically expect in return for their stake.

The contributors' motivation relies on their desire to give purpose to their savings or actions, as well as their desire to help project leaders or entrepreneurs with close ties to their community. Naturally, depending on the projects, the motivation of investors can also be the tax incentives that some countries offer in a crowdinvesting scenario. But this alone is not sufficient.

A project leader who does not restrict the amount of information they post online about a project, which contains a unique and particularly innovative characteristic, may be taking a risk. In contrast, it is often the case that communicating the idea can also protect it.

3. Adhesion

- Ranking supporters as: those that may or may not contribute, those that are certain to contribute, recurring contributors, small or big contributors.
- What is the extent of the support of the members of my three circles of support?
- How do I develop my community from within?

It is necessary to launch with a pre-campaign fundraising phase which also requires evaluating support for the proposal. The first points of communication are the project leaders themselves, and they attract their three circles of support through a snowball effect.

They remain active throughout the campaign process by maintaining the interest of their community of supporters, financial or otherwise. Beyond the time and resources required, the use of crowdfunding is a tremendous opportunity for the project leaders to develop a community, learn more about it and analyse it. Crowdfunding can therefore increase customer loyalty and/or help to identify new customers attracted by the products and services of the company.

During the pre-campaign phase, project leaders should take time to build the minimum community base, actively seeking out their first circle of support (family, friends, or professional acquaintances) and invite them to join the platform either to support them or to invest. The first circle in turn helps to attract the second circle of support (friends of friends), and the project leaders finally use the platform to find their third circle of more widespread support, the "Target Group".

4. Involvement

- How do I work with the first and second circles of my network to reach a significant part of the financing sought, ideally up to 20 or 30 %, before the day of the crowdfunding campaign launch?

The project leader must determine this during the crucial phase which precedes the campaign of fundraising launch. A proactive project leader is essential for success.

5. Interaction

- Evaluation of my proposal following the feedback of my contacts
- Evaluate the amount to raise from my community.
- Did I take into account the suggestions and comments received from Internet users?
- Did I analyse the projects that have been funded?
- What communication channels should I use?
- Does my network support me?

Due to a lack of time and often a lack of understanding or willingness to experiment with Internet crowdfunding platforms, many project leaders sometimes have a very imprecise vision of the segment or territory to be targeted, the profile of desired supporters or the exact amount to be raised. Project leaders can refine their criteria and their strategy by communicating with their community during the fundraising pre-campaign. Intensely testing the proposal is crucial.

6. Readjustment

- Does my proposal allow me to keep my promises to supporters?
- Is the financing goal realistic?
- Do I need to raise funds in phases?
- Have the project's costs of execution been taken into account?

It is important to understand that the terms of the offer of support for the project will not necessarily be permanent, and that they may have to be constantly readjusted. The project leader has to assess the terms and make final adjustments before publishing the project online. Through analysis and triage of the community, between those who have, for example, shown their support by simply clicking on the project page, and those who actually intend to provide the funds sought, the project leader is able to better target the specific profile of members, the territory, or even country, for a successful fundraising campaign. This commandment implies adjusting the project directly to the identified potential contributors. Such an assessment also allows the project leader to apprehend the costs associated with the execution of the fundraising and to readjust the proposal, since honouring the promise is key. The risk of not fulfilling its promise to its supporters is greater than the risk of not achieving its objective of amount raised.

7. Planning

- How and when do I communicate with the appropriate members of my circles of support?
- Did I develop a storytelling for my project?
- How do I transform manifest expressions of interest into confirmed support?
- Have I planned my fundraising goals incrementally?
- Have I planned the costs associated with the implementation of the proposal?
- What is the deadline for the release of funds by the platform?
- Should there be an additional source of funding?

Once the decision to use crowdfunding has been taken following *The Ten Commandments of Crowdfunding* assessment, the project leader enters a second phase. Preparation for success requires the establishment of a real campaign plan. Each circle of support is addressed differently, during the preparation, execution and post-campaign fundraising phases. Further literature from the author has been developed separately. The *Crowdfunding Campaign Planification Dashboard* and the *Crowdfunding Collection Tool*, by FR Prospektiv, assist the project leader in preparing and managing a successful crowdfunding campaign.

8. Confidence

- Am I really open to crowdfunding?
- Am I a communicator and responsive to the visibility provided by the Internet?
- Am I able to meet my commitments?

Confidence is at the heart of this still emerging ecosystem. It is vital and feeds on a mutual transparency of the stakeholders (project leaders, supporters, platforms). The entrepreneurial, creative, innovative and/or social project leader should be a good communicator and should act in a proactive way with the community. Any management team using crowdfunding must be open about the subject and comfortable with the visibility offered by the web. The degree of the project's maturity and the involvement of the management team are naturally a key factor in the establishment of an essential trust. A successful fundraising operation will guarantee confidence among institutional investors and can facilitate the search for additional sources of funding.

9. Transparency

- Did I develop a communication schedule with my supporters?
- Did I anticipate the presentation of how I am going to meet my commitments?
- How am I going to manage the communication about any project delays?
- Does the project have any social impact?

After the execution of the campaign, the project is actually implemented. During the post-crowdfunding phase, it is important to make sure that the contributors continue to be informed according to the schedule established beforehand. It is a question of planning the equivalent of "after-sales service". Contributors are generally curious to know how the project evolves, and are also often inclined to suggest improvements, or even to help if possible.

10. Emotion

- What attitude should I adopt as project leader?
- What is my project's "little bit extra" that makes the difference?

Crowdfunding is based on confidence, strengthened by an underlying emotion. What triggers the desire to support a project is not always rational, but sometimes subjective, due to the emotion conveyed. This commandment requires the project leader to be proactive, empathetic, confident, and communicative: to pass on their emotions to the investors. This will make the difference. This is what I call the "petit plus" or "little bit extra".

3 The Decision to Use Crowdfunding

The above development of *The Ten Commandments of Crowdfunding* explores the elements that should be taken into account when considering the use of crowdfunding.

Am I ready to be positioned within these Ten Commandments when I look at the possible use of crowdfunding to market and finance my project? Am I in tune with this approach? Did I measure the impact of my decision? These are the ultimate questions to answer.

Having assimilated the pre-requisites of the concept and determined that crowdfunding is suitable for the project leader's personality, capabilities and interests, the crowdfunding pre-campaign phase can start with the support of other specific tools developed by the author (Risterucci, 2014a, 2014b).

References

Risterucci, F. (2013a, November). Europe should facilitate the emergence of crowdfunding for a new growth model. *Le Cercle Les Echos*. Retrieved from http://www.lesechos.fr/idees-debats/cercle/cercle-78879-europe-should-facilitate-the-emergence-of-crowdfunding-for-a-new-growth-model-1018765.php

Risterucci, F. (2013b, June). Crowdfunding: comment préparer sa levée de fonds? *Dynamique Entrepreneuriale*. Retrieved from http://www.dynamique-mag.com/article/crowdfunding-preparer-levee-fonds.3934

Risterucci, F. (2014a). *Crowdfunding campaign planification dashboard*. © FR Prospektiv. Retrieved from www.frprospektiv.com

Risterucci, F. (2014b). *Crowdfunding collection tool*. © FR Prospektiv. Retrieved from www.frprospektiv.com

About the Editorial Board and the Editors

Editorial Board

Ralf Beck Ralf Beck teaches Accounting, Controlling and Finance at the University of Applied Sciences and Arts of Dortmund, whereby Crowdfinance is part of his teaching program. His research activities are focused on Crowdfinance topics.

As author of the book *Crowdinvesting—Die Investition der Vielen* he is a recognized expert in this subject in the German-speaking countries. Professor Beck appears regularly in well-known and reputable magazines (*Capital, Euro Magazin, WirtschaftsWoche*), newspapers (*Die Zeit, Süddeutsche Zeitung, Welt am Sonntag, Handelsblatt*) and on the radio (*Deutschlandfunk, SWR 1, SWR 2*). Furthermore, a sequence of an interview with him was broadcasted in TV (*WDR Markt*).

Dan Marom Dan Marom co-authored a pioneering book on crowdfunding—"The Crowdfunding Revolution" alongside Kevin Lawton. A second edition was published in 2012 by McGraw-Hill. Since then he has been fortunate to speak passionately about crowdfunding around the globe, teach students, consult entrepreneurs, corporations and policy makers (for example the World Bank and the European Commission), and hold several advisory board memberships. To these roles, Dan brings insights developed through rigorous analysis of data as part of his research work. Living in Tel Aviv, Israel, Dan holds a Ph.D. in Finance from the Hebrew University of Jerusalem, a Master in Business Administration (Cum Laude), and a Bachelor of Science in Electrical Engineering.

D. Brüntje, O. Gajda (eds.), *Crowdfunding in Europe*, FGF Studies in Small Business and Entrepreneurship, DOI 10.1007/978-3-319-18017-5

Ivana Pais Ivana Pais is assistant professor of Economic sociology at Università Cattolica del Sacro Cuore, Milan (Italy). Her research interest focuses on social networks in labour markets, organizations and entrepreneurship and investigates new ways of working in the sharing economy. She wrote a book about crowdfunding in Italy (Crowdfunding. La via collaborativa all'imprenditorialità, edited by Egea).

Ali Dardour Ali Dardour is Professor of Management Sciences at KEDGE Business School Bordeaux. His research interests include corporate governance, social entrepreneurship, Microfinance, Crowdfunding, and corporate social responsibility. He has published in Management Decision, Revue d'économie financière, Humanisme and Entreprise, Innovations and Management and Avenir.

Andreas Will Andreas Will is professor of Media and Communication Management at Technische Universität Ilmenau, Germany. His research interests include media management, digital media markets, entrepreneurship, crowdsourcing/crowdfunding, and project management. Together with his team, he advises and scientifically supports various crowdfunding platforms, projects and start-ups. He holds a Dr. rer. pol. in Business Administration/ Information Systems from Augsburg University and a Diploma in Industrial Engineering from Karlsruhe University of Technology.

Editors

Dennis Brüntje Dennis Brüntje is research assistant at the Media and Communication Management Group at Technische Universität Ilmenau, Germany. Together with his team he has conducted a wide range of studies related to crowdfunding, media management and entrepreneurship. Furthermore, the Group advises and scientifically supports various crowdfunding platforms, projects and start-ups. Dennis is head of the Scientific Work Group on crowdfunding at the European Crowdfunding Network. In his PhD thesis he focuses on intermediation by platforms in equity-based crowdfunding. He has several years of experience in business financing, from establishing a venture capital company, his research and initiating a local start-up initiative.

Oliver Gajda Oliver Gajda is the founding Chairman and Executive Director at the European Crowdfunding Network, Belgium. He is a member of the European Crowdfunding Stakeholder Forum at the European Commission and Advisory Board member at Förderkreis Gründungsforschung e.V. (FGF). He works as hands-on operational and strategic consultant with innovative businesses. The past decade, Oliver has worked with venture capital, microfinance, technology and social entrepreneurship in both commercial and non-profit settings in Europe and the USA. As former journalist, he started his career in the early 1990s in the publishing and business information industries. Oliver holds Masters degrees from Solvay Business School and from the University of Hamburg and studied at SEESS (UCL) in London.

MIX
Papier aus verantwortungsvollen Quellen
Paper from responsible sources
FSC® C105338

If you have any concerns about our products,
you can contact us on
ProductSafety@springernature.com

In case Publisher is established outside the EU,
the EU authorized representative is:
Springer Nature Customer Service Center GmbH
Europaplatz 3, 69115 Heidelberg, Germany

Printed by Libri Plureos GmbH
in Hamburg, Germany